ADVCOMP 2016

The Tenth International Conference on Advanced Engineering Computing and Applications in Sciences

October 9 - 13, 2016

Venice, Italy

ADVCOMP 2016 Editors

Alexey Cheptsov, High Performance Computing Center - Stuttgart, Germany

Abir Alharbi, King Saud University, Riyadh, Saudi Arabia

Printed from e-media with permission by:

Curran Associates, Inc.
57 Morehouse Lane
Red Hook, NY 12571

Some format issues inherent in the e-media version may also appear in this print version.

Printed by Curran Associates, Inc. (2016)

International Academy, Research, and Industry Association (IARIA)
412 Derby Way
Wilmington, DE 19810

Phone: (408) 893-6407
Fax: (408) 527-6351

petre@iaria.org

Additional copies of this publication are available from:

Curran Associates, Inc.
57 Morehouse Lane
Red Hook, NY 12571 USA
Phone: 845-758-0400
Fax: 845-758-2633
Email: curran@proceedings.com
Web: www.proceedings.com

TABLE OF CONTENTS

ADVCOMP 5 / COMARA: COMPUTATIONAL MATHEMATICS IN REAL-LIFE APPLICATIONS

ADVCOMP 2016

Forward

The Tenth International Conference on Advanced Engineering Computing and Applications in Sciences (ADVCOMP 2016), held between October 9 and 13, 2016 in Venice, Italy, continued a series of events addressing the fundamentals advanced scientific computing and specific mechanisms and algorithms for particular sciences. The conference provided a forum where researchers were able to present recent research results and new research problems and directions related to them.

With the advent of high performance computing environments, virtualization, distributed and parallel computing, as well as the increasing memory, storage and computational power, processing particularly complex scientific applications and voluminous data is more affordable. With the current computing software, hardware and distributed platforms effective use of advanced computing techniques is more achievable.

The event was very competitive in its selection process and very well perceived by the international scientific and industrial communities. As such, it has attracted excellent contributions and active participation from all over the world. We were very pleased to receive a large amount of top quality contributions.

The conference had the following tracks:

- Computation Methods
- Computing Applications in Science
- Computational Mathematics in Real-life Applications
- Geometry and Logic

We take here the opportunity to warmly thank all the members of the ADVCOMP 2016 technical program committee, as well as the numerous reviewers. The creation of such a high quality conference program would not have been possible without their involvement. We also kindly thank all the authors that dedicated much of their time and effort to contribute to ADVCOMP 2016. We truly believe that, thanks to all these efforts, the final conference program consisted of top quality contributions.

Also, this event could not have been a reality without the support of many individuals, organizations and sponsors. We also gratefully thank the members of the ADVCOMP 2016 organizing committee for their help in handling the logistics and for their work that made this professional meeting a success.

We hope ADVCOMP 2016 was a successful international forum for the exchange of ideas and results between academia and industry and to promote further progress in the field of advanced engineering computing and applications.

We also hope that Venice, Italy, provided a pleasant environment during the conference and everyone saved some time to enjoy the unique charm of the city.

ADVCOMP Advisory Committee

Chih-Cheng Hung, Southern Polytechnic State University, USA
Juha Röning, Oulu University, Finland
Erich Schweighofer, University of Vienna, Austria
Paul Humphreys, University of Ulster, UK
Danny Krizanc, Wesleyan University, USA
Ivan Rodero, Rutgers University - Piscataway, USA
George Spanoudakis, City University London, UK
Vladimir Vlassov, KTH Royal Institute of Technology, Sweden
Jerry Trahan, Louisiana State University, USA
Dean Vucinic, Vrije Universiteit Brussel (VUB), Belgium
Rudolf Berrendorf, Bonn-Rhein-Sieg University, Germany
Wenbing Zhao, Cleveland State University, USA
Camelia Muñoz-Caro, Universidad de Castilla-La Mancha, Spain
Laurent Réveillère, Bordeaux Institute of Technology, France
Ewa Grabska, Jagiellonian University - Krakow, Poland

ADVCOMP Industry/Research Chairs

Jorge Ejarque Artigas, Barcelona Supercomputing Center (BSC-CNS), Spain
Helmut Reiser, Leibniz Supercomputing Centre (LRZ)-Garching, Germany
H. Metin Aktulga, Lawrence Berkeley National Lab, USA
Sameh Elnikety, Microsoft Research, USA
Umar Farooq, Amazon.com - Seattle, USA
Alice Koniges, Lawrence Berkeley Laboratory/NERSC, USA
Peter Müller, IBM Zurich Research Laboratory- Rüschlikon, Switzerland
Simon Tsang, Applied Communication Sciences, Basking Ridge, USA
Anna Schwanengel, Siemens AG, Germany
Christoph Fuenfzig, Fraunhofer ITWM, Germany

ADVCOMP 2016

Committee

ADVCOMP Advisory Committee

Chih-Cheng Hung, Southern Polytechnic State University, USA
Juha Röning, Oulu University, Finland
Erich Schweighofer, University of Vienna, Austria
Paul Humphreys, University of Ulster, UK
Danny Krizanc, Wesleyan University, USA
Ivan Rodero, Rutgers University - Piscataway, USA
George Spanoudakis, City University London, UK
Vladimir Vlassov, KTH Royal Institute of Technology, Sweden
Jerry Trahan, Louisiana State University, USA
Dean Vucinic, Vrije Universiteit Brussel (VUB), Belgium
Rudolf Berrendorf, Bonn-Rhein-Sieg University, Germany
Wenbing Zhao, Cleveland State University, USA
Camelia Muñoz-Caro, Universidad de Castilla-La Mancha, Spain
Laurent Réveillère, Bordeaux Institute of Technology, France
Ewa Grabska, Jagiellonian University - Krakow, Poland

ADVCOMP Industry/Research Chairs

Jorge Ejarque Artigas, Barcelona Supercomputing Center (BSC-CNS), Spain
Helmut Reiser, Leibniz Supercomputing Centre (LRZ)-Garching, Germany
H. Metin Aktulga, Lawrence Berkeley National Lab, USA
Sameh Elnikety, Microsoft Research, USA
Umar Farooq, Amazon.com - Seattle, USA
Alice Koniges, Lawrence Berkeley Laboratory/NERSC, USA
Peter Müller, IBM Zurich Research Laboratory- Rüschlikon, Switzerland
Simon Tsang, Applied Communication Sciences, Basking Ridge, USA
Anna Schwanengel, Siemens AG, Germany
Christoph Fuenfzig, Fraunhofer ITWM, Germany

ADVCOMP 2016 Technical Program Committee

Witold Abramowicz, University of Economics - Poznań, Poland
Kenneth Adamson, University of Ulster, UK
H. Metin Aktulga, Lawrence Berkeley National Lab, USA
Abir Alharbi, Science College - King Saud University, Riyadh, Saudi Arabia
Shahrouz Aliabadi, Jackson State University, USA

Sónia Maria Almeida da Luz, Polytechnic Institute of Leiria, Portugal / University of Extremadura, Spain
Daniel Andresen, Kansas State University, USA
Alina Andreica, Babes-Bolyai University, Romania
Sulieman Bani-Ahmad, Al-Balqa Applied University, Jordan
Hocine Bendjama, Welding and NDT Research Centre (CSC), Algeria
Roberto Beraldi, "La Sapienza" University of Rome, Italy
Mario Marcelo Berón, National University of San Luis, Argentina
Rudolf Berrendorf, Bonn-Rhein-Sieg University, Germany
Ateet Bhalla, Independent Consultant, India
Muhammad Naufal bin Mansor, University Malaysia Perlis, Malaysia
Pierre Borne, Ecole Centrale de Lille - Villeneuve d'Ascq, France
Xiao-Chuan Cai, University of Colorado Boulder, USA
Christophe Calvin, CEA/DEN/DANS/DM2S, France
Kenneth P. Camilleri, University of Malta - Msida, Malta
Juan-Vicente Capella-Hernández, Universitat Politècnica de València, Spain
Omar Andres Carmona Cortes, Instituto Federal do Maranhão, Brazil
Antonio Casimiro, Faculdade de Ciências da Universidade de Lisboa, Portugal
Mete Celik, Erciyes University, Turkey
Yeh-Ching Chung, National Tsing Hua University, Taiwan
Robert Clay, Sandia National Laboratories, USA
Marisa da Silva Maximiano, Escola Superior de Tecnologia e Gestão - Instituto Politécnico de Leiria, Portugal
Vieri del Bianco, Università dell'Insubria, Italy
Javier Diaz, Rutgers University, USA
Xing Cai, Simula Research Laboratory, Norway
Yves Caniou, Université de Lyon, France / University of Tokyo, Japan
Cy Chan, Lawrence Berkeley National Laboratory, USA
Vassilios V. Dimakopoulos, University of Ioannina, Greece
Prabu Do, Wipro Technologies, USA
Jorge Ejarque Artigas, Barcelona Supercomputing Center (BSC-CNS), Spain
Sameh Elnikety, Microsoft Research, USA
Javier Fabra, University of Zaragoza, Spain
Simon G. Fabri, University of Malta - Msida, Malta
Umar Farooq, Amazon.com - Seattle, USA
Mehdi Farshbaf-Sahih-Sorkhabi, Azad University - Tehran / Fanavaran co., Tehran, Iran
Mohammad-Reza Feizi-Derakhshi, University of Tabriz, Iran
Dan Feldman, MIT, USA
Mikael Fridenfalk, Uppsala University, Sweden
Bin Fu, University of Texas - Pan American, USA
Cheng Fu, Shanghai Advanced Research Institute, Chinese Academy of Sciences, China
Akemi Galvez Tomida, University of Cantabria, Spain
Javier García Blas, Universidad Carlos III de Madrid, Spain
Rodrigo García Carmona, Universidad Politécnica de Madrid, Spain

Mikel Larrea, University of the Basque Country UPV/EHU, Spain
Rosa Lasaponara, CNR-IMAA, Italy
Luigi Lavazza, Università dell'Insubria - Varese, Italy
Che-Rung Roger Lee, NTHU, Taiwan
Dmitrii Legatiuk, Bauhaus-Universität Weimar, Germany
Clement Leung, Hong Kong Baptist University, Hong Kong
Vitus Leung, Sandia National Labs, USA
Chendong Li, Dell Silicon Valley R&D Center, USA
Dong Liang, York University, Canada
Cheng-Xian (Charlie) Lin, Florida International University - Miami, USA
Juan Pablo López-Grao, University of Zaragoza, Spain
Hatem Ltaief, KAUST Supercomputing Laboratory, SA
Xiaoyi Lu, Ohio State University, USA
Emilio Luque, University Autonoma of Barcelona (UAB), Spain
Lau Cheuk Lung, INE/UFSC, Brazil
Joanna Isabelle Olszewska, University of Gloucestershire, United Kingdom
Stephane Maag, Telecom SudParis / CNRS UMR 5157 - Samovar, France
Anthony A. Maciejewski, Colorado State University - Fort Collins, USA
Shikharesh Majumdar, Carleton University - Ottawa, Canada
Ming Mao, University of Virginia, USA
Marcin Markowski, Wroclaw University of Technology, Poland
Gregorio Martinez, University of Murcia, Spain
Nicola Masini, Institute for Archaeological and Monumental Heritage - National Research Council, Italy
Jose Merseguer, Universidad de Zaragoza, Spain
Tiffany M. Mintz, Oak Ridge National Laboratory, USA
Sanjay Misra, Covenant University, Nigeria
Mohamed A. Mohandes, King Fahd University of Petroleum and Minerals, SA
José Luis Montaña, Universidad de Cantabria, Spain
Peter Müller, IBM Zurich Research Laboratory- Rüschlikon, Switzerland
Adrian Muscat, University of Malta, Malta
Álvaro Navas, Universidad Politecnica de Madrid, Spain
Quang Vinh Nguyen, University of Western Sydney, Australia
Sascha Opletal, University of Stuttgart, Germany
Flavio Oquendo, European University of Brittany - UBS/VALORIA, France
Mathias Pacher, Leibniz Universität Hannover, Germany
Marcin Paprzycki, Systems Research Institute of the Polish Academy of Sciences, Poland
Hugo Parada, Universidad Politécnica de Madrid, Spain
Kwangjin Park, Wonkwang University, Korea
Sonia Pérez-Díaz, Universidad de Alcalá, Spain
Zornitza Petrova, Technical University of Sofia, Bulgaria
Nada Philip, Kingston University, UK
Meikel Poess, Oracle, USA
Radu-Emil Precup, Politehnica University of Timisoara, Romania

Luciana Rech, Universidade Federal de Santa Catarina, Brazil
Helmut Reiser, LRZ, Germany
Michael Resch, HLRS - University of Stuttgart, Germany
Laurent Réveillère, Bordeaux Institute of Technology, France
Dolores Rexachs, Universidad Autónoma de Barcelona (UAB), Spain
Ivan Rodero, Rutgers University - Piscataway, USA
Alexey S. Rodionov, Institute of Computational Mathematics and Mathematical Geophysics - Siberian Division of the Russian Academy of Science, Novosibirsk, Russia
Juha Röning, Oulu University, Finland
Tomasz Rymarczyk, Net-art (Netrix Group), Poland
Iwona Ryszka, Jagiellonian University - Krakow, Poland
Maytham Safar, Focus Consultancy, Kuwait
Julio Sahuquillo, Universitat Politècnica de València, Spain
Francoise Sailhan, Cedric laboratory - Conservatoire National des Arts et Metiers (CNAM), France
Subhash Saini, NASA, USA
Jose Francisco Salt Cairols, Universitat de Valencia-CSIC, Spain
Rainer Schmidt, Austrian Institute of Technology, Austria
Bruno Schulze, National Laboratory for Scientific Computing - LNCC -Petropolis - RJ, Brasil
Erich Schweighofer, Vienna University, Austria
Kewei Sha, Oklahoma City University, USA
Ali Shahrabi, Glasgow Caledonian University, Scotland, UK
Jie Shen, University of Michigan, USA
George Spanoudakis, City University London, UK
Hari Subramoni, Ohio State University, USA
Saïd Tazi, INSA - Toulouse, France
Andrei Tchernykh, CICESE Research Center, Mexico
Parimala Thulasiraman, University of Manitoba, Canada
Jerry Trahan, Louisiana State University, U.S.A.
Simon Tsang, Applied Communication Sciences, Basking Ridge, USA
José Valente de Oliveira, Universidade do Algarve, Portugal
Doru Vatau, University Politehnica of Timisoara, Romania
Vladimir Vlassov, KTH Royal Institute of Technology, Sweden
Dean Vučinić, Vrije Universiteit Brussel (VUB), Belgium
Mohd Helmy Abd Wahab, Universiti Tun Hussein Onn Malaysia, Malaysia
Lixin Wang, Paine College, Augusta, USA
Zhi Wang, Florida State University, USA
Ted Willke, Intel Corporation, USA
Gabriel Wittum, Goethe University Frankfurt, Germany
Mudasser F. Wyne, National University, USA
Yinglong Xia, IBM, USA
Ping Xiong, Zhongnan University of Economics and Law, China
Chao-Tung Yang, Tunghai University, Taiwan
Muneer Masadeh Bani Yassein, Jordan University of Science and Technology, Jordan

Copyright Information

A Non-repetitive Logic for Verification of Dynamic Memory with Explicit Heap Conjunction and Disjunction

René Haberland   Kirill Krinkin
Saint Petersburg Electrotechnical University *"LETI"*
Saint Petersburg, Russia
email: haberland1@mail.ru, kirill.krinkin@fruct.org

***Abstract*—In this paper, we review existing points-to Separation Logics for dynamic memory reasoning and we find that different usages of heap separation tend to be an obstacle. Hence, two total and strict spatial heap operations are proposed upon heap graphs, for conjunction and disjunction – similar to logical conjuncts. Heap conjunction implies that there exists a free heap vertex to connect to or an explicit destination vertex is provided. Essentially, Burstall's properties do not change. By heap we refer to an arbitrary simple directed graph, which is finite and may contain composite vertices representing class objects. Arbitrary heap memory access is restricted, as well as type punning, late class binding and further restrictions. Properties of the new logic are investigated, and as a result group properties are shown. Both expecting and superficial heaps are specifiable. Equivalence transformations may make denotated heaps inconsistent, although those may be detected and patched by the two generic linear canonization steps presented. The properties help to motivate a later full introduction of a set of equivalences over heap for future work. Partial heaps are considered as a useful specification technique that help to reduce incompleteness issues with specifications. Finally, the logic proposed may be considered for extension for the Object Constraint Language.**

Keywords. ***heap logic, points-to heap specification and verification, spatial heap operation ambiguity.***

I. INTRODUCTION

In contrast to automatically allocated memory, which remains in the stack, *dynamic memory* refers to the main memory part that is altered by commands such as `new`, `delete` and heap data assignments. The dynamic memory contains *heaps* (see definition 2.1). Let us first review a few important definitions and discuss issues with heaps afterwards.

Jones et al. [1] define a *heap* as a contiguous subscripted datastructure, and also, alternatively, as an organised graph of "*discontiguous blocks of contiguous words*". All allocated memory cells have a reference and the liveness of a cell is defined by its reachability. The liveness is independent from the program statement that creates a dynamic memory cell.

Reynolds [2] defines *heaps* (not to be mixed up with a single heap) as the union of all mappings of address subsets to non-empty value cells. Following this definition a single heap would be some addresses pointing to some arbitrary data structure. Reynolds mentions his intention goes back to Burstall's model [3]. Both refer to trees as implied data structure - which, at least in Burstall's proposition, denotes a simple *heap graph* (definition 2.2 formally introduces it, for the moment let us assume it is an arbitrary graph where edges represent some relationship between heap vertices) as for instance the expression $x \xrightarrow{a_1,a_2,a_3} y$ denotes some path within the heap graph in Fig. 1. The graph starts at x and stops at a heap cell which is also pointed by some local variable y by visiting a_1, a_2, a_3, which all may have some unspecified content on its way there. Reynolds introduces the "$\star$"-operator for expressing that two heaps do not share common dynamic memory regions. In contrast to Burstall Reynolds' model is slightly different: all except the start of a path from a stacked variable denotes its value rather its cell location. As shown in the graph in Fig. 2 by convention it is agreed that stacked variables, such as x_1, only have outgoing edges, where all other vertices, such as $x_2, x_3, x_4, x_5, x_6, x_7$, denote some concrete heap cell values and may have zero or more incoming and zero or more outgoing edges.

If we like to parameterise a heap graph so it contained *genuine symbolic variables*, we rather have to distinguish between parameterised and fixed variable meanings on each verification step. Reynolds introduces the ","-operator to specify paths in heap graphs. For example, when using "," the above data-structure could be fully specified by $x_1 \mapsto x_2, x_3, x_4, x_7 \wedge x_5 \mapsto x_6, x_7$. For comparison, the same data structure without the path-operator "," would be $(x_2 \mapsto x_3 \star x_4 \mapsto x_7 \star x_5 \mapsto x_6) \wedge (x_1 \mapsto x_2 \star x_3 \mapsto x_4 \star x_6 \mapsto x_7)$ – we excuse ourselves variable locations and content were mixed up in this example for the sake of simplicity. Based on the "$\star$"-operator

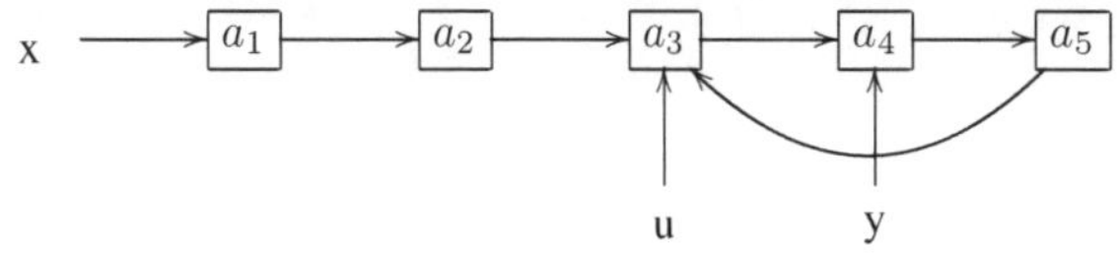

Fig. 1. An arbitrary annotated heap graph with locals x, u and y pointing to cells with some content a_1, a_3 and a_4

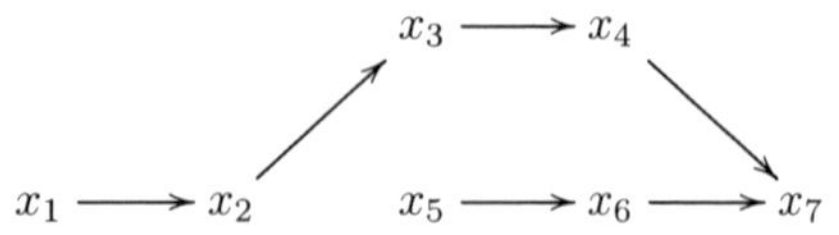

Fig. 2. Heap graph sample consisting of two simply linked lists forming inverted cactuses

and "$\mapsto$" the so-called *Separation Logic* was proposed [2],[4] and implemented [5]. The following example [2] demonstrates the definition of a binary tree predicate (we call a predicate "*abstract*" whenever it depends on parameters):

$tree(l) ::= \texttt{nil} \mid \exists x.\exists y:\ l \mapsto x, y \star tree(x) \star tree(y)$

The abstraction parameter l in Fig. 3 is some variable symbol and $tree$ denotes the recursively defined predicate implying the left branch does not intersect with any part of the right branch, and vice versa. However, strictly speaking this must not always be the case, since in the above specification $tree(y)$ might be substituted by $tree2(x, y)$, which could hypothetically link back to x again and so would breach the convention made previously – luckily, this can be excluded in most cases, except when references to dynamic memory are determined on runtime. For example, `p[13+offset]` where `offset` is decidable on runtime only might be such a scenario. The breach may be avoided for $tree2$ just by not passing x neither recalling it globally. Even if the tree entirely fits into dynamic memory, remember x and y get stacked once the tree is traversed: first x, then y is accommodated at the next available address because of ",". The authors of this paper are aware of dropping unbound heap memory access may induce considerable practical restrictions, however, we think this restriction can in many cases be overcome by a modification to the chosen data model.

By convention, whenever a vertex of the heap graph has at most one outgoing edge, the heap graph is *simple*, e.g. linearly-linked lists, trees and arbitrary heap graphs without multiple edges between two vertices. W.l.o.g. we consider only pointers that refer to particular heap cells or class objects that may union several pointers to heap cells. We will further also consider abstract predicates. In order to decide whether two heaps indeed do not share a common heap, it is necessary to check there exists no path from one heap graph to the other.

One alternative to Separation Logic is *Shape Analysis* [6]. It makes use of transfer functions in order to describe changes to the heap by every program statement. Another approach, as being demonstrated by Baby Modula 3 [7], uses a class-free

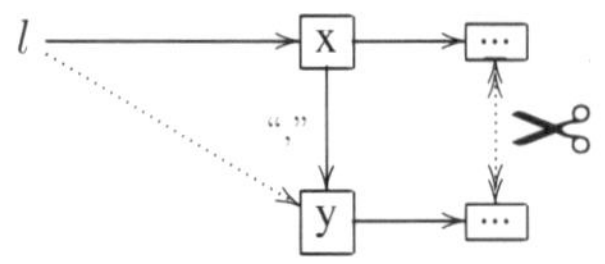

Fig. 3. Heap graph instance for the definition of a binary $tree$. The left x child points to some content which may not interfere with the content pointed to by y

object calculus and a single unique result register. This register stores the result after each single statement and so allows to refer to the state before and after running a particular statement. Class-objects and their typeable theories are discussed in [8],[7].

At this point it is worth noting that a points-to model is considered in this paper due to its *locality property* w.r.t. heap graphs, modifications do not usually require a full specification update due to its edge-based graph representation.

The inspiration for this paper, even if coming from a different context, is [9], where a rather intuitive but incomplete set of "*safe*" symmetry operations on pointers is proposed in order to prove correctness of more complex pointer manipulations. Safe operations, as rotation or shift, raise big practical concerns as hard-to predict pointer behaviour even on very small modifications as well as incompleteness gaps on pointer rotations.

The main purpose of this paper is to present two new *context-free* binary operations for heap conjunction and heap disjunction, to show group properties hold and those can be used for example for proof simplifications on proof rules in the future.

Section I of this paper gave a brief overview of the topic and related problems. Section II introduces briefly Separation Logic, it introduces a concluded definition of heap and heap graph, and it comes with conventions for class objects and heap memory alignment. The main part, section III defines heap terms to be interpreted within heap formulae. Pointers of pointers and arrays are only very briefly discussed, heap conjunction is introduced for basic ("*heaplet*") and generalised heaps (what is later expressed as heap term) as well as path accessors (see observation 3.6). Properties of the conjunction are investigated and established, canonisation steps are demonstrated in order to overcome transient inconsistency, which may occur from references no more alive. Heap inversion is proposed as notational trick. In companion with other properties it may eventually help to define equalities over heaps and so improve the comparison with expected heaps in the future. In particular, defining a partially-ordered set over conjunct heaps w.r.t. sub-graph inclusion, and distributivity along with other properties would eventually help to define for instance a *satisfiability-modulo-theory*. Partial specification is introduced in section IV for objects. Discussions propose an extension with aliases to the *Object Constraint Language*. Finally, conclusions follow a short discussion.

II. Heap Separating Logic

Before going into more detail, let us first ask whether we cannot simply turn all dynamically allocated variables into stacked, as it was proposed, for instance, by [10]. Often this will indeed work, however, sometimes it is not a good idea after all, because of performance issues [11], for instance. More often the nature of the problem forbids general static assumptions on stack bounds. An overview and numerous definitions of dynamic memory may be found in [1].

The essence of Reynolds' heap model and properties was briefly wrapped up in the previous section. So, one central problem seems to be expressibility, which is the main purpose of this paper. This section introduces a heap by referring to a graph, followed by numerous model discussions and property observations.

Definition 2.1. *(concluded from Reynolds) A heap is defined as* $\bigcup_{A \subseteq Addr} A \mapsto Val^n$ *with* $n \geq 1$*, A being some address set and* Val *is some value domain, for instance, integers or inductively defined structures containing A. A heap may be composed inductively by other heaps as following:*

$H_1 \star H_2$*, where* H_1 *describes some heap graph assertion* $H_1 = (V_1, E_1)$ *and in analogy to that* $H_2 = (V_2, E_2)$*, where edges* $E = V \times V$ *and edges are directed, s.t. iff* $\forall v_1 \in V_1$*,* $v_2 \in V_2$ *with* $v1 \neq v2$ *and cases:*

1st *(Separation):* $(v_1, v_2) \notin E_1$*, and* $(v_1, v_2) \notin E_2$.

2nd *(Conjunction):* $\exists s \in V_1, \exists t \in V_2 : (s,t) \in E_1$ *or* $(s,t) \in E_2$ *then* H_1 *or* H_2 *contains some* $\star$*-separated* $s \mapsto t$.

Variables as well as pointers are stored in the stack, where the content pointed to remains in heap memory (the following domain equation [5] holds: $Stack = Values \cup Locals$). Heap graph assertions are assertions about the heap graph constructed by program statements manipulating the dynamic memory. Those assertions are interpreted as *true* or *false* depending on whether an associated concrete heap corresponds or not. Definition 3.2 will introduce the syntax for heap assertions.

Regarding definition 2.1 the overloading of the binary operator "$\star$" happens in two ways: one is to express two heaps do not overlap, and the second way is to express two heaps are somehow linked together by using transient symbols. The "$\star$"-operator is a logical and spatial conjunction, it links two prepositions about heaps together and it describes heap entities which have some configuration in space, both consume different dynamic memory regions. On the one hand, if we link strictly two separate heaps then we have to find a maximal matching in order to describe the given *heap graph* entirely, which is impractical. On the other hand, separation also seems to be a very elegant way to separate specification concerns locally: if there is an assertion regarding a particular data structure in heap, this should involve at most only that data structures and exclude unaffected ones. After all, the above initial definition seems complicated enough, because it is ambiguous and it refers to a single heap definition, which should ideally not be too different from Reynolds' initial and rather intuitive definition of heaps – but as we have seen unfortunately, it is. So, two strict operators would be desired rather a single "$\star$", one operator to strictly separate and one to join heaps. Heaps shall be replaceable with symbolic placeholders in order to beat ambiguity whilst analysing verification conditions. Moreover, syntax and semantic intention of heap expressions shall be unified.

Once both heap operators are defined, properties and equivalences can be established separately. Finally, heap theories and term algebras may eventually be proposed in future over both heap operators. In definition 2.2 we first need to formally define what a heap actually is.

The underpinning theory behind [3] is the so-called *Substructural Logic* [12], which is a higher-order logic, a logic where, for instance, the contraction rule does no more hold, constants have in fact turned into predicates that may be quantified (details can be found in [12]). Contraction-freeness [13] in this context has for our purpose the advantage of non-repeating heap entities within a heap assertion. By repeating we directly refer to points-to expressions as defined later.

Definition 2.2. *A (finite) heap graph is a directed connected graph within the dynamic memory section which may contain cycles, but must remain simple. Each vertex has a type-dependent size and an unique memory address, but may not overlap with other vertices. Every edge represents a relationship, for instance, a pointer to some absolute memory address or a relative jump field displacement.*

The absolute addresses are out of interest to the verification. The heap graph must be pointed by at least one stacked variable, otherwise the so-defined graph is considered as garbage. Stacked variables may also point to one vertex, in this case all except one variable are *aliases* of the variable considered.

The emphasis lies on finite, since only arbitrary big but finite address space shall be considered. The dynamic memory shall be linearly addressable, however some operations `new` and `delete` shall organise themselves how and where to allocate or free heap memory. We restrict ourselves pointers address *correctly* and *sound*, and for the purpose of this paper we neither care too much about an optimal memory coalescing strategy to pointers that is most likely expanded on runtime, nor primarily about garbage collection issues. What we concern about is only that there is a relationship between a pointer and a pointed-by region within the heap memory region, it does not even require a pointer contains an absolute address within the dynamic memory range as it is not the case with bi-directional XOR-calculated jump-fields, which are relative pointer offsets depending on the address provided "somehow" by an actual vertex address.

Conventions 2.3. *Objects are restricted w.l.o.g. to be*

a) *non-inner objects only. Inner objects may always be modelled as with associated outer objects, so that there*

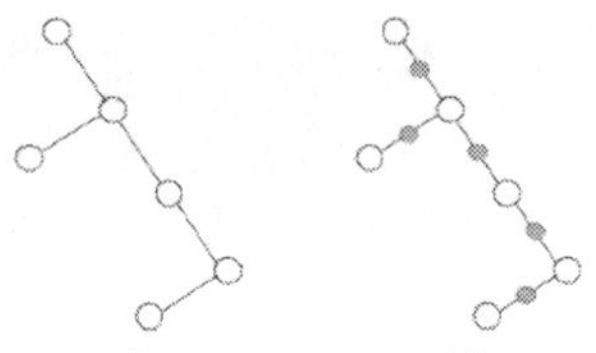

a) b)

Fig. 4. Schematic heap graph a) without direction, b) midpoints represent the substituted graph obtained by encoding source and destination vertices

are references to different locations rather than all objects being accommodated within one contiguous heap chunk.

b) *Object fields and method names have to be all unique w.r.t. to its visibility. W.l.o.g. clashing names, for instance inherited names, are resolved by mangling the origin name with visibility mode and information from the deriving class. All references to mangled names need to be taken into account. This task is primarily done during the semantic program analysis phase.*

c) *Due to encapsulation, objects do not grow in size normally, and due to late binding object references may keep invariant. However, the size of an object may spontaneously change. Sub-class objects may suddenly grow, but they may also shrink, depending on whether the translating compilation phase does align memory for non-used fields or not. If choosing a forced stack-allocated memory alignment for objects, then an object which is bound lately and passed alone to some procedure may better be reordered within its memory chunk, s.t. the growing part rises upwards on the stack. Because the separating heap are non-contractive [3], object fields specified once may not appear again within a conjuncted heap expression.*

d) *Arrays as base type are currently ignored. Multiple edges between the same two vertices are disallowed.*

e) *Sharing of same heap cells by multiple cells is allowed to all object fields.*

In order to stay consistent with the following definitions, a simple check for the incidence relationship for memory cells for a given heap graph needs to be introduced. A given heap graph is composed of points-to heaplets meaning a directed edge represents a location points to a heap address which contains some value. The check requires all these heaplet conjuncts are traversed and the desired heap graph shall be in an edge-centric representation. However, whenever we like to determine if two heap vertices are incident with each other or not, we prefer a vertex-centric model encoding edges. So, we define the following built-in predicates: `reaches(x,y)`, `reaches(x,Y)`, `reaches(X,y)`, `reaches(X,Y)`, where `x` is a vertex and `X` denotes a vertex subset of a given heap graph (`y`, `Y` in analogy).

Both interleaved representations in Fig. 4 (the vertex-centric representation is marked by smaller filled midpoints on every edge) are dual and convertible to each other. Midpoints encode *source* and *destination* as one vertex and link with former neighbouring vertices. Naturally, this mapping is bijective (proof skipped). Since we in general need to interpret predicates of at least first order, we could do this now by describing one heap graph by one conjunction of "$loc \mapsto val$" pairs rather than more complex forms.

Conventions 2.4. *(Heap Alignment) Object fields do not overlap, fields have distinguishing memory addresses. Pointers to objects and its fields may alias. An object is expressed commonly by the points-to expression $x \mapsto object(fld_1, fld_2, ...)$. It is agreed w.l.o.g. that object fields may not be accessed via arithmetic displacements but only by a valid object access path using the ".“-operator and valid subordinate fields. W.l.o.g, but still for the sake of full computability late binding is skipped. A full support would imply the use of only the weakest common heap to be chosen.*

III. Conjunction and Disjunction

Because of definitions 2.1, 2.2 and conventions 2.3, 2.4 we describe a heap now by a term as following.

Definition 3.1. *A heap term describes heap graphs and is syntactically defined as:*

$T ::=$	$loc \mapsto val$	*... points-to heaplet*
	$\mid T \circ T$	*... heap conjunction*
	$\mid T \parallel T$	*... heap disjunction*
	$\mid \underline{true} \mid \underline{false} \mid \underline{emp}$	*... partial heap spec*
	$\mid (T)$	*... subterm expression*

where loc denotes a variable location, a location of a compound object field or a symbol representing some heap variable, and val denotes some value of any arbitrary domain. T describes the current heap state.

T can be considered as a formula since we do not restrict ourselves in not considering variable scopes as long as the syntax definition is obeyed. We further agree on that $\circ$ has lower precedence than $\|$, so $a_1 \circ a_2 \| a_3 \equiv (a_1 \circ a_2) \| a_3$. For the sake of notational simplicity, we do refer to $loc \mapsto val$, which besides is closer to Reynolds' definition rather than Burstall's. However, we really should better refer in practice to the address of the content being pointed to rather than the direct domain value, which naturally may be composed. Hence, we agree without any further notice on some polymorphic notational helpers, like $address(val)$, which will allow us to address given values.

$\underline{true}$ implies certain (remaining) heap term(s) is a tautology, regardless of the actual term(s). In analogy to that stands $\underline{false}$, which implements a contradiction. $\underline{emp}$ is a constant built-in predicate implying a given heap must be empty to be satisfiable. This is why all three may be used to consume all not explicitly listed $\circ$-conjuncted heaplets. The partial specification we get allows us to keep heap formulae simple, since we now may implicitly include all unaffected, but still intended, heaps belonging together. Partial specifications together with abstract predicates raise modularity. This becomes particularly of interest for class objects, where all field heaplets generate its own heaplet scope, which is different from the global non-object scope (see convention 2.4). In fact we just discussed extensions to our heap term definition, which ought to be summarised:

Definition 3.2. *Extended heap terms ET are heap terms with constant formulae, negation and logical conjuncts:*

$ET ::=$	T	*... heap term*
	$\mid p(\alpha)$	*... abstract predicate call*
	$\mid \neg ET$	*... logical negation*
	$\mid ET \wedge ET$	*... logical conjunction*
	$\mid ET \vee ET$	*... logical disjunction*

The logical conjunctions do not really require more explanations than already said. A predicate call to a previously defined predicate may invoke all dependent subcalls, although predicate calls are not classic procedure calls. An brief introduction of Prolog using predicates and reasoning a specific Hoare-calculus may be found in [14]. Predicates may be parameterised by zero or more heap terms bound to the predicate. Heap terms may be used as input or output terms, or even both at the same time. Intentionally, heap terms are used as sub-expressions in logical assertions. The verification of a predicate retrieves a Boolean value depending on if a given formula is obeyed.

Observation 3.3. *Pointers of pointers are syntactic sugar. They do not fundamentally extend the expressibility of heap graph assertions. Their only purpose w.r.t. heap terms is to have an additional indirection level for increased programming language flexibility. They act as placeholder or symbol variable for pointer locations.*

By pointers of pointers neither the heap graph itself gets extended nor the referenced heap in comparison with no pointers of pointers. Symbolic variables and placeholders are useful, because they may select numerous heaplets at once. But, the ",“-operator can do this already for linearly-linked lists and this operator was found superficial in terms of expressibility. In addition to that, it should be noted, that abstract predicates may also perform a selection of numerous heap cells. Although not too useful in a theoretic manner, the above conjecture does not necessarily exclude usability gains in practice.

Definition 3.4. *Heap conjunction $H \circ \alpha \mapsto \beta$ is defined as heap graph, where $G = (V, E)$ is H's heap graph representation, H is a heap graph, and $\alpha \mapsto \beta$ is a points-to heaplet:*

$$\begin{cases} (V \cup \{\alpha, \beta\} \cup \beta', & \text{if } isFreeIn(\alpha, H) \\ E \cup \{(\alpha, \beta)\} \cup \{(\beta, b) | b \in \beta'\}) & \text{if } H = \underline{emp} \\ & (V = E = \emptyset) \\ \underline{false} & \text{otherwise} \end{cases}$$

where $\beta' = vertices(\beta) \subseteq V$ determines all heap graph vertices being directly pointed by β, which in case β is an object includes all of the fields pointing to some vertices. Since α must be a unique location (for instance an object access path) there may be only either one or no heap vertex matching in $isFreeIn$ for a given heap H. The assumption is there is always exactly one matching free vertex for conjunction when building up a heap graph from a scratch, otherwise two heaps are not linkable.

Lets say we would like to join three points-to pairs a, b, c together (see Fig. 5). First, a must be expressed either purely by a itself or by $\underline{emp} \circ a$. Only then b might be connected to a, iff additionally a contains actually a matching destination vertex that is not being assigned elsewhere. Once we have $a \circ b$, only then the edge c may be connected as announced in the previous step, and we finally obtain the heap graph as seen in

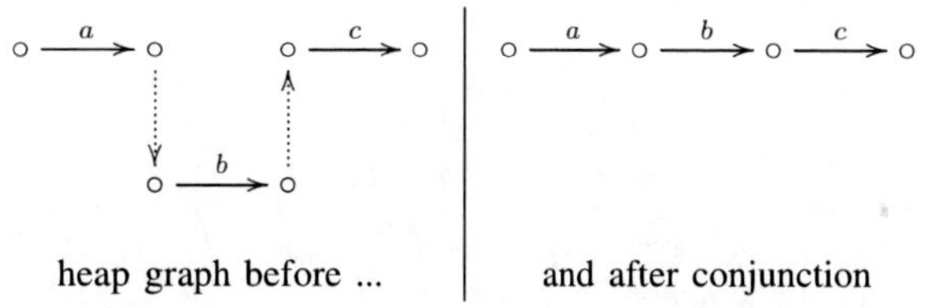

Fig. 5. Heap graph before and after heap conjunction.

Fig. 5. Since we may also conjunct any kind of graphs, e.g., binary trees, we allow to vary the conjunction ordering as long as the resulting graph is connected. For instance, $a \mapsto 5$ would be a valid heap conjunction, but $a \mapsto 5 \circ b \mapsto 5$ would be not. Notice that this way we still may express aliases if we want, for instance the heap graph $x \circ \longrightarrow \circ^z \longleftarrow \circ\ y$ could be expressed as heap term $x \mapsto z \circ y \mapsto z$.

In Fig. 5 all source and target vertices are simple and not annotated. In general the vertices may naturally be simple or compound in case of objects. For the sake of simplicity, only a one-to-one connection is considered further, however assigning multiple objects to fields at once might be a very convenient method as long as the assignment is unambiguous, especially when it comes to arrays where a separator might be needed.

Remark: Let Φ_0 be some heap, then $\Phi = \Phi_0 \circ a_0 \mapsto b_0 \Leftrightarrow \exists (a_m \mapsto b_m) \in \Phi_0 \wedge (a_m = a_0, b_m \neq b_0 \vee a_m \neq a_0, b_m = b_0)$.

Theorem 3.5. *$H_1 \circ H_2$ conjuncts two heaps H_1 and H_2, if there exists at least one common vertex in each heap graph representations. It is agreed by convention $H_1 \circ \underline{emp} = \underline{emp} \circ H_1 = H_1$ holds.*

Proof. This theorem is actually a generalisation of definition 3.4. In contrast to definition 3.4, the term on the right-hand side of the generalisation of $\circ$ is searched for a matching vertex. $H_1 \circ H_2$ represents one connected heap graph. Both, H_1 and H_2 may either be heaplet or a composition of heaplets of kind $a_1 \mapsto b_1 \circ a_2 \mapsto b_2 \circ \cdots \circ a_n \mapsto b_n$. In order to show the correctness of the theorem first we need to show is that if there is no common element in both heap graphs, then by definition 3.4 we obtain $\underline{false}$, which corresponds to what we would obtain from a conjunction. Otherwise, if we do have at least one common element, then inductively we do not bother about further common elements. So, we link both heap graphs up and the conjunction on heaps refers to connectible heaps. Further common elements would meld existing heap graph edges, the melded graph still is simply linked (but with multiple bridges), otherwise this would mean at least source or target of a melded heap graph edge would exclusively be either in H_1 or in H_2, and in both H_1 and H_2 at the same time, which is a contradiction, hence we just showed the theorem holds. □

Regarding the search for a matching element the $a \circ a$-decider mentioned later will resolve this practical issue.

Observation 3.6. *In an abstract predicate locations may be symbols. In order to increase reuse of abstract predicates for* *different locations and different location kinds (primarily for locals and object fields) it is agreed, that the field accessor "." is a left-associative binary operator.*

Left-associativity means $object1.field1.field2.field3$ is internally represented by $(((object1).field1).field2).field3$. This way object access paths may be substituted by variable symbols, which raise modularity and flexibility of access paths expressions.

Lemma 3.7. *$G = (\Omega, \circ)$ is a monoid, where Ω denotes the set of heap graphs and $\circ$ denotes heap conjunction.*

Proof. In order to prove G is a monoid we need to show (i) Ω is closed under $\circ$, (ii) $\circ$ is associative, and (iii) $\exists \varepsilon \in \Omega. \forall m \in \Omega : m \circ \varepsilon = \varepsilon \circ m = m$.

First of all, by $\omega \in \Omega$ we refer to a connected heap graph over "$\mapsto$"-heaplets as being introduced in definition 3.1. According to definition 3.4 $\forall \omega \in \Omega : \omega \circ \omega = \underline{false}$, which is defined. Alternatively, there may be only two cases for some $\omega_1, \omega_2 \in \Omega$: if ω_1 and ω_2 do have at least one joining vertex, then according to theorem 3.5 the resulting heap graph is well-defined, otherwise the result is $\underline{false}$ (meaning ω_1 and ω_2 are disjoint). This way we have just shown that Ω is closed under $\circ$ and that a "*meaningful*" heap graph conjunct may be obtained by connectible heap graphs. The connection is established successively.

Second, associativity needs to be demonstrated, namely that $m_1 \circ (m_2 \circ m_3) = (m_1 \circ m_2) \circ m_3$ holds. When looking at Fig. 5 we can immediately see the validity of both directions of the equation, because it does not matter whether a and b are joined first, or a is connected to connected $b \circ c$, since the joining vertex of b remains invariant when altering the connect ordering.

Now G forms a semi-group, we still need to show there always exists some neutral element ε, so (iii) holds. This follows, however, immediately from the generalised heap theorem 3.5. □

Remark: From (i) follows that $c \notin b \wedge c \neq a$: $a \mapsto b \circ c \mapsto d \equiv \underline{false}$, and that $a \mapsto b \circ a \mapsto d \equiv \underline{false}$ holds. Furthermore, it is intuitively clear that connecting two heap graphs may be done using different joining vertices, regardless of which joints are connected first. The resulting heap graph shall be the same due to *confluence*, due to (ii) and, moreover, due to the property being demonstrated later in definition 3.8.

Remark: Closeness (i) demonstrates the non-repetitiveness property of a Substructural Logic (the Separation Logic as still to be shown later) remains.

Theorem 3.8. *$G = (\Omega, \circ)$ is an Abelian group.*

Proof. Due to lemma 3.7, G is a monoid; hence we still need to show (i) the existence of an inverse element for every heap graph, s.t.

$$\forall \omega \in \Omega . \exists \omega^{-1} \in \Omega : \omega \circ \omega^{-1} = \omega^{-1} \circ \omega = \varepsilon \qquad (1)$$

and (ii) $\circ$ is commutative.

Let us start to prove the induction with (ii): for the base case "$loc_1 \mapsto var_1 \circ loc_2 \mapsto var_2 = loc_2 \mapsto var_2 \circ loc_1 \mapsto var_1$" of definition 3.1 the equivalence holds obviously. The inductive case holds also as long as the conditions on $\circ$ are obeyed, the proof induction can be deduced from Fig. 5, implying commutativity holds for arbitrarily connected heaps. However, when it comes to abstract predicate, the boundaries of a $\circ$-connected heap graph term may vanish. This needs to be taken into consideration by whoever writes the specification.

Now, let us proceed with (i). We do have the problem of finding an inverse for whatever heap we get. The question what it means particularly raises immediately. If we think about natural numbers as operating carrier set and an attempt to invert addition, we factually introduce subtraction on integers. The same happens to complex numbers as an extension of real numbers. Nobody really is not able to count imaginary numbers in practice. Nevertheless, this extension seem to simplify basic calculations significantly in applications. So, why not assume for the moment and postulate equation (1) right until found different?

And so, what does it *intuitively* mean "*to negate a heap*" ? One could think of negating a points-to predicate affects only the state or that there is just no such heap reference. However, it does not really *undo* a heap reference after all. A hypothetical "*not-points-to*" requires primarily some kind of a "*transcendental heap removal*" – at the first glance this may indeed sound like a delicate problem, because up to now we were only specifying what is in the heap. We shall also be able to specify what is not in, but we had no chance whatsoever to specify a predicate which states some heap must be removed "*somehow*". Let us not bother about it too much for the moment and focus instead only on equation (1). What this equation actually states is a *negated points-to* $a \not\mapsto b$ relationship, or more generalised some *negated heap* H^{-1}, s.t. by convention $a \mapsto b \circ a \not\mapsto b = \underline{emp}$ and $a \not\mapsto b \circ a \mapsto b = \underline{emp}$, and more general: $H \circ H^{-1} = H^{-1} \circ H = \underline{emp}$. This means $\omega \circ \omega^{-1}$ removes a heap, and in fact it is an edge removal in addition to an optional heap graph vertex removal in case there are no more edges going to/leaving from the corresponding heap vertex. It is now easy to see why $H \circ H^{-1} \circ H \equiv H$ holds. For demonstration let us have a look at Fig. 6. The heap states before inversion $d \mapsto a \circ a \mapsto b \circ c \mapsto b$, when applied $\circ(a \mapsto b)^{-1}$ we obtain $d \mapsto a \circ a \mapsto b \circ c \mapsto b \circ (a \mapsto b)^{-1}$ equals $d \mapsto a \circ a \mapsto b \circ (a \mapsto b)^{-1} \circ c \mapsto b$ equals $d \mapsto a \circ c \mapsto b$, which may not occur quite plausible at the first view yet, because both pointers do not interfere. Therefore it is required to perform one generic step.

Canonization step I: If a bridge is removed from between sub-heap graphs, then the conjunction needs to be replaced by a heap disjunction.

For the example a bridge is detected between a and b, so $\circ$ may be substituted by $\|$ in the remaining heap term, and so the result appears plausible again. But for sake of completeness heap graph vertices may need to be removed even completely. This becomes urgent especially when it comes to object field locations.

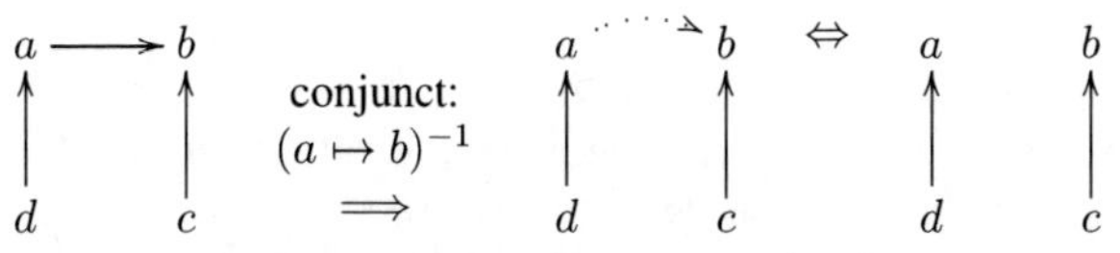

Fig. 6. Heap graph before and after inversion

Canonization step II: Remove some heap graph vertex a entirely whenever there are no more references to it.

Applying those two canonization steps keeps the chosen model sound and confluent (proof skipped here).

Remark: We did not mention heap generalisations explicitly in the previous paragraphs, although it remains to the reader to prove correctness of $H \circ H^{-1} \equiv \underline{emp}$ (proof by induction over $\circ$, use the fact that $(g_1 \circ g_2)^{-1} \equiv g_1^{-1} \circ g_2^{-1}$ holds, so there exists a homomorphism for $.^{-1}$ w.r.t. $\circ$, refer to lemma 3.9).

Convention: Condition (i) implies particularly $\underline{emp} \circ \underline{emp}^{-1} \equiv \underline{emp}$, because we agree on $\underline{emp}^{-1} \equiv \underline{emp}$. □

Subsumption: $H \circ a \mapsto b \circ (a \mapsto b)^{-1}$ denotes:

1) unlink edge between a and b
2) unlink/remove a if there are no more uses in H
3) unlink/remove b as well if no more uses in H

The group properties allow us to define equalities for the separated heap theory. This will allow us, for instance, to define arithmetic equalities, which applied will cause faster convergence to a normalised heap representation. It will lower the risk of highly bloated verification rules and conclusively it will lead us to a smaller logic in combination with partial specification (see section IV). Future work may include heap arithmetics to be implemented by satisfiability-modulo-theory solvers, which will be integrated to the verification process. This approach does not only sound promising, but in fact it was successfully proven concept in several different areas, particularly for bloated and notoriously incomplete Hoare logics.

Lemma 3.9. *$(g_1 \circ g_2)^{-1} \equiv g_1^{-1} \circ g_2^{-1}$ holds for any heaplets g_1 and g_2.*

Proof. Lets generalise this lemma, let $G = g_1 \circ g_2 \circ \cdots \circ g_n$, we need to show $G \circ G^{-1} = \underline{emp}$. This can be shown by induction over n. In the base case ($n = 1$) we have $g_1 \circ g_1^{-1} \equiv \underline{emp}$, which holds because of the existence of an inverse. For the inductive step let $G = \underbrace{(g_1 \circ g_2 \circ \cdots \circ g_k)}_{G_k} \circ g_{k+1}$, then $G \circ G^{-1} = (G_k \circ g_{k+1}) \circ (G_k \circ g_{k+1})^{-1}$ denotes in the inverse part a graph extension. The right part of this equation equals $\underbrace{G_k \circ G_k^{-1}}_{\underline{emp}} \circ \underbrace{g_{k+1} \circ g_{k+1}^{-1}}_{\underline{emp}} \equiv \underline{emp}$ (because of the inductive inversion property). □

Definition 3.10. *Heap disjunction $H \parallel a \mapsto b$ defines heap H and heaplet $a \mapsto b$ which do not interfere, iff G_H is the heap graph of H, $G_H = (V, E)$, and for all edges $(\_, a) \notin E$ and there exists no path from b to H, and there is no path back from H to a.*

That is why $x.b \parallel x.c$ does not hold for any object x with fields b and c, if there exists at least one common vertex on any path from $x.b$ or from $x.c$.

Let $\Sigma = X_0 \| X_1 \| \cdots \| X_n$ with $n > 0$ and X_j is of form $x_j \mapsto y_j$, then $\Sigma = \Sigma_0 \parallel a_0 \mapsto b_0 \Leftrightarrow \forall (a_j \mapsto b_j) \in \Sigma_0 : a_j \neq a_0 \wedge b_j \neq b_0$.

Theorem 3.11. *$G = (\Omega, \|)$ is a monoid and a group, if Ω is the set of heap graphs and $\|$ denotes heap disjunction.*

Proof. In analogy to the previous lemma, first of all, $\forall m_1, m_2 \in \Omega : m_1 \| m_2$, iff m_1 and m_2 have no common joint, which is the case whenever there is no path from m_1 to m_2, and there is not even an indirect heap graph surrounding both m_1 and m_2. If m_1 and m_2 are different, then $m_1 \| m_2$ must be a valid heap $\in \Omega$ again, because m_1 is from a different heap graph part than m_2, and vice versa, so closeness holds. Associativity holds obviously. $\underline{emp}$ may be chosen as neutral element, so $\underline{emp} \| m_1 = m_1 \| \underline{emp} = m_1$, by default let $\underline{emp} \| \underline{emp} = \underline{emp}$ hold. Last, we agree on the convention $s \| s^{-1} = s^{-1} \| s = \underline{emp}$, which behaves similar to $\circ$. Heaps in general obey this rule. □

The heap-wise conjunction and disjunction may be expressed as following:

$$\circ_{[B,C]} \frac{U \circ B \parallel C}{U \circ B \circ C} \qquad \|_{[B,C]} \frac{U \circ B \circ C}{U \circ B \parallel C}$$

$$\|_{[B,C]} ; \circ_{[B,C]} ; \|_{[B,C]} \equiv \|_{[B,C]} \tag{2}$$

$$\circ_{[B,C]} ; \|_{[B,C]} ; \circ_{[B,C]} \equiv \circ_{[B,C]} \tag{3}$$

The operations $\|$ and $\circ$ are dual and self-inverse as can be seen from equations (2) and (3), where ";" is the statement sequentializer. The equations do hold (direct proof, skipped here), because of its self-inverse character and due to the assertion that both specified heap vertices B and C, in fact, exist.

Theorem 3.12. *Distributivity holds for $\forall a, b, c \in \Omega$ for $\circ$ and $\|$:*

(i) $a \circ (b \| c) = (a \circ b) \| (a \circ c)$
(ii) $(b \| c) \circ a = (b \circ a) \| (c \circ a)$

Proof. (direct proof, skipped, take note of Fig. 7). □

Remark: Since the neutral element for both operations, $\circ$ and $\|$, is $\underline{emp}$, there cannot be defined a field over both operations, although lemma 3.7, theorem 3.8 and 3.12 hold, and Ω is finite. Particular heaps would be finite. All operations applied to finite heaps would be finite again.

Remark: In analogy to logical conjuncts $\wedge$ and $\vee$ a $\|$-normalform exists when the previous equalities are applied. Lemma 3.9 can be applied for the inversion of generalised heaps.

In order to optimize reasoning by minimizing graph size, $\|$ should be moved upwards at most in heap terms, e.g., by

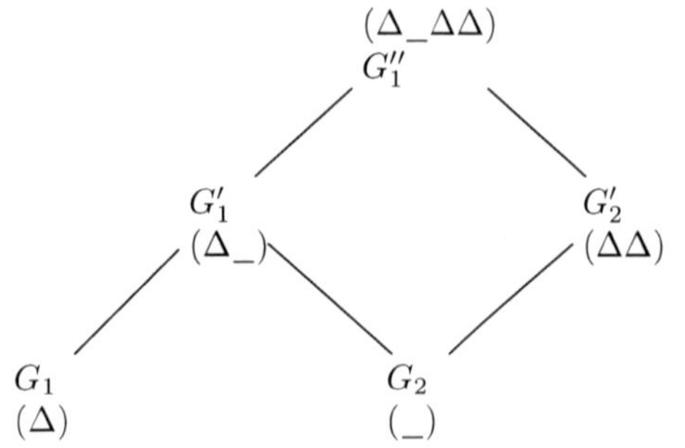

Fig. 7. A partially-ordered set (poset) can be defined for heap graphs under inclusion, the join operator is $\circ$.

applying distributivity rules or by reordering points-to heaps so that the left-hand sides are ordered in lexicographical order by its location. The motivation behind this is, for instance, to optimize incremental verification, so only affected heaps may require re-calculations.

As seen in Fig. 7 a partially-ordered set can always be defined over inclusion of heap graphs. Despite there might be an infimum defined as $\underline{emp}$ and some always existing supremum, the complete heap graph, the structure is still not a (complete) lattice due to non-holding connective properties w.r.t. $\|$ as meet for absorption. The poset G from Fig. 7 contains $\{G_1, G_2, G_1', G_2', G_1''\}$ and can be ordered by the following ascending chains $G_1 \sqsubseteq G_1' \sqsubseteq G_1''$, $G_2 \sqsubseteq G_1'$ and $G_2 \sqsubseteq G_2' \sqsubseteq G_1''$. The supremum is $G_1'', inf(G) = \underline{emp}$, where $\sqsubseteq$ shall be defined as the heap sub-graph relationship. Obviously, if two heaps are not disjoint (this denotes $\underline{emp}$ because of definition 3.4) they may always be connected with each other in the corresponding Hasse-diagram. This join is always valid because of (1st contradiction) $a \mapsto b \circ a \mapsto d$ may not occur after a single heap conjunct, or any composite heap in general (2nd contradiction) $a \mapsto b \| b \mapsto d$ contradicts the definition of $\|$. However, it needs to be taken into consideration that the inclusion-ordering mentioned may be destroyed by applying inverse heaps if used arbitrarily (compare with previous section), but those may usually, at least at the moment, be used only in cases where a difference between expected and actual heap graphs needs to be calculated rather than a desired heap graph specification, so the locality property mentioned from section I remains untouched.

IV. Partial Heap Specification

Having said earlier after definition 3.1 class objects may be considered as containers of fields $obj.f_1 \mapsto .. \circ obj.f_2 \mapsto .. \circ obj.f_n \mapsto ..$, all fields constitute a scoped heap (in analogy to single points-to local variables among abstract predicates). Since class object fields may not exist independently from other fields of the same class, they must by convention be $\circ$-conjuncted. In contrast to locals, object fields too require a possibility to specify only parts, hence constants from definition 3.2 are parameterised to $\underline{true}(obj)$ or $\underline{false}(obj)$. Abstract predicates modularise specifications, they can particularly be used to specify objects from unrelated objects and locals. W.r.t. the proposed stack-based implementation of a "$a \circ a$"-decider incoming and outgoing terms for abstract predicates may be traced in order to skip re-verficiation of unaffected parts.

Definition 4.1. *A partial heap specification $\underline{t}(o)$ for some object o is defined as a $\circ$-conjunction of all remaining fields, possibly none, that are not specified until $\underline{t}$ is used and unfold in the current object scope. When $\underline{t}$ is used all actual fields are unfold into the surrounding heap specification, which are not yet been specified in terms of the current scope of o.*

Example 4.2. *Lets say object a has three fields f_1, g_1 and g_2, and $\mathcal{C}[\![]\!]$ denotes some (implicit) heap term denotation of type $(ET \to ET) \to \{true, false\}$, where the first extended heap is supposed to be the expected and the second extended heap is supposed to be the actual heap term then*

$$\begin{aligned} \mathcal{C}[\![a.f_1 \mapsto x \circ \underline{true}(a)]\!] = \ & \mathcal{C}[\![a.f_1 \circ a.g_1 \circ a.g_2]\!] \\ = \ \mathcal{C}[\![\underline{true}(a) \circ a.f_1 \mapsto x]\!] \neq \ & \mathcal{C}[\![p(a) \circ a.f_1 \mapsto x]\!] \end{aligned}$$

where p is some abstract predicate denoting $\underline{true}(a)$. However, $\mathcal{C}[\![a.f_1 \mapsto x \circ p(a)]\!]$ would denote equality, because the stack-oriented recognition finds all remaining fields even when obfuscated beneath several predicate levels. $\mathcal{C}[\![]\!]$ is a homomorphic mapping regarding $\circ$.

Example 4.3. $\mathcal{C}[\![\underline{true}(a) \circ \underline{true}(a)]\!] = \mathcal{C}[\![a.f_1 \circ a.g_1 \circ a.g_2]\!] \circ \mathcal{C}[\![\underline{true}(a)]\!] = \mathcal{C}[\![a.f_1 \circ a.g_1 \circ a.g_2]\!] \circ \underline{emp}(a)$.

V. Discussions

By exchanging one ambiguous spatial heap operator by two strict operations, the initial and core properties of a Separation Logic did not change essentially, except an unbound and arbitrary heap inversion as discussed in section IV. The introduction of a strict normalform allows a linear and local analysis of the heap terms without an eager comparison of still non-matched conjuncts.

As mentioned in section III there arises the question of inconsistency, whether in remote parts of the same specification, for instance, somewhere up or down relative to the current abstract predicate calling stack, there are in fact two identical heaplets or if there are any two pointers with the same location multiple times. The reason beyond is non-repetitiveness.

This problem may be resolved in general only dynamically during the verification due to the undecidability of abstract predicates due to the undecidability of the Halting-problem. Hence a stack-based analysis for processing abstract predicates is needed very similar to the operational semantics provided by Warren [15] including processing of symbols and back-references to the stack parameters, except that abstract predicates require an adapted reasoning control (see [14]). Applying Warren's approach to strict heap conjunction and disjunction will decide $\forall a.a \circ a$. Because of ungrounded symbols, a memoizer may not cope with global states in abstract predicates.

Prolog is a general purpose logical programming language [16]. We strongly believe Prolog may be used to reason about extended heap terms and abstract predicates in order to resolve key heap verification problems, such as expressibility restrictions [14]. One advantage of Prolog predicates over classic *one-way* functions (as used in [4], for instance) is that input and output terms may be considered as relation, unioning exponentially many different combinations of input and output vectors, skipping only those combinations where a relation is not defined. This is often the case when the corresponding one-way function is either non-invertible, contains cuts or arithmetic evaluations (e.g. by using the built-in predicate `is`). There must be a strong correlation between input and output vectors, s.t. a bijective mapping exists between both vectors for the most common definition. Besides, Prolog predicates containing cuts may always be rewritten w.l.o.g. cut-free. Predicates containing `is` may be rewritten without as ground term, e.g. a Church number, as long as it can be represented as unifiable term, which is feasible even if not too elegantly.

The "*Object Constraint Language*" (OCL) [17] is a specification language for class-instantiated objects in companion with the "*Unified Modeling Language*". It implements a fragment of the predicate logic, it supports some quantification of variables and supports collection types and ad-hoc polymorphism by sub-classing. It allows life-cycle specification of objects and class methods. However, OCL does not know of pointer constraints like aliasing. If pointer constraints were added to OCL and propagated down to code generation when compiling user code, for instance, then code performance could significantly improve (compare with [14]). In combination with abstract predicates the proposed modification of this paper may be used as proposition for an update of the recent OCL recommendation w.r.t. the intrinsic points-to model, particularly referring here to conventions 2.3, and definitions 3.1 and 3.2. Presumably, this would also raise expressibility, abstraction and higher modularity. Previous attempts to demonstrate applications of Separation Logic to Design Patterns can be found for instance in [4].

VI. Conclusions

At the beginning, the problem of verifying dynamic heap was introduced. Related problems and the benefit of the heap separation model were provided. The description of points-to assertions corresponds to heap-manipulating program statements – in the chosen model the generated heap graph is described edge-wise. The problem with the $\star$-operator was that it may be used syntactically and semantically in two different ways: for heap disjunction, but also for heap conjunction. This caused the described issues. The introduction of two strict heap operations allows heap terms to be interpreted simple. In addition to this, partial object specifications make it promising to understand and control better completeness w.r.t. incoming heaps in heap formulae. Properties of both operations were investigated and found restrictive, but still flexible enough for expressing arbitrary heap graphs. The integration of derived rules to a SMT-solver requires further research. Finally an extension of the current OCL was proposed.

Acknowledgement

Some parts of this paper have been prepared within the scope of project part of the state plan of the Board of Education and Science of Russia (task # 2.136.2014/K).

References

[1] R. Jones, A. Hosking, and E. Moss, *The Garbage Collection Handbook: The Art of Automatic Memory Management*, 1st ed. Chapman & Hall/CRC Press, 2011.

[2] J. C. Reynolds, *Separation Logic: A logic for shared mutable data structures*, in Lecture Notes in Computer Science, Springer, pp. 55–74, 2002.

[3] R. M. Burstall, *Some techniques for proving correctness of programs which alter data structures*, in *Machine Intelligence 7*, B. Meltzer and D. Michie (eds.), Edinburgh University Press, Scotland, pp. 23–50, 1972.

[4] M. Parkinson, *Local reasoning for Java*, Ph.D. thesis, Cambridge University, England, 2005, 159p.

[5] J. Berdine, C. Calcagno, and P. W. O'Hearn, *Smallfoot: Modular automatic assertion checking with Separation Logic*, in Lecture Notes in Computer Science, Springer, pp. 115–137, 2005.

[6] M. Sagiv, T. Reps, and R. Wilhelm, *Parametric shape analysis via 3-valued logic*, ACM Transactions of Programming Language Systems, vol. 24(3), pp. 217–298, 2002.

[7] M. Abadi, *Baby Modula-3 and a Theory of Object*, Systems Research Center, Digital Equipment Corporation, Technical Report, 1993. ftp://gatekeeper.research.compaq.com/pub/DEC/SRC/research-reports/abstracts/src-rr-095.html

[8] M. Abadi and K. R. M. Leino, *A Logic of Object-Oriented Programs*, in TAPSOFT '97: Proceedings of the 7th International Joint Conference CAAP/FASE on Theory and Practice of Software Development, Springer, pp. 682–696, 1997.

[9] N. Suzuki, *Analysis of Pointer "Rotation"*, Communications of the ACM, vol. 25(5), pp. 330–335, 1982.

[10] B. Meyer, *Proving pointer program properties - Part 1: Context and overview, Part 2: The overall object structure*, ETH Zürich, Journal of Object Technology, 2003.

[11] A. W. Appel, *Garbage collection can be faster than stack allocation*, Information Processing Letters, vol. 25(4), pp. 275–279, 1987. http://dx.doi.org/10.1016/0020-0190(87)90175-X

[12] K. Dosen, et. al, *Substructural Logics*, K. Dosen and P. Schroeder-Heister (eds.) Clarendon Press, Oxford Science Publications, 1993, 386p.

[13] G. Restall, *On logics without contraction," Ph.D. thesis*, Department of Philosophy, University of Queensland, 1994, 278p.

[14] R. Haberland and S. Ivanovskiy, *Dynamically allocated memory verification in object-oriented programs using Prolog*, in Proceedings of the 8th Spring/Summer Young Researchers' Colloquium on Software Engineering, A. Kamkin, A. Petrenko, and A. Terekhov (eds.), pp. 46–50, 2014.

[15] D. H. Warren, *Applied logic - its use and implementation as a programming tool*, SRI International, Menlo Park, California, USA, Technical Report No. 290, 1983.

[16] L. Sterling and E. Shapiro, *The Art of Prolog (2nd Edition): Advanced Programming Techniques*. MIT Press, Cambridge, Massachusetts, USA, 1994.

[17] Object Management Group (OMG), *Object Constraint Language Specification*, version 2.2, Feb 2010, http://www.omg.org/spec/OCL/2.2.

A Cell-Centered Lagrangian Method Based on Characteristics Theory For Numerically Simulating Condensed Explosive Detonation

Ming Yu
Key Laboratory for Computational Physics, Institute of Applied Physics and Computational Mathematics
Beijing, China
E-mail: yu_ming@iapcm.ac.cn

Zhibo Ma
Institute of Applied Physics and Computational Mathematics
Beijing, China
E-mail: ma_zhibo@iapcm.ac.cn

Abstract—**The paper proposes a cell-centered Lagrangian method for numerically simulating two-dimensional detonation flows in condensed explosives. The main feature of this method is that the velocity and pressure at the mesh vertex are computed using the characteristics theory in terms of the linearized partial differential equations about the detonation flows, and then the velocity and pressure are used to update the grid coordinates and evaluate the numerical flux across the cell interface. This vertex solver gives the instantaneous evolution solutions for velocity and pressure, which is regarded as a generalization of Riemann solver for one-dimensional Godunov scheme in multidimensional flows.**

Keywords-cell-centered Lagrangian method; characteristics theory; condensed explosive; detonation.

I. INTRODUCTION

The staggered-grid Lagrangian (SGL) method, where the kinematic variables are defined at the vertex of the mesh and the state variables are defined at the center of the mesh cell, is currently the most extensive way to numerically simulating explosive detonation flows [1]. However, SGL method has the following main disadvantages: 1) unable to preserve the conservation of the total energy; 2) always smooth the discontinuity of detonation with artificial viscosity; 3) difficult to adopt high precision for temporal and spatial discretization; 4) easy to produce the spurious motion of the mesh; 5) nonsynchronous time advance between the momentum equation and the mass and internal energy equations.

To eliminate these deficiencies, a highly promising alternative to SGL method is to use cell-centered Lagrangian (CCL) method [2][3], where all physical variables are defined at the center of the mesh cell, and the numerical scheme is constructed by integrating directly the conservation system of detonation flows on each moving cell with finite volume discretization. So, the key technique of CCL method lies in the determination of the velocity at the mesh vertex from the physical variables at the center of mesh cell, especially in multidimensional cases. An important contribution of this paper is to give a new idea to determine the physical variables at the mesh vertex in 2D detonation flows using the characteristics theory of partial differential equation.

The paper is organized as follows. In Section 2, we give the cell-centered finite volume method for detonation flows equations in the Lagrangian formulation. In Section 3, the vertex solver to compute velocity and pressure at vertex of the cell by local evolution Galerkin operator is derived. In Section 4 some numerical tests are shown to demonstrate the excellent performance of this new scheme. Some main conclusions are presented in Section 5.

II. THE GOVERNING EQUATIONS OF DETONATION AND THE FINITE VOLUME SCHEME

The governing equations of detonation flows in Lagrangian formulation are as follows:

$$\frac{d}{dt}\int_{\Omega(t)} d\Omega = \int_{\partial\Omega(t)} \boldsymbol{u}\cdot\boldsymbol{n}dl \tag{1.1}$$

$$\frac{d}{dt}\int_{\Omega(t)} \rho d\Omega = 0 \tag{1.2}$$

$$\frac{d}{dt}\int_{\Omega(t)} \rho\boldsymbol{u} d\Omega = -\int_{\partial\Omega(t)} p\boldsymbol{n}dl \tag{1.3}$$

$$\frac{d}{dt}\int_{\Omega(t)} \rho E d\Omega = -\int_{\partial\Omega(t)} p\boldsymbol{u}\cdot\boldsymbol{n}dl \tag{1.4}$$

$$\frac{d}{dt}\int_{\Omega(t)} \rho\lambda d\Omega = \int_{\Omega(t)} \rho r d\Omega \tag{1.5}$$

where ρ is the density, u and v are component velocities, p is pressure, E is specific total energy, $E = e + (u^2 + v^2)/2$, e is specific internal energy, and $\Omega(t)$ is a control volume with the boundary $\partial\Omega(t)$, dl is the differential length of the surface for the control volume, r is the chemical reaction rate of explosives detonation, in which Ignition-Growth model is adopted [4].

On Lagrangian hydrodynamics, a control volume moves along with the fluid particle with the trajectory equations:

$$\frac{dx}{dt} = u,\ \frac{dy}{dt} = v \tag{2}$$

For a given control volume Ω with the mass $m_\Omega = \int_\Omega \rho d\Omega$ and area $A_\Omega = \int_\Omega d\Omega$, the average value of any physical variable f is $\bar{f}_\Omega = \frac{1}{m_\Omega}\int_\Omega \rho f d\Omega$. Thus, for 2D flows, (1.2) becomes an algebraic equation $\bar{\rho}_\Omega A_\Omega = m_\Omega = \text{const}$, and Eqs. (1.1) and (1.3)-(1.5) can be written as the following semi-discrete expression:

$$\frac{d\bar{\boldsymbol{q}}_\Omega}{dt} = -\frac{1}{m_\Omega}\int_{\partial\Omega} \boldsymbol{H}\cdot\boldsymbol{n}dl + \bar{\boldsymbol{r}}_\Omega \tag{3}$$

where $\bar{\boldsymbol{q}}_\Omega = \left(-\bar{\tau}_\Omega, \bar{u}_\Omega, \bar{v}_\Omega, \bar{E}_\Omega, \bar{\lambda}_\Omega\right)^T$, $\boldsymbol{H} = (u, p, 0, pu, 0)^T \boldsymbol{i} + (v, 0, p, pv, 0)^T \boldsymbol{j}$, $\bar{\boldsymbol{r}} = \left(0,0,0,0,\bar{r}_\Omega\right)^T$, $\bar{\tau}_\Omega = 1/\bar{\rho}_\Omega$.

For any non-overlapping structured quadrilateral mesh with sides denoted by l_k (k=1,2,3,4), the semi-discrete finite volume discretization of Eq.(3) can be written as:

$$\frac{d\bar{\boldsymbol{q}}_\Omega}{dt} = -\frac{1}{m_c}\sum_{k=1}^{4}\int_{l_k} \boldsymbol{H}\cdot\boldsymbol{n}\,dl + \bar{\boldsymbol{r}}_\Omega \tag{4}$$

Due to the fact that a semi-discrete model describes the instantaneous behavior of the dynamical system at its initial time, the full discretization of Eq.(4) can be turned into the following form by means of the trapezia rule to evaluate the numerical integration of the interface flux in structured grids:

$$\bar{\boldsymbol{q}}_\Omega^{(n+1)} = \bar{\boldsymbol{q}}_\Omega^{(n)} - \frac{\Delta t}{2m_\Omega}\left\{\sum_{i=1}^{4}\left[\boldsymbol{H}_i\left(\boldsymbol{E}_0\,\bar{\boldsymbol{q}}_\Omega^{(n)}\right) + \boldsymbol{H}_{i+1}\left(\boldsymbol{E}_0\,\bar{\boldsymbol{q}}_\Omega^{(n)}\right)\right]\cdot\boldsymbol{n}_{i,i+1}\Delta l_{i,i+1}\right\} + \boldsymbol{r}\left(\bar{\boldsymbol{q}}_\Omega^{(n+1)}\right) \tag{5}$$

where $\boldsymbol{E}_0$ is the vertex solver to compute the instantaneous solutions at the mesh vertex at time $t_n^+ = t_n + 0$, namely there is $\boldsymbol{q}(t_n^+) = \boldsymbol{E}_0\boldsymbol{q}(t_n)$, and subscript i is the numbering of the vertices counterclockwise for a quadrilateral grid.

From Eq.(2) and Eq.(5), the velocity and pressure of a vertex of a mesh cell must be obtained. Here, the velocity and pressure of a vertex are solved by the characteristics theory of partial differential equation.

III. VERTEX SOLVER $\boldsymbol{E}_0$ BY CHARACTERISTICS THOERY

To obtain the analytical expressions of the vertex solver $\boldsymbol{E}_0$ by means of the characteristics theory of hyperbolic partial differential equations, the quasilinear and heterogeneous detonation equations (6.1) can be transformed into a locally linearized and homogeneous system (6.2) in terms of the primitive variables:

$$\frac{d\boldsymbol{w}}{dt} + \boldsymbol{A}(\boldsymbol{w})\frac{\partial\boldsymbol{w}}{\partial x} + \boldsymbol{B}(\boldsymbol{w})\frac{\partial\boldsymbol{w}}{\partial y} = \boldsymbol{r}_w,\quad \boldsymbol{w}_0 = \boldsymbol{w}(t_n) \tag{6.1}$$

$$\frac{d\hat{\boldsymbol{w}}}{dt} + \boldsymbol{A}(\boldsymbol{w}_0)\frac{\partial\hat{\boldsymbol{w}}}{\partial x} + \boldsymbol{B}(\boldsymbol{w}_0)\frac{\partial\hat{\boldsymbol{w}}}{\partial y} = 0,\quad \hat{\boldsymbol{w}}_0 = \boldsymbol{w}(t_n) \tag{6.2}$$

where $\boldsymbol{w} = \hat{\boldsymbol{w}} = \begin{bmatrix}\rho\\ u\\ v\\ p\\ \lambda\end{bmatrix}$, $\boldsymbol{A}(\boldsymbol{w}) = \begin{bmatrix}0 & \rho & 0 & 0 & 0\\ 0 & 0 & 0 & \frac{1}{\rho} & 0\\ 0 & 0 & 0 & 0 & 0\\ 0 & \rho c_\lambda^2 & 0 & 0 & 0\\ 0 & 0 & 0 & 0 & 0\end{bmatrix}$, $\boldsymbol{r}_w = \begin{bmatrix}0\\ 0\\ 0\\ r\frac{\partial p}{\partial\lambda}\\ r\end{bmatrix}$,

$\boldsymbol{B}(\boldsymbol{w})$ is similar to $\boldsymbol{A}(\boldsymbol{w})$, and c_λ is the sonic speed.

We can prove the equality $\boldsymbol{w}(t_n^+) = \hat{\boldsymbol{w}}(t_n^+)$ as follows.

Proof:

From the Taylor expansion, it holds:

$$\begin{aligned}\boldsymbol{w}(t_n+\tau) &= \boldsymbol{w}(t_n) + \frac{d\boldsymbol{w}}{dt}\tau + O(\tau^2)\\ &= \boldsymbol{w}_0 - \boldsymbol{A}(\boldsymbol{w})\frac{\partial\boldsymbol{w}}{\partial x}\tau - \boldsymbol{B}(\boldsymbol{w})\frac{\partial\boldsymbol{w}}{\partial y}\tau + \boldsymbol{r}_w\tau + O(\tau^2)\end{aligned}$$

$$\begin{aligned}\hat{\boldsymbol{w}}(t_n+\tau) &= \hat{\boldsymbol{w}}(t_n) + \frac{d\hat{\boldsymbol{w}}}{dt}\tau + O(\tau^2)\\ &= \hat{\boldsymbol{w}}_0 - \boldsymbol{A}(\hat{\boldsymbol{w}}_0)\frac{\partial\boldsymbol{v}}{\partial x}\tau - \boldsymbol{B}(\hat{\boldsymbol{w}}_0)\frac{\partial\hat{\boldsymbol{w}}}{\partial y}\tau + O(\tau^2),\end{aligned}$$

There is

$$\begin{aligned}&\boldsymbol{w}(t_n+\tau) - \hat{\boldsymbol{w}}(t_n+\tau)\\ &= \left(\boldsymbol{A}(\boldsymbol{w}_0)\frac{\partial\hat{\boldsymbol{w}}}{\partial x} - \boldsymbol{A}(\boldsymbol{w})\frac{\partial\boldsymbol{w}}{\partial x}\right)\tau + \left(\boldsymbol{B}(\boldsymbol{w}_0)\frac{\partial\hat{\boldsymbol{w}}}{\partial y} - \boldsymbol{B}(\boldsymbol{w})\frac{\partial\boldsymbol{v}}{\partial y}\right)\tau + \boldsymbol{r}_w\tau + O(\tau^2)\end{aligned} \tag{7}$$

A limit operation is carried out for the Eq.(7), and we have:

$$\lim_{\tau\to 0}\left(\boldsymbol{w}(t_n+\tau) - \hat{\boldsymbol{w}}(t_n+\tau)\right) = 0,$$

namely, $\boldsymbol{w}(t_n^+) = \hat{\boldsymbol{w}}(t_n^+)$.

End.

Because of $\hat{\boldsymbol{w}}(t_n^+) = \lim_{\tau\to 0}\hat{\boldsymbol{w}}(t_n+\tau)$, the expression of $\hat{\boldsymbol{w}}(t_n^+)$ may be obtained from $\hat{\boldsymbol{w}}(t_n+\tau)$ firstly, and the limit operation can be carried out secondly.

For convenience, Eq.(6.2) can be transformed into the following quasi-diagonalized system by means of left multiplication of the eigen-matrix:

$$\frac{d\boldsymbol{v}}{dt} + \boldsymbol{\Lambda}_A\frac{\partial\boldsymbol{v}}{\partial x} + \boldsymbol{\Lambda}_B\frac{\partial\boldsymbol{v}}{\partial y} = \boldsymbol{s} \tag{8}$$

where $\boldsymbol{v}$ is the eigenvector, $\boldsymbol{v} = \boldsymbol{R}^{-1}\hat{\boldsymbol{w}}$, $\boldsymbol{R}$ is the right eigen-matrix of a matrix pencil $\boldsymbol{C} = \cos\theta\boldsymbol{A}(\boldsymbol{w}_0) + \sin\theta\boldsymbol{B}(\boldsymbol{w}_0)$ ($\theta\in[0,2\pi]$) and has the right eigenvectors $\boldsymbol{r}_l$ ($l = 1,2,3,4,5$); and there are $\boldsymbol{\Lambda}_A = diag[\lambda_{A,1},\lambda_{A,2},\lambda_{A,3},\lambda_{A,4},\lambda_{A,5}]$ and $\boldsymbol{\Lambda}_B = diag[\lambda_{B,1},\lambda_{B,2},\lambda_{B,3},\lambda_{B,4},\lambda_{B,5}]$.

Obviously, it can be found from the characteristics theory of two-dimensional first-order hyperbolic partial differential equations that, given the physical state $\boldsymbol{w}_0 = \tilde{\boldsymbol{w}} = (\tilde{\rho},\tilde{u},\tilde{v},\tilde{p},\tilde{\lambda})$ at initial time-space point $\tilde{P} = (x,y,t)_{t=t_n}$, the every characteristics variable v_l ($l = 1,2,3,4,5$) at any time-space point $P = (x,y,t)_{t=t_n+\tau}$ would evolve for the time τ along the corresponding bicharacteristics line and then can be written into [5][6]:

$$\begin{aligned}v_l(P,\theta) &= v_l[\tilde{P}(\theta)]\\ &+ \int_{t_n}^{t_n+\tau} s_l[x-\lambda_{A,l}(\theta)(t_n+\tau-\xi),\ y-\lambda_{B,l}(\theta)(t_n+\tau-\xi),\ \xi]d\xi\end{aligned} \tag{9}$$

By left multiplying Eq.(9) through $\hat{\boldsymbol{w}} = \boldsymbol{R}\boldsymbol{v}$ and then integrating with respect to θ from 0 to 2π, it leads to:

$$\hat{\boldsymbol{w}}(P) = \frac{1}{2\pi}\int_0^{2\pi}\left\{\sum_{l=1}^{5}\boldsymbol{r}_l\left[v_l\left(\tilde{P}(\theta)\right) + s_l(\theta)\right]\right\}d\theta \tag{10}$$

For discretized structured grids, $\tilde{P} = (x,y,t)_{t=t_n}$ is assumed to be time-space position of any vertex. Obviously, the vertex is shared by four grid cells, and θ_{ka} and θ_{kb} are respectively assumed to be the starting and ending angles of the kth ($k\le 4$) grid cell of the shared vertex, thus Eq.(10) can be rewritten into:

$$\begin{aligned}u(P) &= \frac{1}{2}u(\tilde{P}) + \frac{1}{2\pi}\sum_{k=1}^{4}\int_{\theta_{ka}}^{\theta_{kb}}\left[-\frac{p(\tilde{Q})}{\tilde{\rho}\tilde{c}_\lambda}\cos\theta + u(\tilde{Q})\cos^2\theta + v(\tilde{Q})\sin\theta\cos\theta\right]d\theta\\ &+ \frac{1}{2\pi}\sum_{k=1}^{4}\int_{\theta_{ka}}^{\theta_{kb}}\int_{t_n}^{t_n+\tau} S[\boldsymbol{z}+\tilde{c}_\lambda(t_n+\tau-\xi)\boldsymbol{n}(\theta),\xi,\theta]\cos\theta\, d\xi\, d\theta\,\frac{1}{2\tilde{\rho}}\int_{t_n}^{t_n+\tau}\frac{\partial p(\boldsymbol{z},\xi)}{\partial x}d\xi\end{aligned} \tag{11}$$

$$v(P)=\frac{1}{2}v(\tilde{P})+\frac{1}{2\pi}\sum_{k=1}^{4}\int_{\theta_{ka}}^{\theta_{kb}}\left[-\frac{p(\tilde{Q})}{\tilde{\rho}\tilde{c}_{\lambda}}\sin\theta+u(\tilde{Q})\cos\theta\sin\theta+v(\tilde{Q})\sin^{2}\theta\right]d\theta$$
$$+\frac{1}{2\pi}\sum_{k=1}^{4}\int_{\theta_{ka}}^{\theta_{kb}}\int_{t_n}^{t_n+\tau}S[\boldsymbol{z}+\tilde{c}(t_n+\tau-\xi)\boldsymbol{n}(\theta),\xi,\theta]\sin\theta d\xi d\theta-\frac{1}{2\tilde{\rho}}\int_{t_n}^{t_n+\tau}\frac{\partial p(\boldsymbol{z},\xi)}{\partial y}d\xi \quad (12)$$

$$p(P)=\frac{1}{2\pi}\sum_{k=1}^{4}\int_{\theta_{ka}}^{\theta_{kb}}\left[p(\tilde{Q})-\tilde{\rho}\tilde{c}_{\lambda}u(\tilde{Q})\cos\theta-\tilde{\rho}\tilde{c}_{\lambda}v(\tilde{Q})\sin\theta\right]d\theta$$
$$-\frac{1}{2\pi}\tilde{\rho}\tilde{c}_{\lambda}\sum_{k=1}^{4}\int_{\theta_{ka}}^{\theta_{kb}}\int_{t_n}^{t_n+\tau}S[\boldsymbol{z}+\tilde{c}(t_n+\tau-\xi)\boldsymbol{n}(\theta),\xi,\theta]d\xi d\theta \quad (13)$$

Equtions.(11)-(13) are the exact evolution solutions of the locally linearized and homogeneous system (6.2). The instantaneous evolution solutions of Eqs.(11)-(13) at time $t_n^+=t_n+0$ can be obtained by means of the limit operations in terms of $\tau\to 0$, and then the analytical expressions of the vertex solver $\boldsymbol{E}_0$ are as follows:

$$u(t_n^+)=\frac{1}{\pi}\sum_{k=1}^{4}\left[-\frac{\tilde{p}_k}{\tilde{\rho}\tilde{c}_{\lambda}}(\sin\theta_{kb}-\sin\theta_{ka})\right.$$
$$\left.+\tilde{u}_k\left(\frac{\theta_{kb}-\theta_{ka}}{2}+\frac{\sin 2\theta_{kb}-\sin 2\theta_{ka}}{4}\right)-\tilde{v}_k\frac{\cos 2\theta_{kb}-\cos 2\theta_{ka}}{4}\right] \quad (14)$$

$$v(t_n^+)=\frac{1}{\pi}\sum_{k=1}^{4}\left[\frac{\tilde{p}_k}{\tilde{\rho}\tilde{c}_{\lambda}}(\cos\theta_{kb}-\cos\theta_{ka})\right.$$
$$\left.-\tilde{u}_k\frac{\cos 2\theta_{kb}-\cos 2\theta_{ka}}{4}+\tilde{v}_k\left(\frac{\theta_{kb}-\theta_{ka}}{2}-\frac{\sin 2\theta_{kb}-\sin 2\theta_{ka}}{4}\right)\right] \quad (15)$$

$$p(t_n^+)=\frac{1}{2\pi}\sum_{k=1}^{4}[\tilde{p}_k(\theta_{kb}-\theta_{ka})-\tilde{\rho}\tilde{c}_{\lambda}\tilde{u}_k(\sin\theta_{kb}-\sin\theta_{ka})+\tilde{\rho}\tilde{c}_{\lambda}\tilde{v}_k(\cos\theta_{kb}-\cos\theta_{ka})] \quad (16)$$

IV. NUMERICAL EXAMPLES

The steady structure of 1D planar detonation wave, unsteady propagation of 1D spherically divergent detonation wave and 2D rectangular diffraction of planar detonation wave in high explosive PBX9502 [1] are investigated. Here, only the results of 1D planar detonation wave are given. The calculating length of explosive takes 5.0cm, and the explosive is initiated by the Chapman-Jougeut condition [1] at its left hand side. The distributions of pressure and velocity in chemical reaction zone are obtained, and comparisons are made with the exact solutions. Figure 1 gives the results where the mesh sizes are $\Delta x=1/100$, $1/200$, $1/500$, $1/1000$ cm respectively. From Figure 1, the shock front of detonation wave is well resolved and the spurious oscillation does not appear in the vicinity of the shock discontinuity. Meanwhile, when the mesh size is less than $1/500$ cm (about 50 meshes in the reaction zone), the calculating solutions agree well with the exact solutions. It means that this method has good resolution and convergence. Figure 2 shows the change of pressure and velocity at several typical times on the course of unsteady propagation of the detonation, in which the discretized mesh is $\Delta x=1/500$ cm and the corresponding time are: t=0.06, 0.12, 0.24, 0.48, 0.96, 1.44, 1.92, 2.40, 2.88, 3.36, 3.84, 4.32, 4.80, 5.28μs. From the results, the pressure grows much faster and the steady state reaches about 3.84μs after initiating by Chapman-Jougeut conditions, and the propagation velocity is about 0.7670 cm/μs after the steady state. The change course is almost identical with the experimental results [7].

These numerical examples demonstrate the excellent performance of the presented cell-centered Lagrangian method.

V. CONCLUSIONS

This paper proposes a cell-centered Lagrangian method for 2D detonation flows in condensed explosives. Its main feature is that the vertex solver is based on the characteristics theory in terms of the linearized partial differential equations of the detonation flows, which is essentially a multidimensional Riemann solver taking "multidimensional effect" into account in a natural way. From the calculated course, the CCL method is able to preserve the conservation of the total energy by solving the total energy equation, to preserve the good resolution of the discontinuity of detonation without artificial viscosity, to eliminate the unphysical motion of mesh, and keep the synchronous time advance between the momentum equation and the mass and internal energy equations. Our future most important works will be on the generalization of high-order precision and high resolution, and the extension to arbitrary Lagrangian-Eulerian method.

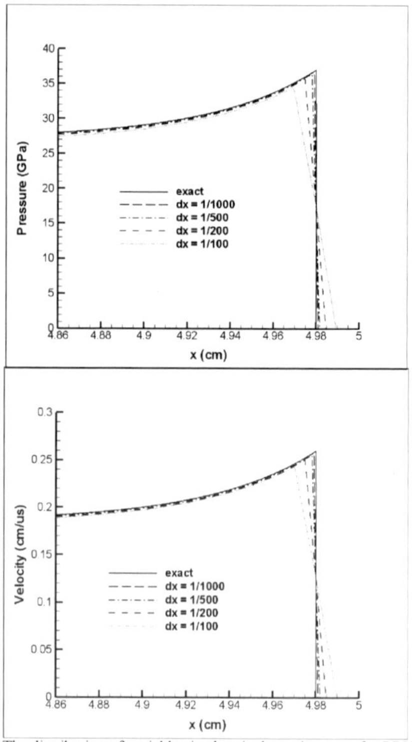

Fig.1 The distribution of variables in chemical reaction zone for PBX9502

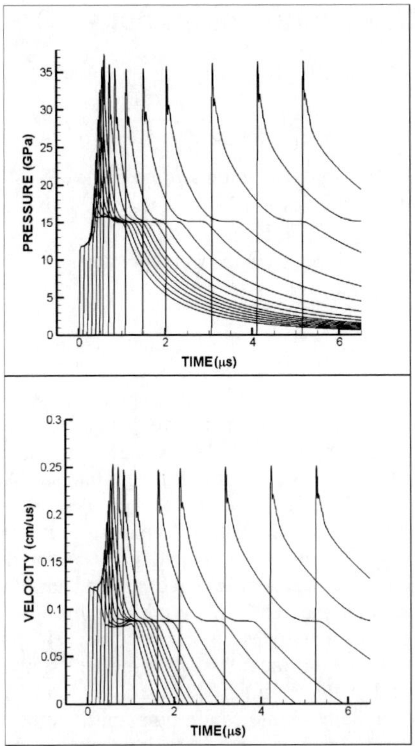

Fig.2 The growth course of one-dimensional planar detonation for PBX9502

ACKNOWLEDGMENT

This research is supported by Natural Science Foundation of China with Grant No. 11272064.

REFERENCES

[1] C. L. Mader, Numerical modeling of explosives and propellants, 2nd edition, CRC Press, New York, 1998.

[2] B. Després and C. Mazeran, Lagrangian gas dynamics in two dimensions and Lagrangian systems, Archive for Rational Mechanics and Analysis, 178: 327–372, 2005.

[3] P.H. Maire, R. Abgrall and J. Breil, A cell-centered Lagrangian scheme for two-dimensional compressible flow problems, SIAM Journal of Scientific Computing, 29(4):1781-1824, 2007.

[4] E.L. Lee and C.M. Tarver, Phenomenological model of shock initiation in heterogeneous explosives. Phys. Fluids, 23:2362–272, 1980.

[5] M. Lukáčová-Medvid'ová and K. W. Morton, Finite volume evolution Galerkin methods: A survey. Ind. J. Pur. Appl. Math., 41: 329-361, 2010.

[6] P. Prasad, Nonlinear Hyperbolic Waves in Multi-Dimensions, Monographs and Surveys in Pure and Applied Mathematics, 121, Chapman & Hall/CRC, New York, 2001.

[7] C.W. Sun, Y.Z. Wei and Z.K. Zhou, Applied Detonation Physics, National Defense Industrial Press of China, 2000 (In Chinese).

Reliability Assessment Based on Modelling and Simulations

Zhibo Ma
Institute of Applied Physics and Computational Mathematics
Beijing, China
E-mail: mazhibo@iapcm.ac.cn

Ming Yu
Key Laboratory for Computational Physics, Institute of Applied Physics and Computational Mathematics
Beijing, China
E-mail: yu_ming@iapcm.ac.cn

Abstract—**Reliability assessments are generally carried out via tests. When a complex system has no opportunity to experience a system-level test, Modelling & Simulations (M&S) will be the only approach to assess the system reliability, and the Uncertainty Quantification (UQ) for M&S becomes one of the most important techniques. With a method named Quantification of Margin and Uncertainty (QMU), reliability could be assessed as to make decisions whether the indices have reached the demands. With our newly proposed UQ method, QMU could be effectively actualized based on M&S. With an example of reliability assessment for a stockpiled product, the main ideas and the implementation of QMU are demonstrated.**

Keywords- modelling & simulation;uncertainty quantification; calibration; verification & validation; reliability assessment.

I. Introduction

Reliability assessment can be regarded as a decision making process in which a decision should be reached whether the reliability of products meets the demands. Traditionally, such decision making is built on tests, which have a solid base of epistemology because of the natural creditability about test data. Owing to the impacts from politics, economy and security, etc., some complicated products can not be subjected to system-level test, so it is necessary to predict their performances by scientific computing [1]. After the moratorium on the testing of nuclear weapons in 1992, National Nuclear Security Administration (NNSA) of the United States developed a Stockpile Stewardship Program (SSP) to assess the nuclear stockpile without nuclear testing, and a new method named QMU was developed for SSP [2]. For QMU implementation, there is an intense divarication how to define the Margin (M) and Uncertainty (U). In 2009, we suggested to choose probability as QMU metric when failure can not be absolutely eliminated due to aleatory uncertainties in products, by which QMU gained an unified decision criterion as confidence factor C=M/U is greater than unity or not [3]. In 2011, Sentz et al. proposed a similar method when failures are inevitable owing to the unbounded stochastic variables [4]. After that, uncertainty quantification for M&S was left to be the main bottleneck in QMU application.

Many literature works exist on UQ of M&S, but the existing methods are roughly falling into two types. One is by comparing the simulation results and the test data [5], the other is by propagating uncertainties from the input variables to the simulation results [6][7][8]. Unfortunately, when system-level test is forbidden, the approach with comparison can not be used. Considering the probability that the systematic deviations may be neglected, and that the uncertainties may be overestimated especially when too many uncertain inputs exist, the propagated uncertainties can not be directly considered as the uncertainties of M&S used for prediction. In order to resolve this problem, we propose a new method to combine the information originating from comparison and propagation [9]. This method has the advantage to observe the true-value-covered and uncertainty-minimized principles of UQ, by which the uncertainties of the predictions made by M&S can be effectively quantified.

The new method includes two important steps, one is to extrapolate the uncertainties obtained by comparison from validation domain to application domain, the other is to fuse the uncertainty information originating from comparison and propagation. This paper aims to display the ideas of QMU, which is supported by the new methods of UQ.

In Section 2, a proposition of reliability assessment is described. Section 3 shows how to predict the performance by M&S. Section 4 shows the UQ of the prediction results. Reliability assessment is fulfilled by QMU in Section 5, and a conclusion is given in Section 6.

II. Description of Proposition

The example we discuss is about reliability assessment for a product which has five parts, namely priming-device, high-explosive, special-metal, frame-material and energetic-material. The lowest demands are $Y^{demand} = 500MJ$ for yield-energy Y and $R^{demand} = 0.99$ for priming-reliability R. Failures may be caused by random errors in the manufacturing process or by aging during stockpile. Available system-level test data are of stock time for 0 year, 3 years, 5 years and 10 years. Test data are unavailable for the products that are stocked for more than 10 years. The energetic-material is designed to be replaced every 5 years for its severe aging rate. We must decide on the proposition that both R and Y are greater than their lowest demands when the product sits in the stockpile for 15 years.

The priming-reliability R is obtained as follows

$$\begin{cases} R = \int_0^{\infty} I\left(\tau, \tau^{upper}\right) f_\tau(\tau) d\tau \\ I\left(\tau, \tau^{upper}\right) = 1, \quad \tau \le \tau^{upper} \\ I\left(\tau, \tau^{upper}\right) = 0, \quad \tau > \tau^{upper} \end{cases} \tag{1}$$

where $f_\tau(\tau)$ is the probability density of characteristic time τ which has an average ${}^{\tau}\mu$. τ^{upper} is the upper limit of τ to guarantee successful priming. As a constant quantity lying on the configuration of products, τ^{upper} remains unchanged during stockpile and its best estimation is $\tau^{upper}=1.2\mu s$ with an epistemic uncertainty ${}^{\tau^{upper}}U^{Modeling}_{whole\text{-}life}=0.05\mu s$.

The epistemic uncertainties can be classified as "known unknowns" and "unknown unknowns", and the requirement to execute the decision making is no "unknown unknowns" existing in M&S. Although the material behaviors in the products stocked 15 years have a further change compared to that stocked less than or equal to 10 years, it can not bring essential changes in the detonation process and there is no "unknown unknowns" in M&S. So it is feasible to assess the reliability for the stock time of 15 years by M&S.

III. PREDICTION BY MODELLING & SIMULATIONS

M&S was first calibrated using the available test data, from which the computing parameters and the physics models including aging models of materials are determined. Then, in keeping with 0 year stock time and the medium values of machining tolerances, we have built a baseline entity model, for which we get the average values via M&S that $\tau^{M\&S}_{0year}=0.364\mu s$ and $Y^{M\&S}_{0year}=605.0MJ$. According to (1) and M&S results of the entity models that sampled from machining tolerances, we have $R^{M\&S}_{0year}=0.99999996$.

Table 1 shows the aging effects of each part after 15 years stocked, from which we have the predictions as $\tau^{M\&S}_{15years}=0.364+0.16=0.524(\mu s)$, $R^{M\&S}_{15years}=0.999995$, and $Y^{M\&S}_{15years}=605.0-55.0=550.0(MJ)$ by M&S and sampling.

IV. QUANTIFICATION OF UNCERTAINTIES

We have some repeated test data for each stock time such as 0 year, 3 years, 5 years, and 10 years. According to the formula in [9] as $U^{M\&S}=\left|y^{M\&S}-\bar{y}^{test}\right|+t_{(1-\beta)/2,v}\cdot s/\sqrt{n}$, and the confidence β=0.95, uncertainties of M&S in validation domain can be quantified by comparison as $U_\tau(t)$=0.123μs, 0.128μs, 0.132μs, 0.143μs and $U_Y(t)$ =9.05MJ, 9.53MJ, 10.20MJ, 12.17MJ for each stock time.

Through optimal square approximations, we have got the relationships between M&S-uncertainties and stock time such as $U_\tau(t)=0.123+0.00158t+0.0000427t^2$ and $U_Y(t)=9.033+0.132t+0.0183t^2$, from which the uncertainties corresponding to 15 years are extrapolated as ${}^{\tau}U^{extrapolaton}_{15years}=U_\tau(15)=0.156(\mu s)$ and ${}^{Y}U^{extrapolaton}_{15years}=U_Y(15)=15.13(MJ)$.

TABLE I. AGING EFFECTS TO SYSTEM PERFORMANCES

Parts or system	$\Delta\tau(\mu s)$	$\Delta Y(MJ)$
Priming-device	0.03	0.0
High-explosive	0.05	-15.0
Special-metal	0.01	-2.5
Frame-material	0.02	-5.5
Energetic-material	0.05	-32.0
Whole system	0.16	-55.0

As stock time increases from 10 years to 15 years, there will be additional epistemic uncertainties in the physics models. From ${}^{\tau}U^{\Delta}_{15years}=\sum_{i=1}^{N}\left|\partial\tau/\partial\xi_i\right|\left({}^{\xi_i}U^{\Delta}_{15years}\right)$ and ${}^{Y}U^{\Delta}_{15years}=\sum_{i=1}^{N}\left|\partial Y/\partial\xi_i\right|\left({}^{\xi_i}U^{\Delta}_{15years}\right)$, we have ${}^{\tau}U^{\Delta}_{15years}=0.05\mu s$ and ${}^{Y}U^{\Delta}_{15years}=20.0MJ$ of additional propagated uncertainties in Table 2.

The UQ method proposed in [9] shows the total uncertainty of prediction should be quantified by fusing the information corresponding to comparison and propagation as $U^{M\&S}_{15years}=U^{extrapolaton}_{15years}+U^{\Delta}_{15years}$. So we have ${}^{\tau}U^{M\&S}_{15years}=0.156+0.05=0.206(\mu s)$ and ${}^{Y}U^{M\&S}_{15years}=15.13+20.0=35.13(MJ)$.

Using (1), the uncertainty of priming-reliability can be obtained as ${}^{R}U^{M\&S}_{15years}=0.003$ just by propagation of the input epistemic uncertainties ${}^{\tau\mu}U^{M\&S}_{15years}={}^{\tau}U^{M\&S}_{15years}=0.206\mu s$ and ${}^{\tau^{upper}}U^{Modeling}_{whole\text{-}life}=0.05\mu s$.

V. RELIABILITY ASSESSMENT WITH QMU

The margins of priming-reliability and yield-energy are ${}^{R}M_{15years}=R^{M\&S}_{15years}-R^{demand}=9.995\times10^{-3}$ and ${}^{Y}M_{15years}=Y^{M\&S}_{15years}-Y^{demand}=50.0(MJ)$ with their uncertainties ${}^{R}U^{margin}_{15years}={}^{R}U^{M\&S}_{15years}+{}^{R}U^{demand}=0.003+0=3.0\times10^{-3}$ and ${}^{Y}U^{margin\,Y}_{15years}=U^{M\&S}_{15years}+{}^{Y}U^{demand}=35.13+0=35.13(MJ)$.

Finally, we have ${}^{R}C_{15years}={}^{R}M_{15years}/{}^{R}U_{15years}=9.995\times10^{-3}/3.0\times10^{-3}=3.33$ and ${}^{Y}C_{15years}={}^{Y}M_{15years}/{}^{Y}U_{15years}=50.0/35.13=1.42$, from which we affirm that the demands to products could be satisfied as the confidence factors $C=M/U$ are all greater than unity.

VI. CONCLUSION

The QMU methods proposed here fit engineering systems in which aleatory and epistemic uncertainties might coexist. Supported by the new methods of UQ for M&S prediction, reliability assessment with unified criterion could be fulfilled based on M&S even when the new system-level test is unavailable. These methods have already been applied in some engineering systems.

ACKNOWLEDGMENT

This research is supported by the National Nature Science Foundation (Grant No. 11371066, 11272064) of China.

TABLE II. ADDITIONAL UNCERTAINTIES FROM PROPAGATION

Parts or system	${}^{\tau}U^{\Delta}_{15years}(\mu s)$	${}^{Y}U^{\Delta}_{15years}(MJ)$
Priming-device	0.01	0.0
High-explosive	0.02	5.5
Special-metal	0.01	9.5
Frame-material	0.01	5.0
Energetic-material	0.00	0.0
Whole system	0.05	20.0

REFERENCES

[1] W. L. Oberkampf and C. J. Roy, "Verification and validation in science computing," Cambridge University Press, 2010.

[2] D. H. Sharp and M. M. Wood-Schultz, "QMU and nuclear weapons certification," J. Los Alamos Science, vol. 28, pp. 47-53, 2003.

[3] Z. B. Ma, Y. J. Ying, and J. S. Zhu, "QMU certifying method and its implementation," Chinese Journal of Nuclear Science and Engineering, vol. 29, no. 1, pp. 1-9, 2009.

[4] K. Sentz and S. Ferson, "Probability bounding analysis in the Quantification of Margins and Uncertainties," Reliability Engineering and System Safety, vol. 96, pp. 1126-1136, 2011.

[5] G. Iaccarino, R. Pecnik, J. Glimm and D. Sharp, "A QMU approach for characterizing the operability limits of air-breathing hypersonic vehicles," Reliability Engineering and System Safety, vol. 96, pp. 1150-1160, 2011.

[6] J. C. Helton, "Conceptual and computational basis for the quantification of margins and uncertainty," Sandia Report, SAND2009-3055.

[7] M. T. Reagan, H. N. Najm, R. G. Ghanem and O. M. Knio, "Uncertainty quantification in reacting-flow simulations through non-intrusive spectral projection," Combustion and Flame, vol. 132, pp. 545-555, 2003.

[8] Q. Liu, R. L. Wang, Z. Lin and W. Z. Wen, "Uncertainty quantification for JWL EOS parameters in explosive numerical simulation," Chinese Journal of Explosion and Shock Waves, vol. 33, no. 6, pp. 647-654, 2013.

[9] Z. B. Ma, J. W. Yin, and H. J. Li, "Uncertainty quantification of numerical simulations subjected to calibration," Chinese J. Comp. Phys., vol. 32, no. 5, pp. 514-522, 2015.

On the Implementation of Novel Velocity-based 3D Beam: Compatibility of Angular Velocities Over the FEM Boundaries

Eva Zupan and Dejan Zupan

Faculty of Civil and Geodetic Engineering
University of Ljubljana
Ljubljana, Slovenia
Email: eva.zupan.lj@gmail.com; dejan.zupan@fgg.uni-lj.si

***Abstract*—In this paper, a new velocity-based finite element approach for non-linear dynamics of beam-like structures is briefly introduced. The additivity of angular velocities in local frame description, which are taken as primary unknowns along with the linear velocities, brings several benefits, such as trivial discretization and update procedure for the primary unknowns and improved stability properties of the time integrator. The novel approach introduces some new issues that need to be treated properly, such as compatibility of angular velocities over the finite element boundaries. A computationally cheap solution of the problem is presented.**

Keywords–non-linear dynamics; spatial beams; finite-element method; velocity-based approach;

I. INTRODUCTION

The total set of equations in solid mechanics consists of non-linear equilibrium, kinematic and constitutive equations that need to be solved for displacements, strains and stresses. Many practical problems in solid mechanics deal with structures that have one dimension larger than the other two, e.g., columns and girders in civil engineering, robotic arms, rotor blades and aircraft wings in mechanical engineering, deoxyribonucleic acid (DNA) molecules in biology and medicine, nanotubes in nanotechnology. Such structures are usually modelled as beams. For beam-like structures the kinematics of a body becomes simplified but the equations remain non-linear, see, e.g., Antman [1]. Additionally, the reduced kinematics introduces the three-dimensional rotations of rigid cross-sections to describe the configuration of a beam. The solution algorithms for beams usually reduce the total set of equations in such a way that the configuration variables (displacements and rotations) become the only unknowns of the problem. For numerical solution methods, such reduction means that the configuration variables need to be discretized with respect to space and time. The three-dimensional rotations, which are important members of configuration variables, represent a demanding mathematical structure, characterized by multiplicative nature (non-additivity), orthogonality and non-commutativity. These properties need to be properly considered in the numerical solution methods to gain a sufficient performance of calculations and accuracy of the results. Such demands highly increase the complexity of algorithms and disable direct applicability of the methods developed for standard Euclidean spaces [2]–[5].

The alternative approach employed here exploits computationally simpler angular velocities as the primary quantities for the description of rotational degrees of freedom. Such approach brings several advantages to non-linear beam dynamics:

- when expressed in local bases, the components of angular velocity vector become additive, which enables the use of standard discretization and interpolation techniques;
- the stability of implicit time integrators is improved by taking the derivative of configuration quantities as the iterative unknowns, see Hosea and Shampine [6];
- the time discretization, linearization of equations and the update procedure are much simpler compared to standard beam elements.

Besides the advantages, this new approach brings some novel issues that need to be properly solved. The crucial idea of the finite element method (FEM) lies in subdivision of a larger structure into smaller parts called finite elements. An important part of the solution procedure is the assembly of equations of finite elements into a larger system of equations that describe the problem at the structural level. The simplest assumption used in the assembly procedure is that the elements are rigidly connected so that the displacements and rotations are continuous over the boundaries. When the displacements and rotations are chosen as the primary variables, a simple Boolean identification of degrees of freedom can be used. This yields that velocities and angular velocities are continuous over the finite element boundaries as well, but only when expressed with respect to a fixed basis.

For the sake of computational advantages at the element level, we express the angular velocities with respect to the moving frame. Because of this choice, the simple identification of degrees of freedom that belong to the joints between elements can no longer be used due to different initial orientations of elements. Thus, the continuity of configuration quantities in a fixed frame leads to a more complicated relation in the local frame. This relation could be introduced at the structural level using the method of Lagrange multipliers, but such an approach would increase the number of degrees of freedom and the computational complexity of the overall algorithm. An elegant and computationally cheap alternative is presented here. Excellent properties of the proposed numerical model are demonstrated by numerical examples.

The rest of the paper is structured as follows. Section II introduces Cosserat beam model. In Section III, we describe a novel numerical solution method for Cosserat beams. The treatment of boundary conditions is presented in Section IV. In Section V, some numerical examples are given. The paper ends with concluding remarks.

II. Cosserat Beam Model

Among beam models, the *Cosserat theory of rods*, [1], is widely used. The numerical implementation of the model is usually attributed to Reissner [7] and Simo [8], where it is also called *the geometrically exact beam*. Only a brief description of the model is presented here.

The centroidal line $\left\{\vec{r}\,(x,t)\,,\ x\in[0,L]\,,\ t\geq 0\right\}$ and the family of cross-sections $\{\mathcal{A}\,(x,t)\,,\ x\in[0,L]\,,\ t\geq 0\}$ of the beam are parametrized by the arc-length parameter x and the time t, where L is the length of the beam in its initial position, see Figure 1. We assume that cross-sections are bounded plane regions that preserve their shape and area during deformation.

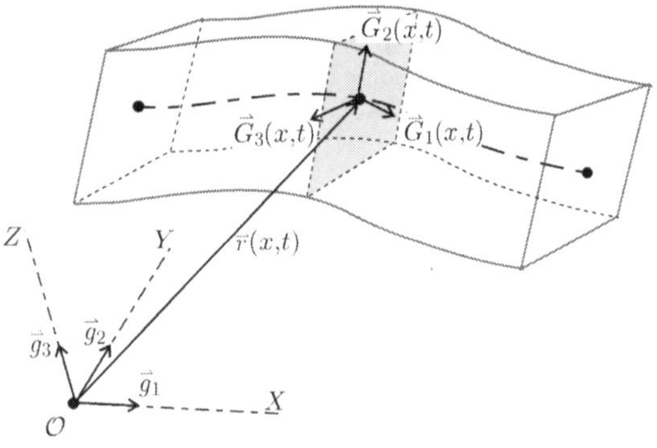

Figure 1. A three-dimensional beam.

For the description of beam equations and the quantities therein, we introduce the *local* orthonormal basis $\left\{\vec{G}_1\,(x,t)\,,\vec{G}_2\,(x,t)\,,\vec{G}_3\,(x,t)\right\}$, which defines the orientation of each cross-section, and the *global* orthonormal basis $\left\{\vec{g}_1,\vec{g}_2,\vec{g}_3\right\}$, which is fixed in time and space. A rotation between the global and the local basis, defined by the quaternion multiplication ($\circ$) reads

$$\vec{G}_i\,(x,t)=\widehat{q}\,(x,t)\circ\vec{g}_i\circ\widehat{q}^{\,*}\,(x,t)\,,\qquad i=1,2,3,\tag{1}$$

where $\widehat{q}$ denotes the rotational quaternion and $\widehat{q}^{\,*}$ its conjugate.

III. Numerical Solution Method

The total set of governing equations describing dynamics of Cosserat rods in terms of quaternions can be found, e.g., in [9] or [10]. Following the classical Galerkin finite-element approach and introducing a family of interpolation functions $I_p\,(x)$, $p=1,2,...,N$, the discretized balance equations of a beam read:

$$\int_0^L\left[\mathbf{n}I_p'-\tilde{\mathbf{n}}I_p+\rho A\ddot{\mathbf{r}}I_p\right]dx-\delta_p\boldsymbol{f}=\mathbf{0}\tag{2}$$

$$\int_0^L\Big[\mathbf{m}I_p'-(\mathbf{r}'\times\mathbf{n})\,I_p-\tilde{\mathbf{m}}I_p+\widehat{\mathbf{q}}\circ\left(\mathbf{J}_\rho\dot{\mathbf{\Omega}}\right)\circ\widehat{\mathbf{q}}^*I_p$$
$$+\boldsymbol{\omega}\times\left(\widehat{\mathbf{q}}\circ(\mathbf{J}_\rho\mathbf{\Omega})\circ\widehat{\mathbf{q}}^*\right)I_p\Big]dx-\delta_p\boldsymbol{h}=\mathbf{0}.\tag{3}$$

The bold-face letters represent vector quantities in the component form. The lower case letters are used when a vector is expressed with respect to the fixed frame and the upper case letters are used for the local basis description. A hat over the letter denotes a four-dimensional vector, a member of the algebra of quaternions. Here, $\mathbf{n}$ and $\mathbf{m}$ are the resultant force and moment vector of the cross-section expressed in fixed frame, i.e.,

$$\mathbf{n}\,(x,t)=\widehat{\mathbf{q}}\,(x,t)\circ\mathbf{N}\,(x,t)\circ\widehat{\mathbf{q}}^*\,(x,t)\,,\tag{4}$$
$$\mathbf{m}\,(x,t)=\widehat{\mathbf{q}}\,(x,t)\circ\mathbf{M}\,(x,t)\circ\widehat{\mathbf{q}}^*\,(x,t)\,,\tag{5}$$

where $\mathbf{N}$ and $\mathbf{M}$ are the same vectors expressed in local basis; $\mathbf{\Omega}$ and $\dot{\mathbf{\Omega}}$ are the angular velocity and angular acceleration; $\ddot{\mathbf{r}}$ is the linear acceleration; ρ is the density of the material; A is the area of the cross-section; $\mathbf{J}_\rho$ is the matrix of mass moments of inertia; $\tilde{\mathbf{n}}$ and $\tilde{\mathbf{m}}$ are vectors of applied distributed force and moment; $\delta_p\mathbf{f}\,(t)$ and $\delta_p\mathbf{h}\,(t)$ are the applied concentrated forces and moments at ends of the beam:

$$\delta_p\mathbf{f}\,(t)\ =\ \begin{cases}\mathbf{f}^0\,(t)\,, & p=1\\ \mathbf{f}^L\,(t)\,, & p=N\\ 0, & \text{otherwise}\end{cases}$$
$$\delta_p\mathbf{h}\,(t)\ =\ \begin{cases}\mathbf{h}^0\,(t)\,, & p=1\\ \mathbf{h}^L\,(t)\,, & p=N\\ 0, & \text{otherwise}\end{cases}\ .$$

Equations (2)–(3) represent a system of $6N$ equations discrete in time but still continuous in space. The dependency of quantities on space x and time t has been omitted for better readability. They need to be solved together with kinematic and constitutive equations. Kinematic equations of Cosserat beam are as follows

$$\mathbf{\Gamma}=\widehat{\mathbf{q}}^*\circ\mathbf{r}'\circ\widehat{\mathbf{q}}+\mathbf{\Gamma}_0,\qquad\mathbf{K}=2\widehat{\mathbf{q}}^*\circ\widehat{\mathbf{q}}',\tag{6}$$

where $\mathbf{\Gamma}$ and $\mathbf{K}$ denote the translational strain vector and the shear strain vector, respectively. For constitutive equations various models could be taken, but here we limit ourselves to the simplest case of linear elastic material, where

$$\mathbf{N}=\mathrm{diag}\left[\ EA\quad GA_2\quad GA_3\ \right]\mathbf{\Gamma}\tag{7}$$
$$\mathbf{M}=\mathrm{diag}\left[\ GI_1\quad EI_2\quad EI_3\ \right]\mathbf{K}.\tag{8}$$

Here, EA/L is the axial stiffness, EI_2 and EI_3 denote the bending stiffness, GI_1/L is the torsional stiffness, GA_2 and GA_3 are the shear stiffnesses.

A. Time discretization

For the time discretization, we use the approximation of displacements at t_{n+1} following from the mean value theorem:

$$\mathbf{r}^{[n+1]}=\mathbf{r}^{[n]}+h\frac{\mathbf{v}^{[n]}+\mathbf{v}^{[n+1]}}{2},$$

which yields

$$\mathbf{r}^{[n+1]}=\mathbf{r}^{[n]}+h\overline{\mathbf{v}},$$

where $\overline{\mathbf{v}}$ denotes the average velocity

$$\overline{\mathbf{v}}=\frac{\mathbf{v}^{[n]}+\mathbf{v}^{[n+1]}}{2}$$

and $h=t_{n+1}-t_n$ is the time step of the scheme.

For accelerations we can similarly employ

$$\frac{\mathbf{a}^{[n]}+\mathbf{a}^{[n+1]}}{2}=\frac{\mathbf{v}^{[n+1]}-\mathbf{v}^{[n]}}{h}.$$

After some rearrangement of terms, the scheme for translational degrees of freedom reads

$$\begin{aligned}\mathbf{r}^{[n+1]} &= \mathbf{r}^{[n]} + h\overline{\mathbf{v}}\\ \mathbf{v}^{[n+1]} &= -\mathbf{v}^{[n]} + 2\overline{\mathbf{v}}\\ \mathbf{a}^{[n+1]} &= -\mathbf{a}^{[n]} - \frac{4}{h}\mathbf{v}^{[n]} + \frac{4}{h}\overline{\mathbf{v}}.\end{aligned} \tag{9}$$

This scheme can be interpreted as a modification of the classical implicit Newmark scheme, where the average velocity becomes the iterative unknown.

A similar approach can be used for rotational degrees of freedom with an important exception stemming from the non-linear relationship between angular velocities and rotational quaternions. The exponential mapping is used to map from incremental angular velocities to incremental rotations. The incremental rotation is then multiplied with the current one. The scheme for rotational degrees of freedom reads

$$\begin{aligned}\widehat{\mathbf{q}}^{[n+1]} &= \widehat{\mathbf{q}}^{[n]} \circ \exp\left(\frac{h}{2}\overline{\boldsymbol{\Omega}}\right)\\ \boldsymbol{\Omega}^{[n+1]} &= -\boldsymbol{\Omega}^{[n]} + 2\overline{\boldsymbol{\Omega}}\\ \boldsymbol{\alpha}^{[n+1]} &= -\boldsymbol{\alpha}^{[n]} - \frac{4}{h}\boldsymbol{\Omega}^{[n]} + \frac{4}{h}\overline{\boldsymbol{\Omega}},\end{aligned} \tag{10}$$

where exp denotes the quaternion exponential

$$\exp(\widehat{\mathbf{x}}) = \widehat{1} + \frac{\widehat{\mathbf{x}}}{1!} + \frac{1}{2!}\widehat{\mathbf{x}} \circ \widehat{\mathbf{x}} + \frac{1}{3!}\widehat{\mathbf{x}} \circ \widehat{\mathbf{x}} \circ \widehat{\mathbf{x}} + \ldots. \tag{11}$$

B. Spatial discretization

In the present time discretization, the average velocities $\overline{\mathbf{v}}$ and $\overline{\boldsymbol{\Omega}}$ are the only unknown functions along the length of the beam at each particular time step. They are replaced by a set of nodal values $\overline{\mathbf{v}}^p$, $\overline{\boldsymbol{\Omega}}^p$ at discretization points x_p, $p = 1, \ldots, N$, with $x_1 = 0$ and $x_N = L$, and interpolated by a set of interpolation functions $I_p(x)$ in-between:

$$\overline{\mathbf{v}}(x) = \sum_{p=1}^{N} I_p(x)\,\overline{\mathbf{v}}^p, \qquad \overline{\boldsymbol{\Omega}}(x) = \sum_{p=1}^{N} I_p(x)\,\overline{\boldsymbol{\Omega}}^p. \tag{12}$$

The same discretization procedure is performed at every finite element of the structure. Thus, boundary nodes x_1 and x_N become members of the global notes important at the structural level, while x_2,... x_{N-1} are internal points of the element, often but not necessarily condensed at the elements level. Angular velocities in local basis description are additive quantities and the standard aditive-type interpolation used is in complete accord with the properties of the configuration space.

C. Newton iteration

After time and space discretization, the governing equations (2)–(3) are replaced by a set of nonlinear algebraic equations that need to be solved at each discrete time for all the nodal values. The non-linear equations are solved iteratively using the Newton-Raphson method

$$\mathbf{K}^{[i]}\delta\mathbf{y} = -\mathbf{f}^{[i]}, \tag{13}$$

where $\mathbf{K}^{[i]}$ is the global Jacobian tangent matrix, $\mathbf{f}^{[i]}$ the residual vector of discretized equations (2)–(3), both in iteration i, and $\delta\mathbf{y}$ a vector of corrections of all nodal unknowns

$$\delta\mathbf{y} = \begin{bmatrix}\delta\overline{\mathbf{v}}_1 & \delta\overline{\boldsymbol{\Omega}}_1 & \cdots & \delta\overline{\mathbf{v}}_M & \delta\overline{\boldsymbol{\Omega}}_M\end{bmatrix}^T$$

A suitable choice of nodal variables allows the kinematically admissible additive update:

$$\overline{\mathbf{v}}^{[i+1]} = \overline{\mathbf{v}}^{[i]} + \delta\overline{\mathbf{v}}, \qquad \overline{\boldsymbol{\Omega}}^{[i+1]} = \overline{\boldsymbol{\Omega}}^{[i]} + \delta\overline{\boldsymbol{\Omega}} \tag{14}$$

at each discrete point of the structure.

IV. CONTINUITY OF BOUNDARY VALUES

Finite elements have equal displacements and rotations at the rigid joints. However, the initial rotations of different elements are not necessarily equal. When the initial orientations differ, we need to distinguish between the initial and the relative rotations. Let us start with two elements having different initial orientations, described by quaternions $\widehat{\mathbf{q}}_0^{\mathrm{I}}$ and $\widehat{\mathbf{q}}_0^{\mathrm{II}}$ at the joint: $\widehat{\mathbf{q}}_0^{\mathrm{I}} \neq \widehat{\mathbf{q}}_0^{\mathrm{II}}$. When the joint is rigid the position vectors are equal, but the total rotations differ

$$\mathbf{r}^{\mathrm{I}} = \mathbf{r}^{\mathrm{II}} \quad \text{and} \quad \widehat{\mathbf{q}}^{\mathrm{I}} \neq \widehat{\mathbf{q}}^{\mathrm{II}}, \tag{15}$$

as shown in Figure 2.

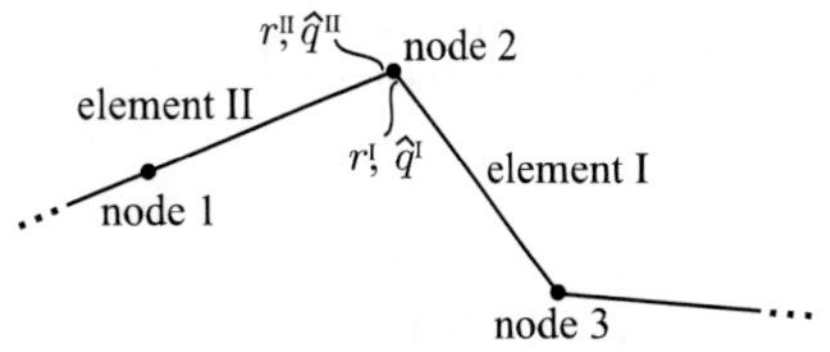

Figure 2. A rigid joint of two differently oriented elements.

The total rotations can be expressed as a composition of initial and relative rotation

$$\widehat{\mathbf{q}}^{\mathrm{I}} = \widehat{\mathbf{q}}_0^{\mathrm{I}} \circ \widehat{\mathbf{k}}^{\mathrm{I}} \quad \text{and} \quad \widehat{\mathbf{q}}^{\mathrm{II}} = \widehat{\mathbf{q}}_0^{\mathrm{II}} \circ \widehat{\mathbf{k}}^{\mathrm{II}}, \tag{16}$$

where the relative rotations are equal:

$$\widehat{\mathbf{k}}^{\mathrm{I}} = \widehat{\mathbf{k}}^{\mathrm{II}}. \tag{17}$$

The continuity condition, which could also be called the compatibility of rotations at the element boundaries, thus reads

$$\widehat{\mathbf{q}}^{\mathrm{I}} \circ \widehat{\mathbf{q}}_0^{\mathrm{I}*} = \widehat{\mathbf{q}}^{\mathrm{II}} \circ \widehat{\mathbf{q}}_0^{\mathrm{II}*}.$$

In configuration based approach we usually avoid enforcing this condition by introducing the relative rotational quaternion $\widehat{\mathbf{k}}$ as the nodal variable. For the velocity-based approach, we can similarly observe that

$$\overline{\mathbf{v}}^{\mathrm{I}} = \overline{\mathbf{v}}^{\mathrm{II}} \quad \text{and} \quad \overline{\boldsymbol{\Omega}}^{\mathrm{I}} \neq \overline{\boldsymbol{\Omega}}^{\mathrm{II}},$$

as the angular velocities are expressed in different local frames. We will derive the compatibility condition for angular velocities at the joints and propose a similar strategy as for rotational quaternions to avoid the use of Lagrange multipliers method by the substitution of the primary unknowns of Newton's iteration at the structural level. The details are presented in the sequel.

A. Relation between boundary angular velocities

The angular velocity vector expressed in the local frame is defined as

$$\boldsymbol{\Omega} = 2\widehat{\mathbf{q}}^* \circ \dot{\widehat{\mathbf{q}}}, \tag{18}$$

which yields the expressions for the nodal angular velocities of elements I and II at the joint

$$\overline{\boldsymbol{\Omega}}^{\mathrm{I}} = 2\mathbf{q}^{\mathrm{I}*} \circ \dot{\mathbf{q}}^{\mathrm{I}} \quad \text{and} \quad \overline{\boldsymbol{\Omega}}^{\mathrm{II}} = 2\mathbf{q}^{\mathrm{II}*} \circ \dot{\mathbf{q}}^{\mathrm{II}}.$$

After considering (16), we have

$$\overline{\mathbf{\Omega}}^{\mathrm{I}} = 2\widehat{\mathbf{q}}_0^{\mathrm{I}*} \circ \widehat{\mathbf{k}}^{\mathrm{I}*} \circ \dot{\widehat{\mathbf{k}}}^{\mathrm{I}} \circ \widehat{\mathbf{q}}_0^{\mathrm{I}} \quad \text{and} \quad \overline{\mathbf{\Omega}}^{\mathrm{II}} = 2\widehat{\mathbf{q}}_0^{\mathrm{II}*} \circ \widehat{\mathbf{k}}^{\mathrm{II}*} \circ \dot{\widehat{\mathbf{k}}}^{\mathrm{II}} \circ \widehat{\mathbf{q}}_0^{\mathrm{II}}.$$

Since the relative rotation $\widehat{\mathbf{k}}$ is continuous over the boundaries of elements, eq. (17), we are able to express the constraint relation between the boundary angular velocities

$$\widehat{\mathbf{q}}_0^{\mathrm{I}} \circ \overline{\mathbf{\Omega}}^{\mathrm{I}} \circ \widehat{\mathbf{q}}_0^{\mathrm{I}*} = \widehat{\mathbf{q}}_0^{\mathrm{II}} \circ \overline{\mathbf{\Omega}}^{\mathrm{II}} \circ \widehat{\mathbf{q}}_0^{\mathrm{II}*}. \tag{19}$$

For the clarity of further derivation, it is convenient to express (19) in terms of rotation matrices:

$$\mathbf{R}_0^{\mathrm{I}}\overline{\mathbf{\Omega}}^{\mathrm{I}} = \mathbf{R}_0^{\mathrm{II}}\overline{\mathbf{\Omega}}^{\mathrm{II}}, \tag{20}$$

where $\mathbf{R}_0^{\mathrm{I}}$ and $\mathbf{R}_0^{\mathrm{II}}$ denote the standard rotation matrices equivalent to quaternion-based rotations expressed with $\widehat{\mathbf{q}}_0^{\mathrm{I}}$ and $\widehat{\mathbf{q}}_0^{\mathrm{II}}$.

B. Algorithmically enforced boundary conditions

A solution of two moment equilibrium equations (3) expressed at the same node, here formally written as

$$\mathcal{M}^{\mathrm{I}}\left(\overline{\mathbf{\Omega}}^{\mathrm{I}}\right) = \mathbf{0} \quad \text{and} \quad \mathcal{M}^{\mathrm{II}}\left(\overline{\mathbf{\Omega}}^{\mathrm{II}}\right) = \mathbf{0}, \tag{21}$$

needs to be found. The solution must also satisfy the algebraic constraint

$$\mathbf{R}_0^{\mathrm{I}}\overline{\mathbf{\Omega}}^{\mathrm{I}} - \mathbf{R}_0^{\mathrm{II}}\overline{\mathbf{\Omega}}^{\mathrm{II}} = 0. \tag{22}$$

Following the method of Lagrange multipliers the constraint equation is multiplied by a multiplier λ and linearized. The corresponding partial derivatives are then added to the initial variational problem to obtain the weak form of Lagrange function. For the present case it reads

$$\mathcal{M}^{\mathrm{I}}\left(\overline{\mathbf{\Omega}}^{\mathrm{I}}\right) + \mathbf{R}_0^{\mathrm{I}}\lambda = \mathbf{0} \tag{23}$$

$$\mathcal{M}^{\mathrm{II}}\left(\overline{\mathbf{\Omega}}^{\mathrm{II}}\right) - \mathbf{R}_0^{\mathrm{II}}\lambda = \mathbf{0} \tag{24}$$

$$\mathbf{R}_0^{\mathrm{I}}\overline{\mathbf{\Omega}}^{\mathrm{I}} - \mathbf{R}_0^{\mathrm{II}}\overline{\mathbf{\Omega}}^{\mathrm{II}} = \mathbf{0}. \tag{25}$$

The method thus increases the size of the system and the computational demands. It introduces three additional scalar unknowns and three additional equations for each rigid joint between two elements. To avoid this, we introduce the following change of variables describing the nodal rotation-related unknowns:

$$\overline{\mathbf{\Omega}}_R^{\mathrm{I}} = \mathbf{R}_0^{\mathrm{I}}\overline{\mathbf{\Omega}}^{\mathrm{I}} \quad \text{and} \quad \overline{\mathbf{\Omega}}_R^{\mathrm{II}} = \mathbf{R}_0^{\mathrm{II}}\overline{\mathbf{\Omega}}^{\mathrm{II}}. \tag{26}$$

Based on the substitution of unknowns (26), the method of Lagrange multipliers gives

$$\mathcal{M}^{\mathrm{I}}\left(\mathbf{R}_0^{\mathrm{I}T}\overline{\mathbf{\Omega}}_R^{\mathrm{I}}\right) + \lambda = 0 \tag{27}$$

$$\mathcal{M}^{\mathrm{II}}\left(\mathbf{R}_0^{\mathrm{II}T}\overline{\mathbf{\Omega}}_R^{\mathrm{II}}\right) - \lambda = 0 \tag{28}$$

$$\overline{\mathbf{\Omega}}_R^{\mathrm{I}} - \overline{\mathbf{\Omega}}_R^{\mathrm{II}} = 0. \tag{29}$$

The system (27)–(29) can be easily reduced since the nodal unknowns are now identical: $\overline{\mathbf{\Omega}}_R^{\mathrm{I}} = \overline{\mathbf{\Omega}}_R^{\mathrm{II}}$. These new variables can be interpreted as the relative angular velocities in a relative local frame. After the summation of the first two equations, we obtain the reduced moment equilibrium equation at the joint:

$$\mathcal{M}^{\mathrm{I}}\left(\mathbf{R}_0^{\mathrm{I}T}\overline{\mathbf{\Omega}}_R^{\mathrm{I}}\right) + \mathcal{M}^{\mathrm{II}}\left(\mathbf{R}_0^{\mathrm{II}T}\overline{\mathbf{\Omega}}_R^{\mathrm{I}}\right) = 0.$$

Translational degrees of freedom are left unchanged. The correction vector of iteration method thus becomes

$$\delta\mathbf{y}_R = \begin{bmatrix} \delta\overline{\mathbf{v}}_1 & \delta\overline{\mathbf{\Omega}}_{R,1} & \cdots & \delta\overline{\mathbf{v}}_M & \delta\overline{\mathbf{\Omega}}_{R,M} \end{bmatrix}^T.$$

Note that the corrections of newly introduced variables (26) can still be directly summed up to the current iterative values. This property follows from the distributivity of multiplication of time-constant matrix $\mathbf{R}_0$ with the sum of angular velocity and its update. The original quantities $\overline{\mathbf{\Omega}}^{\mathrm{I}}$ and $\overline{\mathbf{\Omega}}^{\mathrm{II}}$ remain to be the interpolated quantities at the elements level. Hence in each iteration step i the variables $\overline{\mathbf{\Omega}}^{\mathrm{I}}$ and $\overline{\mathbf{\Omega}}^{\mathrm{II}}$ are extracted from $\overline{\mathbf{\Omega}}_R^{\mathrm{I}} = \overline{\mathbf{\Omega}}_R^{\mathrm{II}}$ and applied for further calculations.

With this procedure only six variables per node are needed and computational complexity is only slightly increased due to reconstruction of average angular velocities at the element's level from the relative ones at the structural level. This procedure is done by applying a simple time-independent rotation. The main advantage, i.e., the additivity of the iterative and the interpolated unknowns, is preserved. The size of the problem for each element thus remains to be $6N$, which means that on the structural level we need to solve $6(N \cdot E - n)$ equations, where E denotes the number of elements and n the number of rigid joints. To enforce the boundary conditions, the proposed method requires additional n matrix products of the initial transposed rotation matrix, $\mathbf{R}_0^T$, and the relative angular velocity, $\overline{\mathbf{\Omega}}_R$. As we will show by numerical example, these costs are negligible with respect to the overall numerical procedure.

V. NUMERICAL STUDIES

The applicability and an excellent performance of the proposed method will be demonstrated on standard examples for flexible beam-like structures with finite strains where the structure undergoes large displacements and rotations. Equidistant discretization points were chosen for spatial discretization and standard Lagrangian polynomials were taken to be interpolation functions. Integrals were evaluated numerically using the Gaussian quadrature rule. The Newton-Raphson iteration scheme was terminated when the Euclidean norm of the vector of corrections of all primary unknowns was under 10^{-9}. The geometric and material data chosen in the examples are

$$EA = GA_2 = GA_3 = 10^6,$$
$$GI_1 = EI_2 = EI_3 = 10^3,$$
$$\rho A = 1.$$

Other data are provided for each example separately .

A. Free flight of a beam: the computational performance

In our first example, we analyse the computational performance of the present approach when solving a problem similar to the one introduced by Simo and Vu-Quoc [2]. The beam is initially inclined and subjected to a piecewise linear point force f_X and point moments h_Y and h_Z at the lower end, as shown in Figure 3. The mass-inertia matrix of the cross-section is taken to be: $\mathbf{J}_\rho = \mathrm{diag}\begin{bmatrix} 10 & 10 & 10 \end{bmatrix}$.

For this particular problem, all elements have equal initial orientations. A simple Boolean identification of degrees of freedom is therefore reasonable even if angular velocities in local frame description are the primary unknowns, which is the case in our approach. This allows us to solve the problem in two different ways: i) with Boolean identification and ii) using the proposed algorithm. By doing so, we will be able to compare the computational times and demonstrate the demands of the presented algorithm. Note that the Boolean identification is not appropriate when solving problems, where elements have different initial inclinations, which limits its applicability and generality.

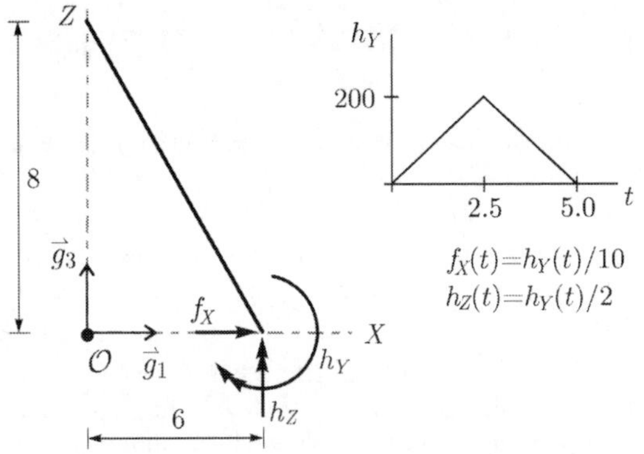

Figure 3. Unsupported beam that is initially straight but inclined.

To compare both methods, a dense mesh of 100 linear elements has been used. For this problem a small number of elements would be sufficient, but by increasing their number the complexity of the overall algorithm raises so the additional demands of the proposed algorithm can be easier observed. The average computational times of the same evaluation in seconds are presented in Table I.

TABLE I. COMPUTATIONAL TIMES OF INITIALLY STRAIGHT BEAM.

Method	*initial time step*	*ten time steps*
Boolean identification	3.415	42.820
proposed algorithm	3.508	34.011

We can observe that computational times of the proposed method are only slightly larger after the first time step. However, in the time stepping procedure the proposed algorithm behaves better since the newly introduced relative velocities seem to be more suitable computational unknowns, which leads to a lower number of total iterations needed and therefore lower computational times.

B. Large deflections of right-angle cantilever

This classical example introduced by Simo and Vu-Quoc [2] was studied by many authors. A right-angle cantilever beam is subjected to a triangular pulse out-of-plane load at the elbow, see Figure 4. Each part of the cantilever is dicretized with two third-order elements. A dynamic responce of the cantilever involves very large magnitudes of displacements and rotations together with finite strains. After removal of the external force, the cantilever undergoes free vibrations and the total mechanical energy of the cantilever should remain constant. Therefore, the stability of the algorithm is here checked through the energy behavior. The centroidal mass-inertia matrix of the cross-section is diagonal: $\mathbf{J}_\rho = \text{diag}\,[\ 20 \quad 10 \quad 10\ ]$. Originally the solution was computed on the time interval $[0, 30]$ with fixed time step 0.25, later the interval was extended to $[0, 50]$ by

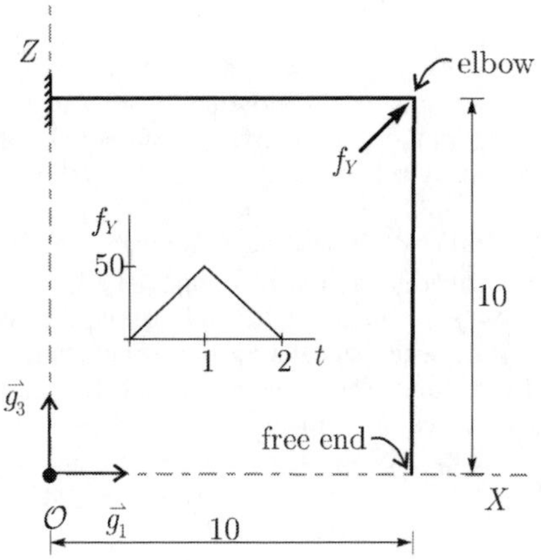

Figure 4. The right-angle cantilever subjected to out-of-plane loading.

Jelenić and Crisfield [11] claiming that most of the algorithms encounter numerical stability problems between times 30 and 50. Here on a longer time interval $[0, 100]$ solution was

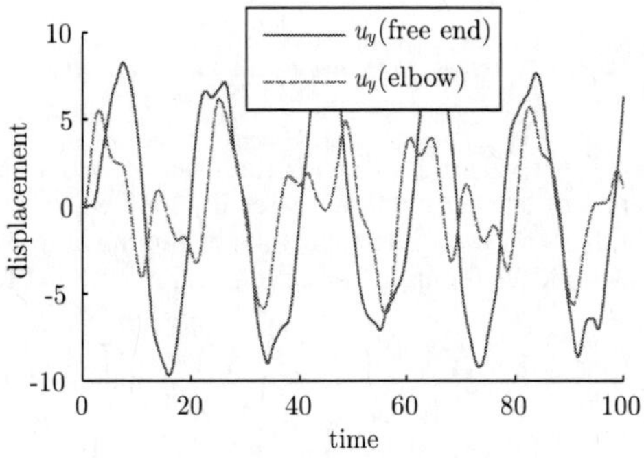

Figure 5. The out-of-plane displacements at free-end and at elbow for the right-angle cantilever.

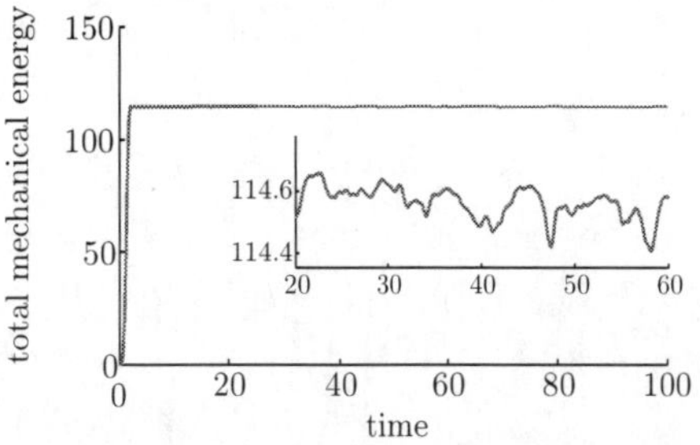

Figure 6. The time history of the total mechanical energy for the right-angle cantilever.

obtained without any numerical problems noticed, see Figure 5. However the time step used had to be reduced by half, $h = 0.125$, otherwise the iteration could not achieve the prescribed tolerance condition at time 51.5. From Figure 6 we can observe almost constant total mechanical energy after time $t = 5$; only slight discrepancy of about 0.2% can be observed, which indicates good stability of calculations. The present results on the time interval $[0, 30]$ agree well with the results reported by other authors.

C. *Large overall motion of a flexible cross-like structure*

The large overall motion of completely free "cross" was first presented by Simo et al. [12] to illustrate the performance of the algorithm when calculating the dynamics response of a reticulated structure. The geometry and the applied external out-of plane forces are depicted in Figure 7. The centroidal mass-inertia matrix of the cross-section is taken to be $\mathbf{J}_\rho = \text{diag}[\ 10 \quad 10 \quad 10\ ]$. The solution was computed on a very

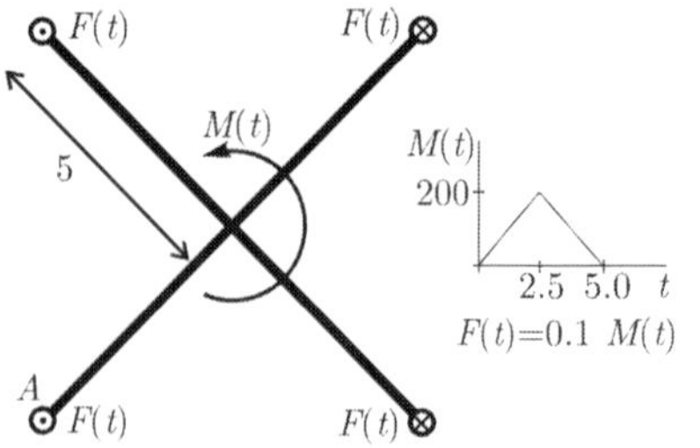

Figure 7. The geometry and the loading of the "cross".

large time interval $[0, 1000]$ with time step $h = 0.1$. Because the interval of calculation is so extremely long we present only displacements on short intervals at the beginning and at the end of calculation, see Figure 8. After removal of external forces at time $t = 5$ the cross vibrates freely in a periodic-like dynamic

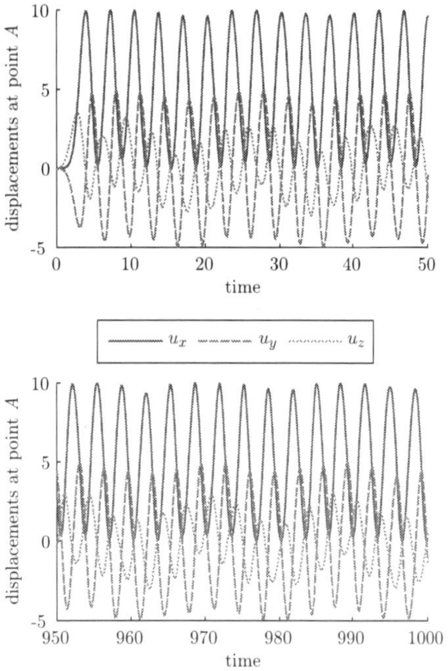

Figure 8. The displacements of the "cross" at point A at the beginning and at the end of calculation.

pattern and the total mechanical energy is almost constant as expected, see Figure 9. The calculations remain stable even after 10 000 time steps.

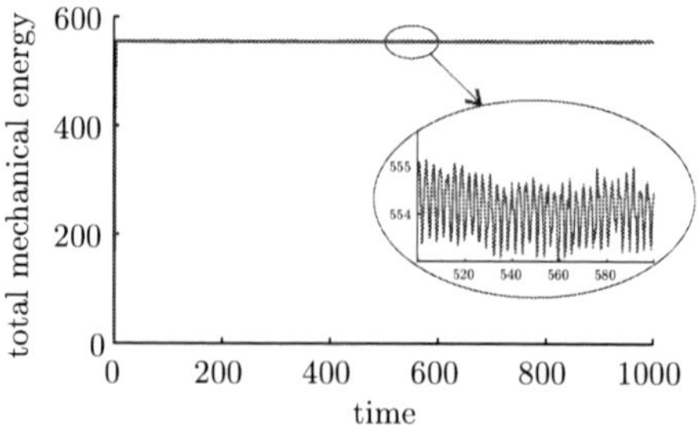

Figure 9. The time history of the total mechanical energy for the "cross".

VI. Conclusion

A novel finite-element approach for the beam dynamics has been presented. The proposed method exploits the benefits of the favourable properties of angular velocity in the local frame description. The issue of the continuity of the structural unknowns over the element boundaries has been resolved with minimal computational cost. The classical benchmark examples demonstrate the accuracy and numerical stability of the proposed method. Its improved behaviour compared to other solution method is evident.

Acknowledgment

This work was supported by the Slovenian Research Agency through the research programme P2-0260. The support is gratefully acknowledged.

References

[1] S. S. Antman, Nonlinear Problems of Elasticity, 2nd ed. Berlin: Springer, 2005.

[2] J. C. Simo and L. Vu-Quoc, "On the dynamics in space of rods undergoing large motions - a geometrically exact approach," Comput. Meth. Appl. Mech. Eng., vol. 66, no. 2, pp. 125–161, 1988.

[3] C. Bottasso and M. Borri, "Integrating finite rotations," Comput. Meth. Appl. Mech. Eng., vol. 164, no. 3-4, pp. 307–331, 1998.

[4] H. Munthe-Kaas, "Runge-Kutta methods on Lie groups," Bit, vol. 38, no. 1, pp. 92–111, 1998.

[5] O. A. Bauchau and S. Han, "Interpolation of rotation and motion," Multibody Syst. Dyn., vol. 31, no. 3, pp. 339–370, 2014.

[6] M. E. Hosea and L. F. Shampine, "Analysis and implementation of TR-BDF2," Appl. Numer. Math., vol. 20, no. 1-2, pp. 21–37, 1996.

[7] E. Reissner, "On finite deformations of space-curved beams," Z. Angew. Math. Phys., vol. 32, no. 6, pp. 734–744, 1981.

[8] J. C. Simo, "A finite strain beam formulation - the three-dimensional dynamic problem. Part I." Comput. Meth. Appl. Mech. Eng., vol. 49, no. 1, pp. 55–70, 1985.

[9] H. Lang, J. Linn, and M. Arnold, "Multi-body dynamics simulation of geometrically exact Cosserat rods," Multibody Syst. Dyn., vol. 25, no. 3, pp. 285–312, 2011.

[10] E. Zupan, M. Saje, and D. Zupan, "Dynamics of spatial beams in quaternion description based on the Newmark integration scheme," Comput. Mech., vol. 51, no. 1, pp. 47–64, 2013.

[11] G. Jelenić and M. A. Crisfield, "Geometrically exact 3D beam theory: implementation of a strain-invariant finite element for statics and dynamics," Comput. Meth. Appl. Mech. Eng., vol. 171, no. 1-2, pp. 141–171, 1999.

[12] J. C. Simo, N. Tarnow, and M. Doblare, "Nonlinear dynamics of 3-dimensional rods - exact energy and momentum conserving algorithms," Int. J. Numer. Methods Eng., vol. 38, no. 9, pp. 1431–1473, 1995.

An Algorithm for Expensive Optimization Problems

Yoel Tenne

Department of Mechanical and Mechatronic Engineering
Ariel University, Israel
email: y.tenne@ariel.ac.il

***Abstract*—Computer simulations are used extensively in engineering and science to evaluate candidate designs, as a partial substitute for real-world experiments. *Metamodels*, which are computationally cheaper approximations of the simulation, are often used in these settings to alleviate various issues arising in such simulation-driven design processes. However, due to the high computational cost of running the simulation only a small number of designs can be evaluated, and hence the resultant metamodel will be inaccurate. To achieve a more accurate approximation, *ensembles* employ multiple metamodel variants concurrently, and aggregate their individual predictions into a single one. Nevertheless, the optimal ensemble topology, namely, which types of metamodels should be incorporated, is typically not known a-priori, while using a fixed topology may degrade the search effectiveness. To address this issue, this study proposes a new metamodel-assisted algorithm with *dynamic topology adaptation*, namely, which autonomously adapts the ensemble topology during the search, and dynamically selects the most suitable topology as the search progresses. An extensive performance analysis shows the effectiveness of the proposed algorithm, and highlights the merit of the proposed topology adaptation.**

Keywords–expensive optimization problems; metamodels; ensembles; computational intelligence

I. INTRODUCTION

The current availability of high performance computing allows engineers and researchers to evaluate candidate designs with computer simulations instead of using laboratory experiments, thereby reducing the duration and cost of the design process. In this setup, a candidate design is parameterized as a vector of design of variables, and is sent to the simulation for evaluation. Such computer simulations, which still need to be validated with laboratory experiments, transform the design process into an optimization problem having several distinct features [20]:

- The simulation acts as the objective function as it assigns objective values to candidate designs (input vectors), but it is a 'black-box', namely, the analytic expression of this mapping is unknown. This can occur since the simulation involves intricate calculations, or the simulation's code might be inaccessible to the user. In any case, the lack of an analytic expression presents an optimization challenge.
- Each simulation run is often computationally expensive, and hence only a small number of designs can be evaluated.
- Both the real-world physics being modelled, and the numerical simulation process itself, can yield a black-box function with complicated features, such as multiple optima or discontinuities, which add an additional optimization challenge.

An established solution methodology in such scenarios is to incorporate a *metamodel* into the optimization search. The latter is a mathematical approximation of the true expensive function which provides predicted objective values at a much lower computational cost [20]. A variety of metamodels have been proposed, but the optimal type is problem-dependant and is typically not known a-priori. To alleviate this issue, *ensembles* use several metamodels concurrently and aggregate their predictions into a single one [6, 10, 11]. However, the effectiveness of ensembles depends on their topology, namely, which metamodels they incorporate, but again, the optimal topology is typically unknown. To address this issue, this paper proposes an optimization algorithm which dynamically adapts the ensemble topology during the search, such that an optimal ensemble topology is continuously being selected and used. Also, since metamodels are inherently inaccurate, the proposed algorithm operates within a Trust Region (TR) approach to ensure convergence to an optimum of the true expensive function. Performance analysis using both mathematical test functions and a simulation-driven engineering problem shows the effectiveness of the proposed algorithm, and highlights the merit of the proposed dynamic topology adaptation.

The remainder of this paper is organized as follows: Section II provides the pertinent background information, Section III describes in detail the proposed algorithm, and Section IV provides an extensive performance evaluation. Lastly, Section V concludes this paper.

II. BACKGROUND

As mentioned in Section I, metamodels (also termed in the literature as *response surfaces* or *surrogates*) are used as computationally cheaper approximations of the numerical simulation. Metamodels are trained with previously evaluated vectors, and variants include Artificial Neural Networks (ANNs), Kriging, polynomials, and radial basis functions (RBFs), to name a few [11, 17]. A typical metamodel-assisted optimization search begins by sampling an initial set of vectors, followed by a main loop in which a metamodel is trained by using the vectors evaluated so far, seeking an optimum of the metamodel, and evaluating the latter vector, and possibly additional ones, with the true objective function. The process repeats until the number of simulation calls reaches the user-defined limit. Fig. 1 gives a pseudocode of a typical metamodel-assisted algorithm, while more involved frameworks have also been proposed [14, 18].

While metamodels offer several merits, they also introduce new optimization challenges:

- *Prediction inaccuracy*: Since only a small number of vectors can be evaluated with true expensive function the

Figure 1: A typical metamodel-assisted algorithm.

sample an initial set of vectors;
while *stopping criterion not met* **do**
  train a metamodel with the cached vectors;
  seek an optimum of the metamodel;
  evaluate the found solution, and possibly additional vectors, with the true expensive function;
return the best solution found;

resultant metamodel will inherently be inaccurate, and it is therefore necessary to *manage* it to avoid convergence to a poor final result [9]. This can be achieved with the established *Trust Region* (TR) framework [2, 12], in which the search is performed by a series of trial-steps, each confined to the region in which the metamodel is assumed to be sufficiently accurate. The TR is then updated based on the success of the optimization trial step. A strong merit of the TR approach is that it ensures asymptotic convergence to an optimum of the true expensive function [3]. Section III gives a detailed description of the TR approach implemented in this study.

- *Metamodel suitability*: Various metamodel variants have been proposed, but the optimal type is problem-dependant and is typically unknown [7, 18]. Metamodel *ensembles* address this by using multiple metamodels concurrently and aggregating their individual predictions [10, 19]. However, the ensemble topology itself is also problem dependant, and an inadequate topology can degrade the prediction accuracy. As an example, ensembles were generated based on three metamodels: RBFs, radial basis functions neural network (RBFN), and Kriging, as shown in Table I. The respective prediction accuracies of each ensemble was estimated based on the Root Mean Square Error (RMSE) measure across four test functions in dimensions ranging from 5 to 30. It follows that the optimal topology, namely, that having the lowest RMSE, varied across the functions, and that no single topology was the overall best. This suggests that using a fixed ensemble topology is inoptimal, and the following section proposes an algorithm which addresses this issue.

III. Proposed Algorithm

The algorithm proposed in this study uses *dynamic topology adaption*, namely, during the search it continuously selects and uses the topology deemed as optimal. The algorithm operates in five main steps, as follows:

Step 1) Initialization: An initial sample of vectors is generated with the Optimal Latin Hypercube Sampling (OLHS) method to obtain a space-filling sample, which in turn improves the prediction accuracy of the metamodels [21].

Step 2) The set of sampled vectors is split into a training and testing set, and the RMSE of each of the $j = 1 \dots n$ metamodel variants is calculated based on the testing set as follows

$$e_j = \sqrt{\frac{1}{l}\sum_{i=1}^{l}\left(m_j(\boldsymbol{x}_i) - f(\boldsymbol{x}_i)\right)^2}, \tag{1}$$

where $m_j(\boldsymbol{x})$ is a metamodel trained based on the training set, and $\boldsymbol{x}_i, i = 1 \dots l$ are the testing vectors.

Step 3) The set of sampled vectors is re-split again into training and testing sets, the metamodels are retrained, and the RMSE of each candidate ensemble topology is calculated as follows

$$\varepsilon(\boldsymbol{x}) = \sum_{j=1}^{n} u_j \hat{m}_j(\boldsymbol{x}), \quad u_j = \frac{e_j^{-1}}{\sum_{j=1}^{n} e_j^{-1}}, \tag{2a}$$

$$e_\varepsilon = \sqrt{\frac{1}{l}\sum_{i=1}^{l}\left(\varepsilon(\boldsymbol{x}_i) - f(\boldsymbol{x}_i)\right)^2} \tag{2b}$$

where $\varepsilon(\boldsymbol{x})$ is the ensemble prediction, $\hat{m}_j(\boldsymbol{x})$ is a metamodel trained with the current training set and is active in the topology being evaluated, u_j is the metamodel's weight in the ensemble, while $\boldsymbol{x}_i, i = 1 \dots l$ are the testing vectors in the current testing set, and e_ε is the RMSE of the ensemble being examined.

Step 4) The ensemble topology with the best (lowest) RMSE is selected for the current iteration. A corresponding ensemble is re-trained based on the selected topology but using all the evaluated vectors.

Step 5) A TR is defined around the current best vector ($\boldsymbol{x}_\text{b}$), and a search is performed to locate the best vector in the TR, based on the ensemble prediction. The search is performed by an evolutionary algorithm (EA) followed by an SQP solver. During this trial search only the ensemble is used, and no calls are made to the expensive function.

Step 6) The best vector found ($\boldsymbol{x}^\star$) is evaluated with the true objective function, and the following updates take place:

- If $f(\boldsymbol{x}^\star) < f(\boldsymbol{x}_\text{b})$: The trial step was successful since the new vector found is indeed better than the current best vector. This implies that the ensemble is accurate, and so the TR is centred at the new vector found and the TR radius is doubled.
- If $f(\boldsymbol{x}^\star) \geqslant f(\boldsymbol{x}_\text{b})$ *and* there are sufficient vectors inside the TR: The trial step failed since the vector found is not better than the current best. This implies that the ensemble is inaccurate, and since there are sufficient vectors in the TR the failure is attributed to the TR being too large. Therefore, the TR radius is halved.
- If $f(\boldsymbol{x}^\star) \geqslant f(\boldsymbol{x}_\text{b})$ *and* the number of vectors in the TR is deemed as too low: As above, the trial step failed but now the failure is attributed to the small number of vectors in the TR. Accordingly, a new

TABLE I. The Root Mean Square Error (RMSE) of Different Ensembles Topologies

Function	Ensemble topology			
	R+RN	R+K	RN+K	R+RN+K
Ackley-5D	4.258e-01	3.702e-01	4.151e-01	**2.967e-01**
Rastrigin-10D	1.223e+02	**8.198e+01**	1.312e+02	1.097e+02
Rosenbrock-20D	1.791e+06	1.666e+06	**1.648e+06**	1.693e+06
Schwefel 2.13-30D	**1.882e+06**	2.179e+06	2.343e+06	2.079e+06

R:RBF, RN:RBF neural network, K:Kriging.

vector is sampled in a section of the TR which is sparse with vectors.

As a change from the classical TR framework, the proposed algorithm reduces the TR radius only if the number of vectors in the TR is sufficient, which is done to avoid premature convergence. This threshold value was calibrated with numerical experiments. Also, it is important to note that while in this study the metamodels RBF, RBFN, and Kriging were used, the proposed algorithm can accommodate any other type or number metamodels. To complete this section, Fig. 2 presents the pseudocode of the proposed algorithm.

Figure 2: Proposed algorithm with dynamic ensemble adaptation.

```
/* initialization                                          */
generate an initial Optimal Latin Hypercube sample and
evaluate the vectors with the true function;
/* main optimization loop                                  */
repeat
    /* generate a metamodel ensemble                       */
    estimate the prediction error of individual
    metamodels with cross-validation;
    split the vectors evaluated again into a training
    subset and a testing subsets;
    for each candidate ensemble topology do
        calculate the ensemble weights of each
        metamodel in the topology;
        estimate the ensemble accuracy by using the
        testing set;
    select the optimal (most accurate) topology, and
    train an ensemble with all the vectors evaluated;
    /* perform a TR trial step                             */
    set the TR centre to the best vector found so far;
    perform a trial step (using an EA+SQP) in the TR;
    evaluate the obtained vector with the true expensive
    function;
    /* update the TR                                       */
    if the new solution is better than the current best then
        double the TR radius
    else if the new solution is not better than the current
    best and there the number of vectors in the TR is
    sufficient then
        halve the TR radius;
    else if the new solution is not better than the current
    best and the number of vectors in the TR is
    insufficient then
        add new vectors in the TR to improve the
        prediction accuracy;
until maximum number of simulation calls;
```

IV. Performance analysis

A. Benchmark tests based on mathematical test functions

To assess the effectiveness of the proposed algorithm, it was applied to a well-established set of mathematical test functions [16] which are shown in Table II, in dimensions ranging from 5 to 40.

For a rigorous evaluation, the proposed algorithm was benchmarked against four reference algorithms:

TABLE II. MATHEMATICAL TEST FUNCTIONS

Function	Definition, $f(\boldsymbol{x}) =$	Domain
Ackley	$-20\exp\left(-0.2\sqrt{\sum_{i=1}^{d} x_i^2/d}\right) - \exp\left(\sum_{i=1}^{d}\cos(2\pi x_i)/d\right) + 20 + e$	$[-32, 32]^d$
Griewank	$\sum_{i=1}^{d}\{x_i^2/4000\} - \prod_{i=1}^{d}\{\cos\left(x_i/\sqrt{i}\right)\} + 1$	$[-100, 100]^d$
Rastrigin	$\sum_{i=1}^{d}\{x_i^2 - 10\cos(2\pi x_i) + 10\}$	$[-5, 5]^d$
Rosenbrock	$\sum_{i=1}^{d-1}\{100(x_i^2 - x_{i+1})^2 + (x_i - 1)^2\}$	$[-10, 10]^d$
Schwefel 2.13	$\sum_{i=1}^{d}\{\sum_{j=1}^{d}\left[(a_{i,j}\sin(\alpha_j) + b_{i,j}\cos(\alpha_j)) - (a_{i,j}\sin(x_j) + b_{i,j}\cos(x_j))\right]\}^2$	$[-\pi, \pi]^d$
Weierstrass	$\sum_{i=1}^{d}\{\sum_{k=0}^{20} 0.5^k\cos(2\pi 3^k(x_i + 0.5))\} - d\sum_{k=0}^{20} 0.5^k\cos(\pi 3^k)$	$[-0.5, 0.5]^d$

- *V1*: A variant of the proposed algorithm which is identical to it in operation, *except* that it used a single metamodel (RBF), and no ensembles. This algorithm was used to highlight the impact of the ensemble adaptation in comparison to using a fixed metamodel without an ensemble.
- *V2*: A variant of the proposed algorithm which is identical to it in operation, *except* that it used a fixed ensemble which consisted of RBF, RBFN, and Kriging metamodels. This algorithm was used to highlight the impact of the ensemble adaptation in comparison to using a fixed ensemble (no topology adaptation).
- *EA with Periodic Sampling* (EA–PS): A metamodel-assisted algorithm which leverages on the concepts in [4, 13]. The algorithm combines a Kriging metamodel and an EA, and safeguards the metamodel accuracy by periodically evaluating a small subset of the population with the true objective function and incorporating them into the metamodel. This algorithm is representative of many other metamodel-assisted algorithm in the literature.
- *Expected Improvement with Covariance Matrix Adaptation Evolutionary Strategy* (CMA-ES) (EI–CMA-ES): The algorithm combines a CMA-ES optimizer with Kriging metamodels, and uses the expected improvement framework to update the metamodels [1]. This algorithm represents more advanced metamodel-assisted implementations.

These algorithms were chosen as they allowed to evaluate: i) the contribution of dynamic ensemble adaptation (by comparing to the V1 and V2 algorithms), and ii) how the proposed algorithm compares with existing algorithms from the literature. For each algorithm–test function combination 30 runs were repeated so that there were sufficient runs on which a valid statistical analysis could be made. The number of simulations calls, namely, evaluations of the expensive function, was limited to 200, to represent a tight limit on the number of evaluations of the true objective function. Table III gives the resultant test statistics of mean, standard deviation (SD), median, minimum (best) and maximum (worst) objective value in each optimization test case. It also gives the statistic α which indicates the significance level (either 0.05, 0.01) at which the performance of the proposed algorithm was better than that of the other algorithms, where an empty entry indicates that there was no statistically significant performance advantage. The α statistic was determined with the Mann–Whitney nonparametric test [15].

Test results show that the proposed algorithm performed well, as it obtained the best mean statistic in all six cases, and the best median statistic in five out of six cases (all except for the Rastrigin-5 case where it obtained the second best median). Also, its performance had a statistically significant advantage in 13 out of 24 comparisons, namely over 50% of the cases, which further demonstrates its performance advantage. The proposed algorithm also performed well in terms of the SD statistic: it achieved the best (lowest) SD in 3 cases, and was comparable to the best performing algorithms in other cases, which shows that it typically maintained a low level of variability in its performance, which is also desirable.

The test results also highlight the merits of the dynamic topology adaptation approach of adapting the ensemble topology, as evident from the performance gains with respect to using a single metamodel (V1 algorithm) or a fixed ensemble (V2 algorithm). The proposed algorithm also outperformed the two reference algorithms from the literature, which shows that it was competitive with existing approaches.

The analysis also examined the pattern of updates of the ensemble topology to study if one specific topology was mainly selected, or if various topologies were used. Accordingly, Fig. 3 shows plots of the dynamic ensemble adaptation from a run with the Ackley-10D function and another with the Rosenbrock-20D function. While a Kriging metamodel topology was selected more frequently than the other topologies, in both tests the optimal topology varied consistently throughout the search. This further highlights the merit of the proposed topology adaptation approach over that of using a fixed topology.

B. Engineering test problem

Beyond the tests with mathematical test functions, the numerical experiments also included a test based on a simulation-driven engineering problem, to more closely represent real-world problems. The optimization goal here was to find an airfoil shape which maximizes the lift produced while minimizing the drag (aerodynamic friction) at some prescribed flight conditions. Candidate airfoils were represented with the method of Hicks and Henne [8], such that an airfoil profile was given by

$$y = y_b + \sum_{i=1}^{h} \alpha_i b_i(x)\,, \tag{3a}$$

$$b_i(x) = \left[\sin\left(\pi x^{\frac{\log(0.5)}{\log(i/(h+1))}}\right)\right]^4\,, \tag{3b}$$

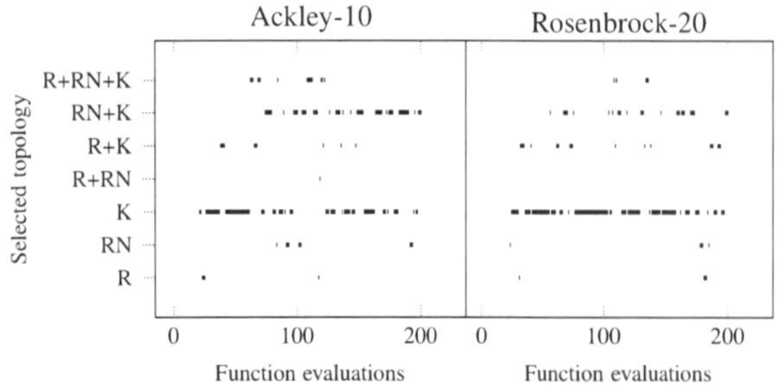

Figure 3. Selected ensemble topologies (R:RBF, RN:RBFN, K:Kriging).

where y_b is a baseline airfoil profile, taken here to be the NACA0012 symmetric airfoil, b_i are geometric basis functions [22], and $\alpha_i \in [-0.01, 0.01]$ are weights whose optimal values need to be found, namely, those which define the best performing airfoil. To visualize the problem formulation, Fig. 4 shows the layout of the airfoil problem.

Two optimization scenarios were examined: i) a low dimensional case where each of the upper and lower airfoil profiles were defined by three basis functions, thereby resulting in a total of six design variables, and ii) a high dimensional case where 10 basis were used per profile, thereby resulting in a total of 20 design variables. The lift and drag coefficients of candidate airfoils were obtained by using *XFoil*, a computational fluid dynamics simulation for analysis of subsonic isolated airfoils [5]. To ensure structural integrity of the airfoil, the minimum airfoil thickness (t) between 20% to 80% of the airfoil chord line needed to be no less than a critical value $t^\star = 0.1$. Accordingly, the objective function used was

$$f = -\frac{c_l}{c_d} + p\,,\quad p = \begin{cases} \frac{t^\star}{t} \cdot \left|\frac{c_l}{c_d}\right| & \text{if } t < t^\star \\ 0 & \text{otherwise} \end{cases} \tag{4}$$

where p is a penalty for violation of the thickness constraint. The prescribed flight conditions were a cruise altitude of 30,000 ft, a cruise speed of Mach 0.7, namely 70% of the speed of sound, and an angle of attack (AOA) of 2°, which is the angle between the airfoil chord line and the aircraft velocity.

Tests were performed following the setup in Section IV-A, and Table IV gives the resultant test statistics. It follows that the results obtained here are consistent with those of the previous section, and that the proposed algorithm again outperformed the others algorithms, as evident from the test statistics.

Also following Section IV-A, Fig. 5 shows the ensemble topologies which were selected during one run from the 6D scenario and one from the 20D scenario, respectively. As before, the optimal topology varied continuously during the

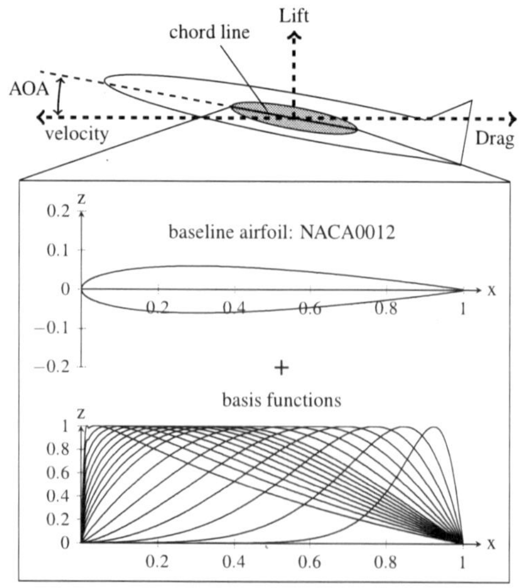

Figure 4. The layout of the airfoil optimization problem.

TABLE III. TEST STATISTICS–MATHEMATICAL TEST FUNCTIONS

		Proposed	V1	V2	EA-PS	EI-CMA-ES
Ackley-10	Mean	**7.705e+00**	1.455e+01	1.356e+01	5.241e+00	1.796e+01
	SD	8.359e+00	4.649e+00	8.051e+00	5.590e-01	1.529e+00
	Median	**2.314e+00**	1.592e+01	1.908e+01	5.408e+00	1.797e+01
	Min(best)	9.007e-02	2.383e+00	3.457e+00	4.098e+00	1.443e+01
	Max(worst)	1.836e+01	1.825e+01	2.048e+01	6.010e+00	1.988e+01
	α			0.01		0.01
Griewank-10	Mean	**1.304e-01**	1.972e-01	2.078e-01	9.579e-01	9.338e-01
	SD	1.851e-01	1.714e-01	2.213e-01	1.076e-01	2.435e-01
	Median	**7.747e-02**	1.294e-01	1.357e-01	9.862e-01	1.007e+00
	Min(best)	9.350e-03	3.569e-02	2.290e-02	7.146e-01	2.441e-01
	Max(worst)	6.505e-01	5.661e-01	7.601e-01	1.046e+00	1.050e+00
	α				0.01	0.01
Rastrigin-5	Mean	**6.377e+00**	9.360e+00	8.018e+00	7.631e+00	2.131e+01
	SD	3.728e+00	7.852e+00	8.349e+00	4.811e+00	4.890e+00
	Median	5.980e+00	7.464e+00	**4.298e+00**	7.226e+00	2.139e+01
	Min(best)	1.997e+00	1.005e+00	3.369e+00	1.621e+00	1.353e+01
	Max(worst)	1.195e+01	2.787e+01	3.076e+01	1.456e+01	3.006e+01
	α					0.01
Rosenbrock-20	Mean	**5.839e+02**	1.031e+03	8.186e+02	8.435e+02	3.967e+03
	SD	2.094e+02	5.818e+02	3.823e+02	3.012e+02	9.406e+02
	Median	**5.956e+02**	8.665e+02	7.932e+02	7.782e+02	3.685e+03
	Min(best)	2.143e+02	5.483e+02	3.078e+02	4.676e+02	3.141e+03
	Max(worst)	8.905e+02	2.517e+03	1.521e+03	1.439e+03	6.144e+03
	α		0.01		0.05	0.01
Schwefel-40	Mean	**7.727e+05**	8.981e+05	1.935e+06	1.774e+06	1.667e+06
	SD	2.219e+05	2.571e+05	6.789e+05	2.509e+05	6.520e+05
	Median	**7.243e+05**	8.622e+05	2.032e+06	1.744e+06	1.528e+06
	Min(best)	5.130e+05	5.885e+05	8.715e+05	1.415e+06	8.933e+05
	Max(worst)	1.131e+06	1.362e+06	3.065e+06	2.104e+06	2.871e+06
	α			0.01	0.01	0.01
Weierstrass-40	Mean	**2.824e+01**	4.160e+01	4.394e+01	3.045e+01	3.598e+01
	SD	4.401e+00	4.261e+00	3.885e+00	1.645e+00	1.463e+01
	Median	**2.547e+01**	4.227e+01	4.461e+01	2.995e+01	2.597e+01
	Min(best)	2.421e+01	3.353e+01	3.726e+01	2.878e+01	2.100e+01
	Max(worst)	3.482e+01	4.794e+01	4.867e+01	3.337e+01	5.817e+01
	α		0.01	0.01		

entire search. These results, combined with the test statistics, show that dynamically adapting the ensemble topology during the search improved the search effectiveness also in these simulation-driven problems.

V. CONCLUSION AND FUTURE WORK

The use of simulations in engineering design defines a unique optimization problem which is termed in the literature as an *expensive black-box* problem. Metamodels are used in such settings to approximate the computationally expensive simulation, and to allow a more efficient optimization search. Since the optimal metamodel variant is problem-dependant and is typically unknown a-priori, ensembles use multiple metamodels concurrently, and aggregate their predictions to a single output, in an attempt to improve the prediction accuracy. However, the ensemble topology itself is also problem-dependant, and the optimal topology is also typically unknown. To address this issue, this study has proposed an ensemble based optimization algorithm which dynamically adapts the ensemble topology during the search, so that an optimal topology is used at each stage. Furthermore, the proposed algorithm operates within a TR framework to ensure convergence to an optimum of the true expensive function in spite of the inherent metamodel prediction inaccuracies. In a detailed performance analysis the proposed algorithm was benchmarked against various algorithms with no dynamic topology adaptation. It consistently outperformed the other algorithms across the different test problems, and the optimal topology varied continuously throughout the search. Overall, results show that the proposed algorithm performed well across a range of test problems, and that the effectiveness of metamodel-assisted search was improved with the proposed dynamic topology adaption. Based on the promising results obtained, future work will examine additional topology selection mechanisms, for example, such as those based on other error measures or other sampling approaches.

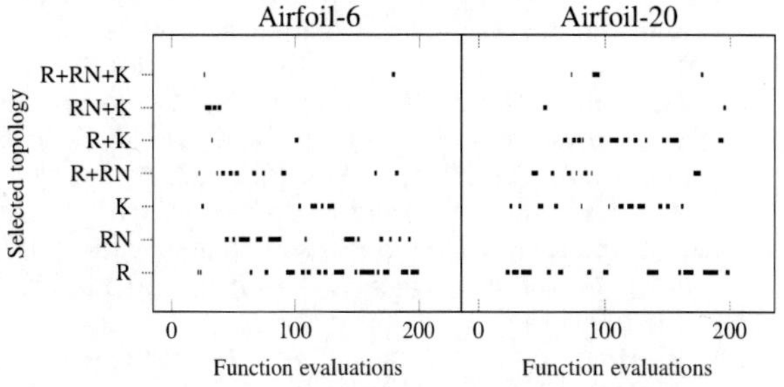

Figure 5. Selected topologies for the airfoil problems (R:RBF, RN:RBFN, K:Kriging).

TABLE IV. TEST STATISTICS–AIRFOIL PROBLEM

		Proposed	V1	V2	EA–PS	EI–CMA-ES
6D	Mean	**-8.360e+01**	-8.048e+01	-8.203e+01	-7.799e+01	-7.231e+01
	SD	1.320e+01	1.659e+01	2.261e+01	2.250e+00	7.159e-01
	Median	**-7.567e+01**	-7.533e+01	-7.554e+01	-7.831e+01	-7.264e+01
	Min(best)	-1.068e+02	-1.268e+02	-1.436e+02	-8.036e+01	-7.290e+01
	Max(worst)	-7.488e+01	-7.174e+01	-6.405e+01	-7.238e+01	-7.099e+01
	α					0.01
20D	Mean	**-3.247e+00**	-3.202e+00	-3.239e+00	-3.174e+00	-3.212e+00
	SD	6.421e-02	6.991e-02	8.932e-02	8.887e-02	9.405e-02
	Median	**-3.231e+00**	-3.208e+00	-3.206e+00	-3.142e+00	-3.202e+00
	Min(best)	-3.354e+00	-3.303e+00	-3.414e+00	-3.348e+00	-3.327e+00
	Max(worst)	-3.151e+00	-3.098e+00	-3.134e+00	-3.070e+00	-3.036e+00
	α				0.05	

REFERENCES

[1] D. Büche, N. N. Schraudolph, and P. Koumoutsakos, "Accelerating evolutionary algorithms with Gaussian process fitness function models," *IEEE Transactions on Systems, Man, and Cybernetics–Part C*, vol. 35, no. 2, pp. 183–194, 2005.

[2] A. R. Conn, K. Scheinberg, and P. L. Toint, "On the convergence of derivative-free methods for unconstrained optimization," in *Approximation Theory and Optimization: Tributes to M.J.D. Powell*, A. Iserles and M. D. Buhmann, Eds. Cambridge; New York: Cambridge University Press, 1997, pp. 83–108.

[3] A. R. Conn, N. I. M. Gould, and P. L. Toint, *Trust Region Methods*. Philadelphia, Pennsylvania: SIAM, 2000.

[4] K. A. de Jong, *Evolutionary Computation:A Unified Approach*. Cambridge, Massachusetts: MIT Press, 2006.

[5] M. Drela and H. Youngren, *XFOIL 6.9 User Primer*, Department of Aeronautics and Astronautics, Massachusetts Institute of Technology, Cambridge, MA, 2001.

[6] T. Goel, R. T. Haftka, W. Shyy, and N. V. Queipo, "Ensembles of surrogates," *Structural and Multidisciplinary Optimization*, vol. 33, pp. 199–216, 2007.

[7] D. Gorissen, T. Dhaene, and F. De Turck, "Evolutionary model type selection for global surrogate modeling," *The Journal of Machine Learning Research*, vol. 10, pp. 2039–2078, 2009.

[8] R. M. Hicks and P. A. Henne, "Wing design by numerical optimization," *Journal of Aircraft*, vol. 15, no. 7, pp. 407–412, 1978.

[9] Y. Jin, M. Olhofer, and B. Sendhoff, "A framework for evolutionary optimization with approximate fitness functions," *IEEE Transactions on evolutionary computation*, vol. 6, no. 5, pp. 481–494, 2002.

[10] J. Muller and R. Piché, "Mixture surrogate models based on dempster-shafer theory for global optimization problems," *Journal of Global Optimization*, vol. 51, no. 1, pp. 79–104, 2011.

[11] J. Muller and C. A. Shoemaker, "Influence of ensemble surrogate models and sampling strategy on the solution quality of algorithms for computationally expensive black-box global optimization problems," *Journal of Global Optimization*, vol. 60, pp. 123–144, 2014.

[12] M. J. D. Powell, "On trust region methods for unconstrained minimization without derivatives," *Mathematical Programming, Series B*, vol. 97, pp. 605–623, 2003.

[13] A. Ratle, "Optimal sampling strategies for learning a fitness model," in *The 1999 IEEE Congress on Evolutionary Computation–CEC 1999*. Piscataway, New Jersey: IEEE, 1999, pp. 2078–2085.

[14] R. G. Regis and C. A. Shoemaker, "A quasi-multistart framework for global optimization of expensive functions using response surface models," *Journal of Global Optimization*, vol. 56, pp. 1719–1753, 2013.

[15] D. J. Sheskin, *Handbook of Parametric and Nonparametric Statistical Procedures*, 4th ed. Boca Raton, Florida: Chapman and Hall, 2007.

[16] P. N. Suganthan, N. Hansen, J. J. Liang, K. Deb, Y. P. Chen, A. Auger, and S. Tiwari, "Problem definitions and evaluation criteria for the CEC 2005 special session on real-parameter optimization," Nanyang Technological University, Singapore and Kanpur Genetic Algorithms Laboratory, Indian Institute of Technology Kanpur, India, Technical Report KanGAL 2005005, 2005.

[17] Y. Tenne, "A computational intelligence algorithm for simulation-driven optimization problems," *Advances in Engineering Software*, vol. 47, pp. 62–71, 2012.

[18] ——, "An optimization algorithm employing multiple metamodels and optimizers," *International Journal of Automation and Computing*, vol. 10, no. 3, pp. 227–241, 2013.

[19] ——, "An algorithm for computationally expensive engineering optimization problems," *International Journal of General Systems*, vol. 42, no. 5, pp. 458–488, 2013.

[20] Y. Tenne and C. K. Goh, Eds., *Computational Intelligence in Expensive Optimization Problems*, ser. Evolutionary Learning and Optimization. Berlin: Springer, 2010, vol. 2.

[21] F. A. C. Viana, G. Venter, and V. Balabanov, "An algorithm for fast optimal Latin hypercube design of experiments," *International Journal of Numerical Methods in Engineering*, vol. 82, no. 2, pp. 135–156, 2009.

[22] H.-Y. Wu, S. Yang, F. Liu, and H.-M. Tsai, "Comparison of three geometric representations of airfoils for aerodynamic optimization," in *Proceedings of the 16th AIAA Computational Fluid Dynamics Conference*. Reston, Virginia: American Institute of Aeronautics and Astronautics, 2003, AIAA 2003-4095.

Parallel Program Complex "Express-3D" for 3D Flows Simulation on Hybrid Computer Systems

Alexander A. Davydov and Evgeny V. Shilnikov
Keldysh Institute of Applied Mathematics RAS
Moscow, Russia
e-mail: alexander.a.davydov@gmail.com, shiva@imamod.ru

***Abstract*—The paper presents a program complex for solving computational fluid dynamics problems, oriented on heterogeneous computer systems. Based on finite volumes method, an explicit difference scheme is constructed for Quasi Gas Dynamic equations system in 3D formulation on arbitrary hexagonal non-orthogonal structured index grid. The use of multi block grids is proposed. To improve the stability condition, the flux relaxation approach is used. The algorithm efficiency was verified on a set of test problems with wide variety of flow types. The speed-up for different computing units was investigated.**

Keywords-quasi gas dynamic equations; explicit scheme; finite volume method, nonorthogonal grid; hybrid supercomputer architecture.

I. INTRODUCTION

The development of modern hybrid computer systems is connected with massively parallel multicore processors with powerful accelerators, such as general purpose graphics processing units (GP-GPUs). They open possibilities for reducing the cost of a computer system per unit of performance and significantly reduce power consumption. These systems bring new opportunities to mathematical modeling and simulation. However, the difficulties in the efficient use of such hybrid systems are much greater than those in using conventional cluster-type high performance computers. Many of the existing sophisticated numerical methods are often not sufficient for modern high performance computer (HPC) systems. Such systems require software being created to take into account different types of processing units and a hybrid structure of memory. Experience shows that, for an effective application, it is preferable to apply algorithms as simple as possible from the logic point of view. In this regard very promising are the explicit schemes, which can be easily adapted to the computer systems with different architectures.

This paper presents further development of a program complex "Express-3D" [1], oriented on heterogeneous GPU-based computer systems. The program complex uses the explicit variant of kinetically consistent finite difference schemes based on quasi gas dynamic (QGD) equation system [2][3]. These schemes belong to the class of kinetic or Boltzmann schemes which are presently often used in the computational fluid dynamics (CFD) [4][5]. They are an effective approach to the numerical simulation of continuous media problems. The use of previous version of our program complex showed good results in solving a large number of gas dynamic problems. However, its use was limited by rectangular grids. Here, we present a new version of this program complex, which uses multi block, non orthogonal curvilinear structured hexahedral grids. Such grids give the opportunity to solve problems with complicated geometry and, on the other hand, the computational algorithm for structured grid is usually much simpler than for widely used unstructured tetrahedral grids.

In Section 2, the QGD equations system is presented and analyzed, the method of difference scheme construction is described, the stability conditions and the method of their improving are discussed. In Section 3, the results of a set of test problems simulation are presented. In Section 4, the parallel implementation of our program complex is described. The comparison is presented of speedups achieved on different GPU types. In Section 5, some conclusions are drawn based on our experience in using the program complex presented.

II. NUMERICAL METHOD

QGD equation system [2] differs from Navier-Stokes equations in some additional dissipative terms. These terms are small compared to the terms of natural viscosity and conductivity and equal to zero in flow regions where the solution satisfies the stationary Euler equations. They can be interpreted as efficient numerical stabilizers, which provide smoothness of the solution at distances of the order of mean free path. The successful use of kinetic schemes for solving a wide range of fluid dynamics problems shows that they describe viscous heat conducting flows, as well as the Navier–Stokes equations in the regions where the latter equations are applicable.

For a 3D ideal polytrophic gas flow, this system in traditional notation may be written in the form of conservation laws approximation, as follows:

$$\frac{\partial \mathbf{U}}{\partial t} - \left(\nabla \mathbf{W}_{QGD}\right)^T = 0. \quad (1)$$

Here $\mathbf{U} = \left(\rho, \rho u_1, \rho u_2, \rho u_3, E\right)^T$ – the vector of conservative variables, $E = \rho\left(\varepsilon + \mathbf{u}^2/2\right)$ – total energy,

$\mathbf{W}_{QGD}$ – is the matrix consisting of the conservative variables fluxes:

$$\mathbf{W}_{QGD} = \left(-\mathbf{j}_m, \Pi - \mathbf{j}_m \otimes \mathbf{u} - pI, \Pi\mathbf{u} - \mathbf{q} - \mathbf{j}_m (E+p)/\rho\right). \quad (2)$$

I - is the unity matrix, vectors of mass flux ($\mathbf{j}_m$), heat flux ($\mathbf{q}$) and viscous stress tensor (Π) are defined as follows:

$$j_{mi} = \rho(u_i - w_i), \quad w_i = \frac{\tau}{\rho}\left(\frac{\partial}{\partial x_j}\rho u_j u_i + \frac{\partial}{\partial x_i} p\right), \quad (3)$$

$$q_i = q_i^{NS} - \tau\rho u_i u_j \left(\frac{\partial}{\partial x_j}\varepsilon + p\frac{\partial}{\partial x_j}\frac{1}{\rho}\right), \quad q_i^{NS} = -\kappa\frac{\partial}{\partial x_i}T, \quad (4)$$

$$\Pi_{ij} = \mu\left(\frac{\partial u_j}{\partial x_i} + \frac{\partial u_i}{\partial x_j} - \frac{2}{3}\delta_{ij}\frac{\partial u_k}{\partial x_k}\right) + $$
$$+\tau\rho u_i\left(u_k\frac{\partial u_j}{\partial x_k} + \frac{1}{\rho}\frac{\partial p}{\partial x_j}\right) + \tau\delta_{ij}\left(u_k\frac{\partial p}{\partial x_k} + \gamma p\frac{\partial u_k}{\partial x_k}\right). \quad (5)$$

Closing equations are:

$$p = \rho\varepsilon(\gamma - 1), \quad T = \frac{p}{\rho R}, \quad \tau = \frac{\mu}{p\mathrm{Sc}}, \quad (6)$$

$$\mu = \mu_0 \frac{C + T_0}{C + T}\left(\frac{T}{T_0}\right)^{3/2}, \quad \kappa = \mu\frac{\gamma R}{(\gamma - 1)\mathrm{Pr}} \quad (7)$$

Here γ – specific ratio, Pr and Sc – Prandtl and Schmidt numbers, τ is a relaxation parameter having a dimension of time, summation is implied over repeated indices. Parameters in the Sutherland formula for viscosity may be taken from the tables. For example, for nitrogen C = 111 K, T_0 = 300.55 K, μ_0 = 17.81 μPa·c.

In order to achieve computational stability, an item proportional to the spatial step size is usually added to the expression for relaxation parameter in (6)

$$\tau = \frac{\mu}{p\mathrm{Sc}} + \alpha\frac{h}{c}, \quad (8)$$

where c – is a local speed of sound, α – is a number of the order of unity, which is adjusted experimentally. Note that for high Reynolds numbers and not very fine grids the first term in (8) is much less than the second one and may be neglected.

When the flow of non viscid gas is simulated, we have $\mu = 0$ and $\tau = \alpha h/c$. So, all dissipative terms in QGD equations system are artificial regularizers, corresponding to the artificial viscosity $\mu_{art} = \tau \cdot p \cdot Sc$. In the case of viscous flows, equations contain both terms with natural viscosity and terms with artificial one. However, this combined viscosity may be insufficient for the computational stability when hypersonic flows with strong shock waves are simulated. In this case we correct the natural viscosity by some artificial additive proportional to the spatial step size. It means that the natural viscosity μ is replaced in all Navier-Stokes terms by corrected value $\mu' = \tau \cdot p \cdot Sc$, where τ is taken from (8).

To construct difference scheme we use the control volume method. Let some regular index grid be done, which consists of arbitrary convex hexahedrons in the computational domain. Let all gas dynamic parameters be addressed to cell centers and equal to $\bar{\mathbf{U}} = V^{-1}\int_V \mathbf{U}dV$, where V is a cell volume (we will omit the dash over variables in the following text). Integrating (1) over cell volume we obtain integral form of conservation laws. Replacing time derivative by finite difference, we have the following expression for conservative variables at the next time level (here summation is held over cell faces S_l with normal vectors $\mathbf{n}_l$):

$$\hat{\mathbf{U}} = \mathbf{U} + \frac{\Delta t}{V}\sum_{l=1}^{6}\int_{S_l}(\mathbf{W}^T, \mathbf{n}_l)dS \quad (9)$$

To calculate the integrals in (9), we suppose the gas dynamic values be constant on the cell faces. These values may be calculated by linear interpolation between values in the centers of the cells adjacent to the face. The approximation of spatial derivatives in the fluxes of conservative variables is also based on the finite volume method. The control volume is constructed connected with each face of grid cells. Let this volume be the octahedron with the vertices in the four centers of the face edges and two centers of the adjacent cells. The values of gas dynamic variables in the edge center may be calculated as a quarter of the sum of their values in the centers of four adjacent cells. Consider the vector-function $\mathbf{A} = (f(x, y, z), 0, 0)$ and integrate its divergence over the volume $\mathbf{\Omega}$ of the octahedron. By use of Gauss-Ostrogradsky formula, we have:

$$\int_{\Omega} div\mathbf{A}dV = \int_{\partial\Omega}(\mathbf{A}, \mathbf{n})dS = \sum_{m=1}^{8} n_{mx}\int_{S_m} fdS. \quad (10)$$

If we suppose the function $f(x,y,z)$ is linear at each octahedron face, we may calculate last integral. It is equal to the product of the face square and the arithmetic mean of function values in the face vertices. On the other hand, the volume integral in (10) is equal to the product of the octahedron volume by some average value of the derivative $\partial f/\partial x$. Addressing this value to the cell face center we obtain it after algebraic transformations as a linear combination of the function values in six octahedron vertices. The coefficients of this combination only depend on the grid points coordinates. Derivatives $\partial f/\partial y$ and $\partial f/\partial z$ may be expressed similarly. As a result, we have a 19-point stencil for the space approximation.

Usually, the explicit schemes impose stringent stability limitations on a time step, especially when the parabolic equations are solved, $\Delta t \sim h^2$, which is not appropriate for fine grids used in HPC calculation. Theoretical investigation of QGD based explicit schemes showed that, for numerical modeling of inviscid gas flows (when all dissipative terms in (1) – (7) are the artificial regularizers), the stability condition has a Courant type $\Delta t \sim h$, and the time step may be defined by the formula

$$\Delta t = \beta \cdot \min_i \frac{h_i}{c_i + |u_i|}, \tag{11}$$

where h_i, c_i, u_i are the spatial step, local speed of sound and gas velocity in i-th grid cell, β is a coefficient (Courant number), which does not depend on spatial step size. In the case of viscous gas flow simulation the situation is more complicated. Computational experience shows that these schemes have Courant-like stability condition with β close to unity for high and medium Mach number ($Ma \geq 0.3$) flow simulation, giving the opportunity to use very fine meshes to study the fine flow structure. However, with the Mach number diminishing the stability condition tends to $\Delta t \sim h^2$, which is typical for parabolic equations. A similar situation takes place in the case of hypersonic flow simulation ($Ma > 5$), when Courant number acceptable for calculation stability does not exceed 0.1.

To improve this situation we used the flux relaxation approach, proposed in [6]. The main idea of this method is a statement that the fluxes of conservative variables at any time moment cannot achieve new values instantly. They have to relax to them, starting from the previous values with some characteristic time of flux relaxation τ_f. Thus, the system (1) is transformed to

$$\frac{\partial}{\partial t}\mathbf{U} = (\nabla \mathbf{W})^T, \quad \tau_f \frac{\partial}{\partial t}\mathbf{W} = \mathbf{W}_{QGD} - \mathbf{W}. \tag{12}$$

For small values of τ_f or for slow processes (12) practically coincides with (1). But the new system has a hyperbolic type and, consequently, the Courant stability condition for the explicit schemes. So, we may construct finite difference scheme based on system (12) and use τ_f as a regularizing parameter. This parameter must be large enough to provide the best stability and small enough to receive the solution close to the solution of system (1). In [7], such transformation was investigated on the sample of heat conductivity equation. It was proved that, if the solution of the hyperbolic problem has no sufficient oscillations (second time derivative is not very large), then difference between solutions of parabolic and hyperbolic problems is small for small values of τ_f. Note that introducing the relaxation of fluxes, we remove the global defect of parabolic equations – infinite speed of disturbances propagation.

The second equation in (12) is the first order linear ODE, so, its solution on a time step Δt may be written, as follows:

$$\hat{\mathbf{W}} = \mathbf{W}D + \mathbf{W}_{QGD}(1-D), \quad D = \exp\left(-\Delta t / \tau_f\right). \tag{13}$$

So, a time step consists of three parts. At first, using the known values of gas dynamic parameters we calculate fluxes $\mathbf{W}_{QGD}$. Then we find a time step from (11) and, according to (13), correct fluxes values and find $\hat{\mathbf{W}}$. At last, we calculate new values of density, velocity components and energy from (9).

III. Test Problems Simulation

The program complex was tested on a set of problems including subsonic, supersonic and hypersonic flows. Some test results were presented in [8]. Here, we present some new simulations.

The first test problem is a nitrogen flow simulation over 2D edge compression corner described in [9]. This 2D problem was solved by means of 3D program with small number of cells in the third direction (y). The free stream parameters were $Ma_\infty = 9.22$, $Re_\infty = 47{\cdot}10^6$ per meter, $T_\infty = 64.5$ K, stagnation temperature $T_s = 1070$ K, without boundary layer tripping ahead of the flip. The compression corner angles were taken as 15° and 38°. The distance between the left border and angle edge is 76 cm. The boundary conditions are: constant inflow parameters on the left bound, no slip conditions on the bottom, zero normal derivatives on the upper and right bounds, and periodic boundary conditions in the third direction.

The calculation results are presented in Fig. 1 and Fig. 2. Fig. 1 demonstrates stream lines on the background of the pressure distributions in the central section of the computational region. For the case of 15° angle we have an attached flow with the shock wave attached to the corner edge. If the angle is equal to 38°, the separated flow is formed with a vortex and a chock wave in front of it. It is in agreement with the experimental results [9]. The calculated maximum values of pressure in flow field also coincide with experimental data.

Fig. 2 presents the comparison of calculated wall pressure distribution in the middle section with the experimental results. The calculations were held with different values of α coefficient in (8). One can see that the results obtained with α = 0.2 are better than for α = 0.5. This effect is natural because the coefficient α is responsible for the artificial members in equations. Further diminishing of this coefficient leads to the computational instability.

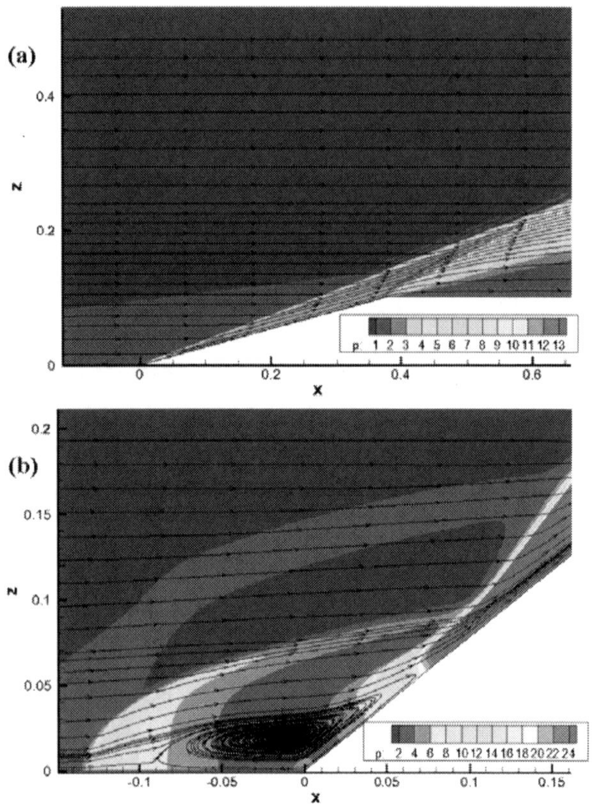

Figure 1. Stream traces near the compression corner with angle of 15° (a) and of 38° (b)

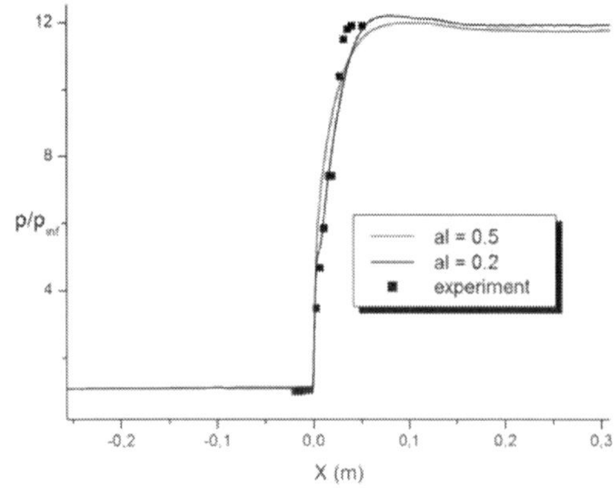

Figure 2. Wall pressure distribution for the corner angle of 15°.

The next problem was a subsonic (Ma = 0.1) flow around a hill. The Reynolds number was taken to be Re = 10^4. For such parameters a flow must be turbulent. A complicated 3D flow arises behind the hill with the separations and reattachments. Volume stream traces on the background of a density distribution are presented in Fig. 3.

Note that, according to [3], boundary conditions for subsonic flow differ from conditions for supersonic ones. This difference concerns only the inflow and outflow conditions for pressure. We state constant pressure $p = p_\infty$ at the right bound (outflow) and $\partial p/\partial n = 0$ at the left bound (inflow).

The third problem was a simulation of the wind load on a launch vehicle standing on the launch pedestal. Unlike previous problems, complicated geometry of this problem forced us to use multi block grid. The computational region was divided into a number of blocks with different index grids in each one. The grid vertices of neighbor blocks coincide on their boundary surface. The volume stream traces and pressure distribution on the vehicle surface in a stationary flow are presented in Fig. 4. The ascending vortices are clearly visible near pods.

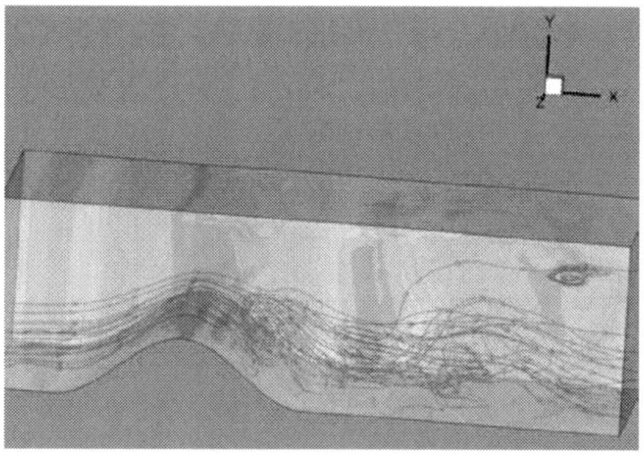

Figure 3. Volume instant stream traces behind the hill.

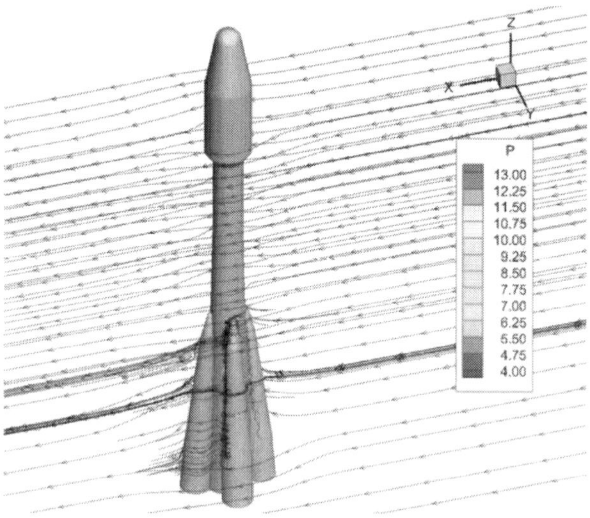

Figure 4. Flow around standing Soyuz launch vehicle.

IV. Parallel Implementation

There are two levels of parallelism in CFD program complex "Express-3D" [1][6]:

- The first level — geometrical decomposition. The computation domain is divided into blocks with the indexed grid in each. Blocks are distributed on MPI (Shmem) to processes so that to provide load balancing of all processes. Each MPI (Shmem) process can process one or several blocks.
- The second level — small-grain parallelism. Each mesh cell is processed by one Compute Unified Device Architecture (CUDA) stream [10].

Each face and edge have additional layers of ghost cells for organization of data exchange between blocks. We also add some additional arrays for sending and receiving data for each face and edge. The depth of additional arrays and ghost layers depends on the scheme stencil.

The orientation of faces of neighbor blocks may be arbitrary. Therefore, they are reordered before data transmission. All transferred values are packed into one array for each face and each edge.

We will call "computing process" one of the following tasks:

- The CPU core task — if calculation goes without use of GPU
- The GPU + CPU core task — if calculation goes on GPU under management of CPU

A Shmem (MPI) process corresponds to each computing process.

The data transfer is asynchronous. After processing each block new data are transferred to the neighbor blocks. If blocks are in the same computing process, there is simply a data copying from the sending array of one block to the receiving array of another one. If, on the contrary, the blocks are in different computing processes, we use shmem_put() procedure to asynchronously copy data from the sending array of one block to the receiving array of another one. Addresses of the sending and receiving arrays in each block are adjusted just after the application launch and reading the configuration file. The exchange between computing processes is executed under the control of the CPU-core. In the case of calculation on GPU it is necessary at first to copy data to corresponding CPU memory, then exchange data through Shmem (MPI) and finally copy data to GPU, if needed.

Blocks in computing process are sorted by diminishing the number of cells. For example, the big blocks are processed at first. In combination with asynchronous data transmission it is possible to assume that the main volume of data is already transferred, when processing the last (the smallest) block. The exchange procedure is finished by barrier synchronization. Actually, data exchange consists of two stages with synchronization after each of them. At the first step we exchange information from faces. After obtaining the updated information from faces, at the second step, data from edges are formed and transferred.

In [1][11], efficiency experiments were conducted with program complex "Express-3D". A set of test problems was solved based on QGD equations system on rectangular grids on a large number of graphic processors. Transition to curvilinear structured grids in addition to complication of computing algorithms, demands storage of large volumes of additional information and ensuring access to it.

Explicit finite-volume schemes are quite suitable for realization on CUDA architecture, and we will not dwell on this separately. We will note only some aspects connected with transition to non orthogonal grids.

Graphic processors of CUDA architecture with compute capability 2.0 (such as Tesla C20xx) have small number of registers on thread. As a result, a significant increase in the number of data access operations leads to a loss of efficiency. Acceleration of calculations on such processors is only 5-7 times in comparison with modern CPU cores. However, upon transition to more modern graphic processors with architecture of Kepler and compute capability 3.5 it is possible to achieve the acceptable acceleration without any changes in program code.

The results of the comparison of productivity of various devices are presented in the Table 1. The calculation times were measured for a fixed number of time steps.

TABLE I. DIFFERENT DEVICES PERFORMANCES

Computing Device	Intel Xeon E5-2670 1xCore	Nvidia Tesla C2050	Nvidia Kepler K20	Nvidia Kepler K40	Nvidia Kepler K80
Time (s)	592	175	49,70	39,85	26,81
Speedup	1	3,38	11,91	14,86	22,08

Unfortunately, there was only a small cluster containing only 4 K80 processors at the author's disposal. That's why we had no opportunity to make full research of scalability. However the efficiency received on 4 accelerators (more than 95%) and our previous experience in parallel computing allow to suggest that transition to a large number of GPU will be also effective in a case of non orthogonal grids as well.

V. Conclusion

The efficiency of using modern multicore systems including those based on NVidia GPUs largely depends on the properties of computational algorithms. On one hand, these algorithms must be logically simple; on the other hand, they must be efficient. These stringent requirements are satisfied by the algorithms based on the use of the hyperbolic variant of the quasi gas dynamic equations system.

Use of multi-block non orthogonal index hexahedral grids allows simulating gas flows in the regions with very complicated geometry as well as multiscale problems extremely close to their real behavior.

Numerical simulation of a set of test problems by use of QGD based algorithm demonstrated its good efficiency. This fact opens wide perspectives for modeling real scientific and engineering problems on modern high performance hybrid computer systems by use of explicit schemes, which are very convenient for parallel implementation.

ACKNOWLEDGMENT

This work was partially supported by Russian Foundation for Basic Research (grants No 15-01-03654-a, 15-01-03445-a and 16-07-00206-a).

REFERENCES

[1] B. N. Chetverushkin, E. V. Shilnikov, and A. A. Davydov, "Numerical Simulation of Continuous Media Problems on Hybrid Computer Systems," Advances in Engineering Software, vol. 60-61, pp. 42–47, 2013, http://dx.doi.org/10.1016/j.advengsoft.2013.02.003.

[2] B. N. Chetverushkin, Kinetic Schemes and Quasi-Gasdynamic System of Equations. Barcelona: CIMNE, 2008.

[3] T. G. Elizarova, Quasi-Gas Dynamic Equations. Berlin Heidelberg New York: Springer-Verlag, 2009.

[4] E. Oñate and M. Manzam, "Stabilization techniques for finite element analysis for convective-diffusion problem, " Barcelona: Publication CIMNE 183, (2000).

[5] S. Succi, The lattice Boltzmann equations for fluid dynamics and beyond, Oxford: Clarendon, 2001.

[6] A. A. Davydov, B. N. Chetverushkin, and E. V. Shilnikov, "Simulating Flows of Incompressible and Weakly Compressible Fluids on Multicore Hybrid Computer Systems," Computational Mathematics and Mathematical Physics, vol. 50, No 12, pp. 2157–2165, 2010.

[7] S. I. Repin and B. N. Chetverushkin, "Estimates of the Difference between Approximate Solutions of the Cauchy Problems for the Parabolic Diffusion Equation and a Hyperbolic Equation with a Small Parameter," Doklady Mathematics, vol. 88, No 1, pp. 417–421, 2013.

[8] A. A. Davydov and E. V. Shilnikov, "Program complex for fluid dynamic problems simulation on GPU-based computer systems," Proc. ICNAAM-2014, AIP Conference Proceedings, vol. 1648, 850071, 2015, AIP Publishing LLC, http://dx.doi.org/10.1063/1.4913126.

[9] J. G. Marvin, J. L. Brown, and P. A. Gnoffo, "Experimental Database with Baseline CFD Solutions: 2-D and Axisymmetric Hypersonic Shock-Wave/Turbulent-Boundary-Layer Interactions," NASA/TM–2013–216604, November, 2013.

[10] N. Wilt, CUDA Handbook: A Comprehensive Guide to GPU Programming. Reading MA: Addison-Wesley Professional, 2013. Available from: http://www.cudahandbook.com/.

[11] E. V. Shilnikov and A. A. Davydov. "Numerical Simulation of the Low Compressible Viscous Gas Flows on GPU-based Hybrid Supercomputers," In: Computing: Accelerating Computational Science and Engineering (CSE). Advances in Parallel Computing, M. Bader, A. Bode, H.-J. Bungartz, M. Gerndt, G.R. Joubert, F. Peters eds. IOS Press, vol. 25, pp. 315-323, 2014.

Mathematical Modeling of Water Purification Process of Iron Containing Impurities

Tatiana Kudryashova and Sergey Polyakov
Keldysh Institute of Applied Mathematics RAS
Moscow 125047, Russia
e-mail: kudryashova@imamod.ru, sergepol@mail.ru

Abstract—**This paper is devoted to mathematical modeling processes of water treatment from iron impurities. This problem is relevant for many applications, including the preparation of ultrapure water for medicine. The paper deals with a process of removing iron ions and iron oxides from water by means of a magnetic field. The two-dimensional formulation of the model problem is examined through the incompressible flow approximation in a channel with rectangular cross section. A special numerical method and parallel program were designed to solve the problem. The distributions of the concentration of the iron ions under the effect or lack of transverse magnetic field were obtained in numerical experiments.**

Keywords-mathematical modeling; numerical methods; parallel algorithms; water treatment processes.

I. INTRODUCTION

This paper deals with modeling the processes of magnetic treatment of water. The processing can be applied to many industries, such as heat energetics and related industries. Water treatment of impurities and hardness salts (carbonate, chloride and sulfate salts of Ca^{2+}, Mg^{2+}, Fe^{2+} and Fe^{3+}) is used in the heat exchangers, piping and plumbing systems in various ways, including mechanical, chemical, electrophysical ones, etc. Nowadays, one of the most acute problems deals with obtaining drinking water and ultrapure water for pharmacology. For these purposes, all possibilities of water purification are used (water structuring and catching finely dispersed salts of heavy metals by a magnetic field). Magnetic water treatment is widely implemented in different industries, such as construction industry and agriculture. In the construction industry, the use of magnetic water in the hydration phase of cement processing reduces the time of solidification of cement clinker components with water. A fine-grained structure of the generated solid hydrates makes the product far stronger and increases its resistance to aggressive environmental influences [1]. In agriculture, five-hour seed soaking in magnetized water improves seed germination and can significantly increase the yield. Watering with magnetized water stimulates 15-20% growth and yield of soybean, sunflower, corn, tomatoes [2]. In medicine, the use of magnetized water helps to dissolve kidney stones and has a bactericidal effect.

It is well known that the effect of magnetic fields on water is of a complex multifactorial nature. It results in water structure changes, its physical and chemical properties and dissolved inorganic salts behavior in water [1]. Chemical reactions in water have different speeds under the influence of amagnetic field. Magnetic treatment water softening appears to be very promising. Scale-forming salts accelerated crystallization in water occurs during such processing. This leads to a significant reduction of concentrations of dissolved ions Ca_2^+, Mg_2^+, and other metals. The crystals size reduction under heating is also the result of water magnetic treatment. The magnetized water can change the aggregate stability and accelerate coagulation (adhesion and sedimentation) of suspended particles with subsequent formation of finely dispersed sediment. This ability is implemented to remove sediments from water. Magnetization of water can also be applied for water supply plants with significant turbidity of natural waters. Such magnetic treatment of industrial waste water allows us to precipitate fine dirt quickly and effectively. Magnetic treatment of water helps to prevent the scale-forming salts precipitation and significantly reduces the organic substances deposits, such as paraffin. Magnetic treatment is useful for the high paraffin crude oil production. The influence of magnetic field increases provided the oil contains water.

In this work, the influence of the magnetic field on water is studied. A water stream contains ions of iron and/or iron salts ions and flows through a nonmetallic pipe. A magnetohydrodynamic model was created for this problem. The model takes into account the magnetic induction direct effect on the stream of water. In this case, the ion flux generates a secondary electric field. The paper deals with the two-dimensional plane-parallel flow. The flow is formed in the middle section of a rectangular tube with a strong anisotropy of sides. A magnetic field is applied in the transverse direction of the flow and generates circular motions in this section of the tube. In this case, the flow structure is similar to the two-dimensional model and can be seen as an initial approximation for the three-dimensional problem [3] [4]. The isothermal laminar flow of fluid is examined to simplify the analysis. The drift-diffusion approximation is used to describe the behavior of the finely dispersed impurities.

This paper is organized as follows. In Section 2, we describe the mathematical model of the problem. We then present, in Section 3, some details of the numerical algorithm. In Section 4, the main results obtained for the steady state distribution in the stream are shown, including distribution of electrical potential, distribution of impurity concentration, and distribution of electrical field.

This paper discusses water purification of iron impurities processes. We propose some approaches to the issue in question, and finally we offer some conclusions.

II. Mathematical Description

An isothermal variant of water flow with impurity of iron is considered. The flow is studied in the non-conductive pipe with rectangular cross-section and with a big difference between the sizes of sides (Fig. 1).

The impurities are finely dispersed and we do not take into account the processes of association and dissociation of individual ions in clusters.

The basic equations describe water motion with impurity in the computational domain Ω [5]. This area is section z=0 of the original three-dimensional domain and its size is $L \times H$. The equations (1)-(3) in dimensional variables have form [6]:

$$\rho \frac{\partial \mathbf{u}}{\partial t} + \rho(\mathbf{u}\nabla)\mathbf{u} = -\nabla p + \eta \Delta \mathbf{u}, \quad div\,\mathbf{u} = 0, \qquad (1)$$

$$\frac{\partial n}{\partial t} = div(D\nabla n - q\mu \mathbf{F} n) + (u, \nabla n), \qquad (2)$$

$$div(\varepsilon \mathbf{E}) = q(n - n_*), \quad \mathbf{E} = -\nabla \varphi, \qquad (3)$$

where $\mathbf{u} = (u_x, u_y, 0)$ – velocity vector of water stream, $\rho = \rho_0 \rho(T)$ – water density at the specified temperature T, p – pressure in water stream, $\eta = \eta_0 \eta(T)$ – dynamic viscosity coefficient of water stream at the specified temperature, n_* and n – equilibrium and non-equilibrium concentrations of impurity ions in water, $D = D_0 D(T)$, $\mu = \mu_0 \mu(T)$ – diffusion coefficient and coefficient of ion mobility, q – ion charge, $\mathbf{F} = \mathbf{E} + [\mathbf{u} \times \mathbf{B}]$ – the total vector field acting on the ions, $\mathbf{E}$ and φ – strength and potential of the electric field, $\mathbf{B} = B_0 \mathbf{e}_z$ – vector of magnetic field strength ($\mathbf{e}_z = (0,0,1)$), div and ∇ – operators of divergence and gradient in the spatial coordinates (x, y), ε – dielectric constant of water.

Initial conditions (4):

$$\mathbf{u} = \mathbf{u}_0, \quad n = n_0, \quad t = 0, \quad (x, y) \in \Omega. \qquad (4)$$

Boundary conditions (5) - (7):

$$x = 0: \quad u_x = u_n(y), \quad u_y = 0, \quad n = n_0, \quad \frac{\partial \varphi}{\partial x} = 0; \qquad (5)$$

$$x = L: \quad \frac{\partial u_x}{\partial x} = 0, \quad \frac{\partial u_y}{\partial x} = 0, \quad \frac{\partial n}{\partial x} = 0, \quad \frac{\partial \varphi}{\partial x} = 0; \qquad (6)$$

$$y = 0, H: \quad \frac{\partial u_x}{\partial y} = 0, \quad u_y = 0, \quad \frac{\partial n}{\partial y} = 0, \quad \frac{\partial \varphi}{\partial y} = 0. \qquad (7)$$

At low speeds, the flow becomes stationary and can be determined by the transition to the variables ψ (current function) and ω (vortex). If we assume that the flow is irrotational, the Laplace's equation (8), (9) can be used to calculate water stream [7]:

$$\Delta \psi \equiv \frac{\partial^2 \psi}{\partial x^2} + \frac{\partial^2 \psi}{\partial y^2} = 0, \quad (x, y) \in \Omega; \qquad (8)$$

$$u_x = \frac{\partial \psi}{\partial y}, \quad u_y = -\frac{\partial \psi}{\partial x}, \quad (x, y) \in \Omega. \qquad (9)$$

The boundary conditions for the current function are expressed as follows (10), (11):

$$\psi(0, y) = \int_0^y u_n(y)\,dy; \quad \frac{\partial \psi}{\partial x}(L, y) = 0; \qquad (10)$$

$$\frac{\partial \psi}{\partial x}(x, 0) = 0; \quad \frac{\partial \psi}{\partial x}(x, H) = 0. \qquad (11)$$

The equation for the concentration can be written in form (12):

$$\frac{\partial n}{\partial t} = div\,\mathbf{W} + (\mathbf{R}, \mathbf{W}) + Qn, \qquad (12)$$

where $\mathbf{W} = D(\nabla n - \mathbf{P} n)$, $\mathbf{P} = q\mu D^{-1}\mathbf{F}$, $\mathbf{R} = D^{-1}\mathbf{u}$, $Q = q\mu D^{-1}(\mathbf{u}, \mathbf{F})$.

For solving of the problem we used the dimensionless variables $x' = x/H$, $y' = y/H$, $t' = t/t_0$, $\psi' = \psi/u_0$, $\mathbf{u}' = \mathbf{u}/u_0$, $n' = n/n_0$, $\varphi' = \varphi/\varphi_0$, $\mathbf{E}' = \mathbf{E}/E_0$, $\Omega' = \{(x', y') \in (0, L) \times (0, 1)\}$, $t_0 = H/u_0$, $\varphi_0 = q n_0 H^2/\varepsilon$, $E_0 = \varphi_0/H$.

We neglect the temperature dependence of the diffusion coefficient and the mobility coefficient.

Then, the resulting formulation of the problem (13) - (15) is written as [3], [4]:

$$\Delta \psi = 0, \quad u_x = \frac{\partial \psi}{\partial y}, \quad u_y = -\frac{\partial \psi}{\partial x}, \qquad (13)$$

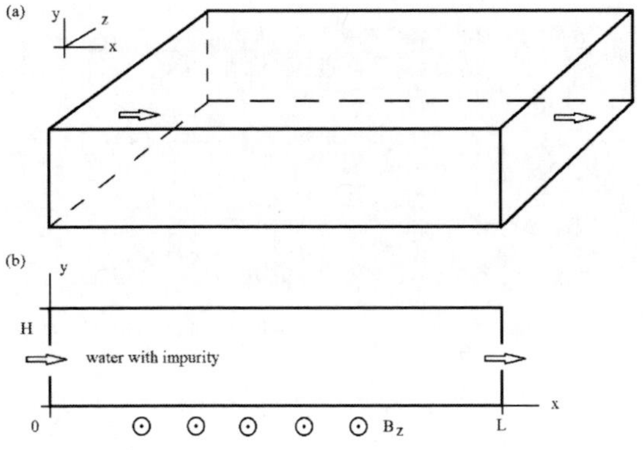

Figure 1. 3D (a) and 2D (b) computational domains.

$$\frac{\partial n}{\partial t} = div\,\mathbf{W} + (\mathbf{u},\mathbf{W}) + Qn, \qquad (14)$$

$$\Delta\varphi = -(n - n_*), \quad E = -\nabla\varphi, \qquad (15)$$

where $\mathbf{W} = D_n(\nabla n - P_n\mathbf{F}n)$, $D_n = D_0/(Hu_0)$, $P_n = q\mu_0 E_0 u_0^{-1}$, $Q = Q_n(\mathbf{u},\mathbf{F})$, $Q_n = q\mu_0 E_0 H D_0^{-1}$, $\mathbf{F} = \mathbf{E} + B_n[\mathbf{u}\times\mathbf{e}_z]$, $B_n = u_0 B_0 E_0^{-1}$. The basic dimensionless parameters of the problem are: L, D_n, P_n, Q_n, B_n.

The initial conditions take the form:

$$\mathbf{u} = \mathbf{u}_0 = u_n(y)\times(1,0),\ n = 1,\ u_n(y) \equiv 1-(2y-1)^2. \qquad (16)$$

The boundary conditions for $x = 0$ (17):

$$\psi = \int_0^y u_n(y')dy',\ u_x = u_n(y),\ u_y = 0,\ n = 1,\ \frac{\partial\varphi}{\partial x} = 0. \qquad (17)$$

The boundary conditions for $x = L$ take the form (18):

$$\frac{\partial\psi}{\partial x}, \frac{\partial u_x}{\partial x}, \frac{\partial u_y}{\partial x}, \frac{\partial n}{\partial x}, \frac{\partial\varphi}{\partial x} = 0. \qquad (18)$$

The boundary conditions for $y = 0, 1$ are formulas (19):

$$\frac{\partial\psi}{\partial x}, \frac{\partial u_x}{\partial y}, u_y, \frac{\partial n}{\partial y}, \frac{\partial\varphi}{\partial y} = 0. \qquad (19)$$

III. NUMERICAL ALGORITHM

The finite difference method is proposed to solve the problem. To do this, we introduce a uniform grid $\Omega_h = \omega_x \times \omega_y$ in domain Ω. The grid is multiplication of 1D grids $\omega_x = \{x_i = h_x \cdot i, i = 0,...,N_x, h_x = L/N_x\}$ and $\omega_y = \{y_j = h_y \cdot j, j = 0,...,N_y, h_y = 1/N_y\}$, where N_x, N_y – the number of network segments on x and y. We introduce also grid $\bar{\Omega}_h = \bar{\omega}_x \times \bar{\omega}_y$, where we use 1D grids $\bar{\omega}_x = \{x_{i-1/2} = 0.5(x_{i-1} + x_i), i = 1,...,N_x\}$, and $\bar{\omega}_y = \{y_{j-1/2} = 0.5(y_{j-1} + y_j), j = 1,...,N_y\}$, and uniform grid on time $\omega_t = \{t_k = \tau\cdot k, k = 0,...,N_t\}$ (τ – the time step, N_t – number of steps). The current function is defined on Ω_h grid (in grid nodes), other functions – on the grid $\bar{\Omega}_h$ (in the centers of the cells).

Standard differential equations are written for the current function, of the velocity vector and the potential of electric field [5][6]. They can be supplemented with boundary conditions (20), (21), if it is necessary:

$$\Lambda_h\psi_h \equiv (\psi_h)_{x\bar{x}} + (\psi_h)_{y\bar{y}} = 0, \quad (x,y)\in\Omega_h; \qquad (20)$$

$$\begin{cases} u_{x,h} = +0.5(\psi_{h,y} + \psi_{h,\bar{y}}), \\ u_{y,h} = -0.5(\psi_{h,x} + \psi_{h,\bar{x}}), \end{cases} \quad (x,y)\in\bar{\Omega}_h;$$

$$\Lambda_h\varphi_h \equiv (\varphi_h)_{x\bar{x}} + (\varphi_h)_{y\bar{y}} = -(n_h - n_*), \quad (x,y)\in\bar{\Omega}_h; \qquad (21)$$

$$E_h = -\nabla_h\varphi_h, \quad (x,y)\in\bar{\Omega}_h.$$

To approximate the equation for the concentration, we write it in a modified form (22), using a double integral transformation [7][8]:

$$\frac{\partial n}{\partial t} = \frac{1}{g_x}\frac{\partial}{\partial x}(g_x W_x) + \frac{1}{g_y}\frac{\partial}{\partial y}(g_y W_y) + Qn, \qquad (22)$$

where $Q = Q_n(u_x F_x + u_y F_y)$, $F_x = E_x + B_n u_y$, $F_y = E_y - B_n u_x$, $g_x = \exp\left[\int_0^x u_x dx'\right]$, $g_y = \exp\left[\int_0^y u_y dy'\right]$, $W_x = D_n\frac{1}{e_x}\frac{\partial}{\partial x}(e_x n)$, $W_y = D_n\frac{1}{e_y}\frac{\partial}{\partial y}(e_y n)$, $e_x = \exp\left[-\int_0^x P_n F_x dx'\right]$, $e_y = \exp\left[-\int_0^y P_n F_y dy'\right]$.

Explicit-implicit difference scheme is written, supplemented by appropriate boundary conditions (23), (24):

$$\frac{\hat{n}_h - n_h}{\tau} = \bar{\Lambda}_h\hat{n}_h + Q_h\hat{n}_h, \quad n_h|_{t=0} = 1, \qquad (23)$$

$$\bar{\Lambda}_h \hat{n}_h = \frac{1}{g_{x,h}}\left(\left(g_{x,h}W_{x,h}\right)_x\right)_{\bar{x}} + \frac{1}{g_{y,h}}\left(\left(g_{y,h}W_{y,h}\right)_x\right)_{\bar{x}}, \quad (24)$$

where $g_{x,h} = \exp\left[\sum_{0\le x'\le x} u_x h_x\right]$, $\quad g_{y,h} = \exp\left[\sum_{0\le y'\le y} u_y h_y\right]$,

$$W_{x,h} = D_n \frac{1}{e_{x,h}}\left(e_{x,h} n_h\right)_x, \qquad W_{y,h} = D_n \frac{1}{e_{y,h}}\left(e_{y,h} n_h\right)_y,$$

$$e_{x,h} = \exp\left[-\sum_{0\le x'\le x} P_n F_{x,h} h_x\right], \quad e_{y,h} = \exp\left[-\sum_{0\le y'\le y} P_n F_{y,h} h_y\right].$$

The implementation of schemes is performed by using iterative algorithms of alternating directions [9] and methods of non-monotonic sweep.

The parallel realization of the algorithm is based on the methods of domain decomposition [10] [11], and [12] and a sweep parallel algorithm. Computer implementation is performed by using Message Passing Interface (MPI) and Open Multi-Processing (OpenMP) technologies [13], [14].

There are both advantages and disadvantages of the proposed mathematical approach.

Firstly, the proposed model, of course, is incomplete because it does not take into account the reverse influence of changes of the ions concentration on flow characteristics. However, in many cases, these corrections are of little significance. At the same time, the rejection enables us to calculate relatively easily the basic process of an electromagnetic treatment of water.

Secondly, the transition to the current function enables us not to worry about condition $div\,\mathbf{u} = 0$, that (in alternative numerical algorithms) is a big problem.

Thirdly, the rejection of the calculation of the vortex structure of flow at low speeds does not have much value, but saves computation time.

Fourthly, the use of staggered grids enables us to reduce errors during interpolation of solution from one grid to another.

Fifthly, the application of exponential schemes releases from the problem of stability of the solution equation algorithm for the concentration and separation of boundary layers. Of course, the implementation of an exponential scheme increases the computation time. However, this increase is not catastrophic and can be compensated by using parallel computing.

Thus, the proposed approach has the following advantages: low time-consuming and highly stable calculations.

IV. COMPUTATIONAL RESULTS

In this section of the paper, the data on numerical experiments are described. To test the numerical algorithm, we chose the calculation variant with values of the dimensionless parameters $L = 6$, $D_n = 1$, $P_n = 1$, $Q_n = 1$, $B_n = 1$. Grid parameters are equal: $N_x = 300$, $N_y = 50$, $h_x = h_y = 0.02$, $\tau = 10^{-4}$.

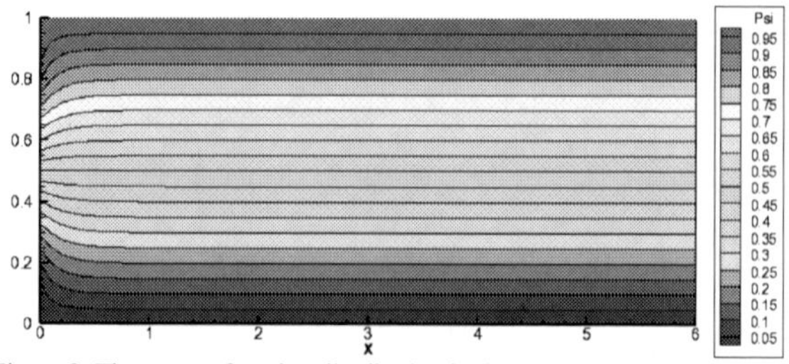

Figure 2. The stream function distribution in the computational domain.

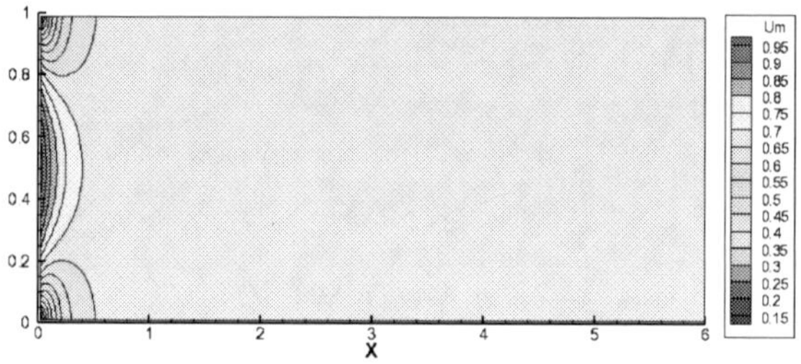

Figure 3. The velocity modulus distribution in the computational domain.

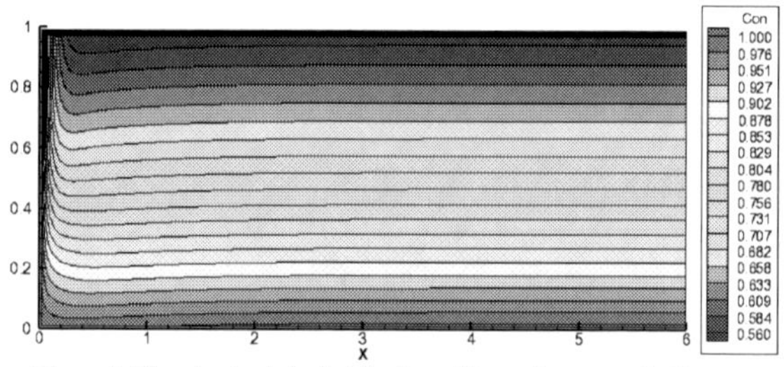

Figure 4. The steady state distribution of impurity concentration.

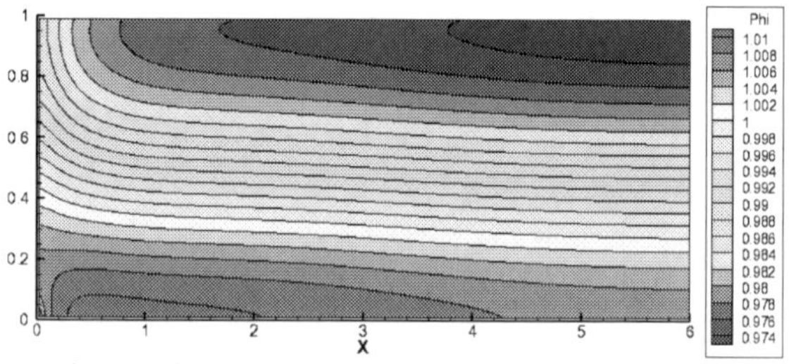

Figure 5. The steady state distribution of electrical potential.

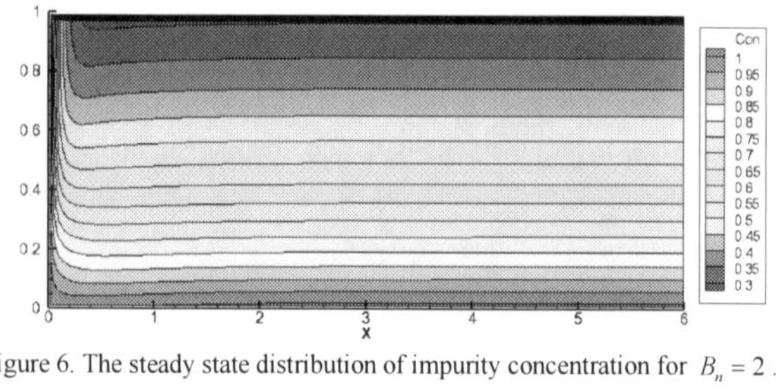

Figure 6. The steady state distribution of impurity concentration for $B_n = 2$.

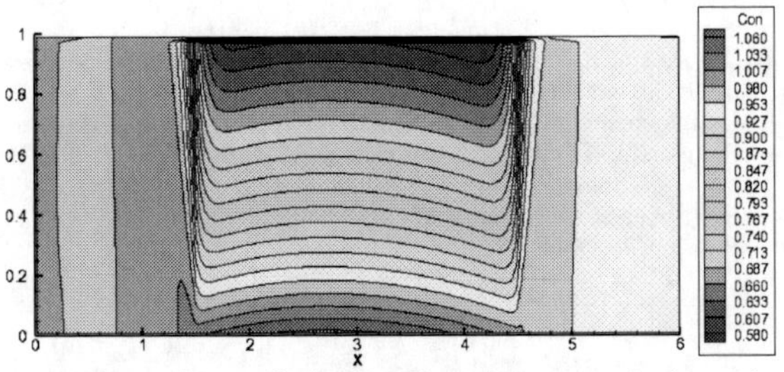

Figure 7. The steady state distribution of impurity concentration into and near localized area for $B_n = 1$.

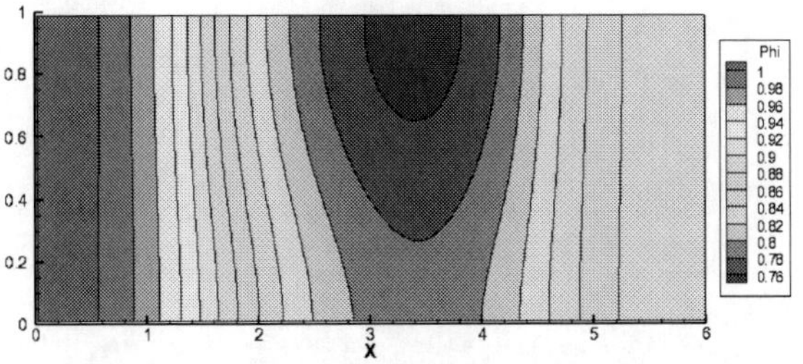

Figure 8. The steady state distribution of electrical potential into and near localized area for $B_n = 1$.

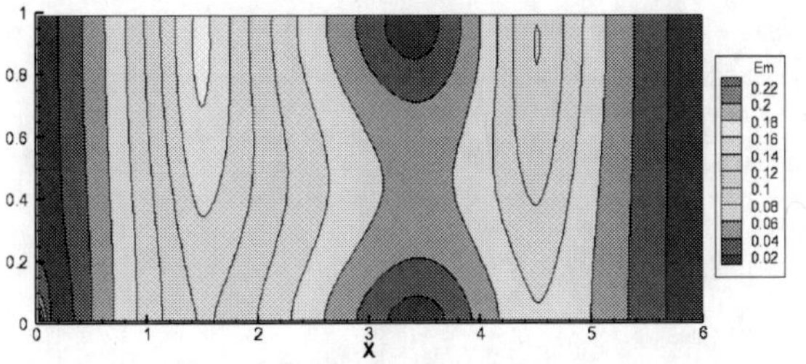

Figure 9. The steady state distribution of electrical field into and near localized area for $B_n = 1$.

The results of calculations are shown in several figures. Fig. 2 presents the stream function distribution in the computational domain. The velocity modulus distribution in the computational domain is displayed in Fig. 3. The steady state distribution of impurity concentration is given in Fig. 4. We can estimate the distribution of electrical potential from Fig. 5.

Analysis of the data shows the following. The influence of the magnetic field leads to decreasing ions concentration at the top of the area for positive values of B_n parameter and formation of increased ion concentration at the bottom layer. Thus, the purification effect of the upper liquid layer is realized.

The value of cleaning depends on the B_n parameter. It becomes noticeable when the Lorentz force is comparable to the hydrodynamic pressure forces, that is $B_n = 1$. Our executed calculations show that reduction of impurity concentration is achieved approximately 2 times for $B_n = 1$. If parameter $B_n = 2$, the reduction of impurity concentration at the upper liquid layer is about 3.5 times (Fig. 6).

The space localized effect of magnetic field is implemented in industrial purification systems. In our work, we introduce B_n parameter dependence on the longitudinal coordinate x. For example, we consider a localization of a magnetic field in the area $x \in [1.5, 4.5]$ and value $B_n = 1$. The calculation results are presented in Fig. 7 and Fig. 8. They show that the layer of purified water is situated in the upper part of the localized area. Water taking may be done from the region, for example, through a special membrane. The steady state distribution of electrical field into and near localized area for $B_n = 1$ is shown in Fig. 9.

V. Conclusions

The issue of water purification of iron impurities by means of electro-magnetic methods is discussed in this paper. A simplified mathematical model was developed for the model problem, describing the the purification process. A numerical algorithm was proposed and the parallel code was constructed for computer experiments. Tests of the code with various sets of parameters confirmed the operability of the proposed computational approach.

Acknowledgment

This work was supported by Russian Foundation for Basic Research (grants №№ 15-01-04620-a, 16-07-00206-a).

References

[1] O. V. Mosin, E. N. Karnaukhova, A. B. Pshenichnikova, and O. S. Reshetova, "Electron impact spectrometry in bioanalysis of stable isotope labeled bacteriorhodopsin." Sixth International Conference on Retinal Proteins. Leiden. The Netherlands. . P.115, 19-24 June 1994.

[2] V. I. Shvets, A. M Yurkevich, O. V Mosin., and D. A Skladnev, "Preparation of deuterated inosine suitable for biomedical application." Journal of Medical Sciences. V. 8. № 4. Pp. 231-232, 1995.

[3] B.N. Chetverushkin, "Kinetic Schemes and Quasi-Gasdynamic System of Equations," Barcelona: CIMNE, 2008.

[4] T.G. Elizarova, "Quasi-Gas Dynamic Equations," Berlin Heidelberg New York: Springer-Verlag, 2009.

[5] A.A. Samarskii, "The Theory Of Difference Schemes," New York: Marcel Dekker, Inc., pp. 1-762, 2001.

[6] A.A. Samarskii and P.N. Vabishchevich, "Numerical methods for solving inverse problems of mathematical physics," Walter de Gruyter, pp. 1-438, 2007.

[7] S.V. Polyakov, "Exponential Difference Schemes with Double Integral Transformation for Solving Convection-Diffusion Equations," Mathematical Models and Computer Simulations, Vol. 5, No. 4, pp. 338-340, 2013.

[8] A.A. Samarskii and E.S. Nikolaev, "Numerical Methods for Grid Equations," Vol. I: Direct Methods, Vol. II: Iterative Methods, Basel-Boston-Berlin, Birkhäuser Verlag, pp. 1-502, 1989.

[9] I.A. Graur, T.G. Elizarova, T.A. Kudryashova, and S.V. Polyakov, "Numerical investigation of jet flows, using multiprocessor computer systems." Mathematical Modelling, 14(6), pp. 51-62., 2002.

[10] T.A. Kudryashova, S.V. Polyakov, V. Podryga, and Yu. Karamzin, "Multiscale modeling of nonlinear processes in technical microsystems." Mathematical modelling, № 7, V 27, pp. 65-74, 2015.

[11] A. Toselli and O. Widlund, "Domain Decomposition Methods" - Algorithms and Theory. Springer, 2004.

[12] N. Wilt, CUDA Handbook: "A Comprehensive Guide to GPU Programming," 2013, [Online]. Available from: http://www.cudahandbook.com/..

[13] Official documentation and manuals on OpenMP. [Online]. Available from: http://www.openmp.org, http://www.llnl.gov/computing/tutorials/openMP

[14] Yu. Karamzin, T. Kudryashova, V. Podryga, and S. Polyakov, "Two-Scale Computation of N2-H2 Jet Flow Based on QGD and MMD on Heterogeneous Multi-Core Hardware, Advances in Engineering Software," Engineering Computational Technology (ECT 2014): Book of Summaries of The Ninth International Conference, 2-5 September 2014, Naples, Italy. - Stirlingshire, Scotland: Civil-Comp Press, p. 28, 2014.

Optimum Angle-Cut of Collimator for Dense Objects in High-Energy Proton Radiography

Haibo Xu
Institute of Applied Physics and Computational Mathematics, Beijing, China
e-mail: 13641017929@163.com

***Abstract*—The use of minus identity lenses with an angle-cut collimator can achieve high contrast images in high-energy proton radiography. This article presents the principles of choosing the angle-cut aperture of the collimator for different energies and objects. Numerical simulation using the Monte Carlo code Geant4 has been implemented to investigate the entire radiography for the French test object. The optimum angle-cut apertures of the collimators are also obtained for different energies.**

Keywords-proton radiography; multiple Coulomb scattering; angualr collimator; Geant4.

I. INTRODUCTION

High-energy proton radiography could provide a new, quantitative, and much more capable diagnostic technique to analyze the aspects for hydrotest experiments [1]. The three most important effects on the protons as they go through an object are absorption, multiple Coulomb scattering (MCS), and energy loss. The key technology that led to the development of proton radiography is a magnetic imaging lens system located between the object and the image, which forms a point-to-point focus of the proton beam and provides good position resolution over the entire field of view required for radiography.

The lens is a minus identity lens. Mottershead and Zumbro [2] demonstrated that it is possible to sort the scattered beam in terms of how it has been scattered. This always occurs in the mid-plane (Fourier plane) of a chromatically matched identity lens, where the trajectory position depends only on the MCS angle, independent of the initial position. If one places an angular collimator at this intermediate Fourier plane where the rays are completely sorted by MCS angle, it is possible to apply an angle-cut to the proton beam, removing part of the scattered beam.

It is a very important to improve the diagnostic technique. By using a single magnetic lens with just an angle-cut, one can achieve high contrast images in proton radiography. The angle-cut must be different for different proton energies and objects. In order to obtain the best image, it is desirable to choose the matching angular collimator and give an optimum angle-cut for that collimator [3].

This paper is organized as follows. The basic principles of proton radiography and choosing collimator angle-cut aperture are presented in Sections II and III, respectively. In Section IV, the numerical results are obtained with the Geant4 toolkit. Finally, the conclusion is given in Section V.

II. BASIC PRINCIPLES OF PROTON RADIOGRAPHY

The processes of proton radiography can be described by assuming a simple exponential formula for nuclear attenuation and the angular distribution of scattering as Gaussian MCS [4]. In this approximation, the transmission of protons through the magnetic lens and angle-cut collimators has the following form:

$$T(L) = \exp\left(-\sum_i \frac{L_i}{\lambda_i}\right)\left[1 - \exp\left(-\frac{\theta_{\text{cut}}^2}{2\theta_0^2}\right)\right] \tag{1}$$

Here, L is the sum of the areal densities of all materials of the object, and L_i is the areal density of the *i'th* material and λ_i is the nuclear attenuation factor for the *i'th* material. θ_{cut} is the angle-cut imposed by the angular collimator and θ_0 is the MCS angle given approximately by

$$\theta_0 \approx \frac{14.1\,\text{MeV}}{pc\beta}\sqrt{\sum_i^n \frac{L_i}{X_{0i}}} \tag{2}$$

Here, p is the beam momentum, $\beta = v/c$ where v is the beam velocity and c is the speed of light, and X_{0i} is the radiation length for the *i'th* material given by

$$X_{0i} = \frac{716.4A_i}{Z_i(Z_i+1)\ln\left(287/\sqrt{Z_i}\right)} \tag{3}$$

The first term of (1) in the attenuation is the nuclear attenuation and is analogous to X-ray attenuation processes, but the second term is due to angular attenuation and makes proton radiography unique. Angular attenuation provides another way of distinguishing material properties.

III. PRINCIPLES OF CHOOSING COLLIMATOR ANGLE-CUT APERTURE

Different collimator apertures will permit the obtaining of different radiographs per proton pulse in the image plane. In order to obtain the best image, which can produce an intensified effect between the special points or structures in transmission; it is desirable to choose a matching angular collimator. The MCS θ_0 is proportional to the beam energy, so that the angle-cut θ_{cut} must be different for different proton energies. By placing an aperture restriction at the Fourier plane that removes scattered beam with large angles, the image contrast can be enhanced to give optimal images.

The transmission along ray j can be expressed by

$$T(L_j) = \exp\left(-\sum_i \frac{L_{ij}}{\lambda_i}\right)\left[1-\exp\left(-\frac{\theta_{cut}^2}{2\theta_{0j}^2}\right)\right] \quad (4)$$

Suppose that a and b are two important pixels needed for observation in the image plane, and the contrast between them is correlated with the quality in proton radiography; the difference of transmission between them can be written as

$$\Delta T = \exp\left(-\sum_i \frac{L_{ia}}{\lambda_i}\right)\left[1-\exp\left(-\frac{\theta_{cut}^2}{2\theta_{0a}^2}\right)\right] - \exp\left(-\sum_i \frac{L_{ib}}{\lambda_i}\right)\left[1-\exp\left(-\frac{\theta_{cut}^2}{2\theta_{0b}^2}\right)\right] \quad (5)$$

The value of the optimal cut angle can be determined by Eq. 5. At high energies where the mean free path λ_i for the *i'th* material is approximately constant, by setting the derivative of ΔT with respect to θ_{cut} to zero, the optimum angle-cut can be obtained.

IV. GEANT4 SIMULATION

The simulations of the transport of protons have been implemented with the Geant4 toolkit [5] in proton radiography. The central part of the collimator designed in the simulation was the same as that in the experimental setup used at Brookhaven National Laboratory. In experiment 955 [6], the protons were provided by the Alternating Gradient Synchrotron, and the momentum of the protons was 24 GeV/c. The collimators approximated multiple-scattering angle acceptance cuts of 6.68 mrad. We have taken data on a thick test object, the so-called French Test Object (FTO), which was designed to allow French and U.S. experimenters to collaborate on high-energy X-ray radiography methods and analysis, and their detection [7]. The FTO consisted of three concentric spherical shells. The inner shell was uranium with an inside radius of 1 cm and an outside radius of 4.5 cm. This was surrounded by a copper shell of outside radius of 6.5 cm, and this was surrounded by a shell of foam plastic with an outside radius of 22.5 cm.

The transmissions for the FTO are taken with different angle-cut apertures of the collimators. The transmission versus angle-cut aperture for 10 GeV, 23 GeV and 50 GeV proton radiography are plotted in Fig. 1. The highest points of the curves are the optimum angle-cut apertures. From Fig. 1, we can see that the optimum angle-cut apertures of the collimators are 13.09 mrad for 10 GeV, 6.68 mrad for 23 GeV and 2.56 mrad for 50 GeV for the FTO.

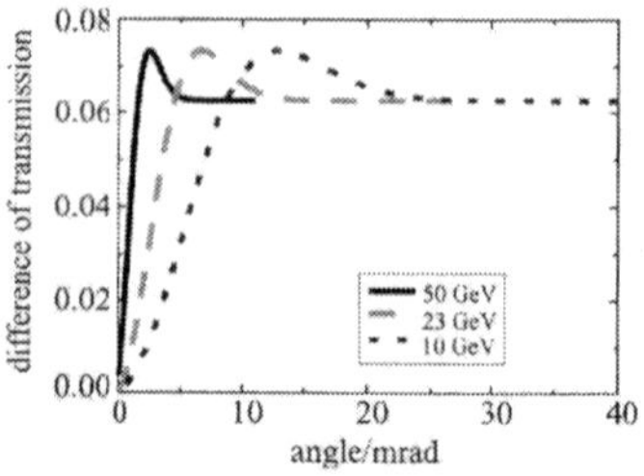

Figure 1. The difference in transmission between central point and the inner shell of uranium as a function of angle-cut aperture.

The simulation results of the proton radiograph image plane of the FTO are shown in Fig. 2. The image in Fig. 2(a) corresponds to the normal angle-cut apertures of the 6.68 mrad collimator, and the image in Fig. 2(b) corresponds to the optimum angle-cut apertures of the 13.09 mrad collimator for 10 GeV, respectively. Fig. 2(c) is the radial distribution for the FTO radiograph where the highest outer dosage is 1.

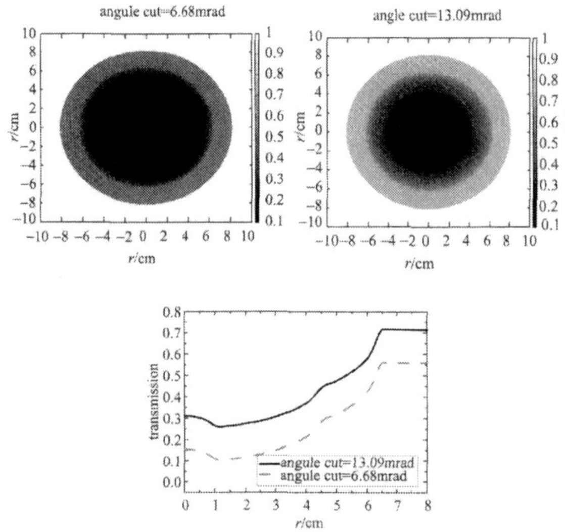

Figure 2. Simulation results from image plane of FTO at 10 GeV protons with angle-cut.

It can be seen that with the increase of angle-cut, there are more protons received in the image plane, and the image becomes lighter. It is obvious that the whole structure of the object can be seen from the image of angle-cut at 13.09 mrad but the core of the object cannot be distinguished if the angle-cut is at 6.68 mrad. This conclusion is consistent with Fig. 1.

V. CONCLUSIONS

The ability of proton radiography to adjust the image contrast by adjusting the angle-cut aperture of the collimator has been demonstrated. There is an optimum angle-cut aperture of the collimator for a given object and a given energy. The angle-cut aperture of the collimator is chosen according to the optical thickness of the object. In this article, using the Monte Carlo code Geant4, the optimum angle-cut apertures of the collimators are obtained as 13.09 mrad for 10 GeV, 6.68 mrad for 23 GeV and 2.56 mrad for 50 GeV respectively for the FTO. The numerical results indicate that the image resolution can be improved by choosing the optimum angle-cut apertures of collimators. Thus, the study is beneficial for the design of the magnetic imaging lens in high-energy proton radiography.

REFERENCES

[1] C. L. Morris, J. W. Hopson, and P. Goldstone, "Proton radiography," Los Alamos National Laboratory, LA-UR-06-0331, 2006.

[2] C. T. Mottershead and J. D. Zumbro. "Magnetic optics for proton radiography." Proceedings of the 1997 Particle Accelerator Conference, pp. 1397-1402, 1997.

[3] H. Xu and N. Zheng, "Optimum angle-cut of collimator for dense objects in high-energy proton radiography," Chinese Physics C, vol.40, pp. 028201, 2016.

[4] C. L. Morris, et al., "Flash radiography with 24GeV/c protons," Journal of Applied Physics, vol. 109, pp. 104905, 2011.

[5] S. Agostinelliae, et al., "Geant4 –a simulation toolkit," Nucl. Instrum. Methods Phys. Res. A, vol. 506, pp. 250-303, 2003.

[6] J. D. Zumbro, "Angle-cuts for the Brookhaven proton radiography experiments E955 and E963 calculated with MCNP TM (U)," Los Alamos National Laboratory, LA-UR-05-7370, 2005.

[7] K. H. Mueller, "Collimation techniques for dense object flash radiography," SPIE High Speed Photography, vol. 491, pp. 130-136, 1984.

Study of Search Optimization Opportunities of Heuristic Algorithms for Solving Multi-Extremal Problems

Rudolf Neydorf, Ivan Chernogorov, Victor Polyakh
Orkhan Yarakhmedov, Yulia Goncharova
Department of Software Computer Technology and Automated Systems and Department of Scientific-Technical Translation and Professional Communication
Don State Technical University
Rostov-on-Don, Russia
Email: ran_pro@mail.ru, hintaivr@gmail.com, silvervpolyah@gmail.com, orhashka@gmail.com, jl.goncharova@gmail.com

Dean Vucinic
Department of Mechanical Engineering and Department of Electronics and Informatics
Vrije Universiteit Brussel
Brussel, Belgium
Email: dean.vucinic@vub.ac.be

Abstract— **The investigated objective of this paper is the search optimization task of multiextremal objects, which is considered to be more complicated than the optimization tasks of mono-extremal objects. This work postulates that in order to achieve this goal, the heuristics algorithms are the only ones able to provide suitable solutions. Therefore, 3 of the most popular and devised approaches have been considered: (1) the method of swarming particles, (2) evolutionary-genetic approach and (3) ant algorithm. The conducted research has established the common test environment for comparing the multi-extremal Rastrigin function, with the 3 investigated methods. It is clearly shown that all of these 3 methods are quite appropriate for solving the multiextremal tasks. However, in each of the addressed heuristic algorithms, we have applied their own specific characteristics to solve the problem of detection and identification of the global and local extrema. These approaches have been combined together due to the general need of data clustering. It is illustrated that, when solving an extremal task, each of these methods can provide the desired solution for a fairly wide range of imposed accuracies and available resource times.**

Keywords: searching optimization; multi-extremal; genetic algorithm; swarm algorithm; ant algorithm

I. INTRODUCTION

The most advanced state-of-the-art issues in science, technology, economics, military affairs and other applied modern trends are somehow connected with the solving tasks of achieving an optimum in designs, technologies, models and environments, through the possibility of controlling the dynamic and static states, as well as, other requirements put forward in the specifications of the design objects. In other words, the developers have to solve the problems of searching optimization (SO) [1][2][3]. It is very typical that most of the current known SO methods are developed and effectively used to find only one extremum, which is often the global one [3][4]. However, many design tasks in solving complex technological systems and transportation problems require optimization. Especially, the objects of discrete nature are characterized by multiextremal (ME) properties [4][5][6][7][8][9][10][11]. A significant distinctive property for solving such tasks requires specific methods to reach the solution. It is unlikely that these methods should be sought in the class of the SO deterministic methods, though such attempts are already well known. These methods are too sensitive to the sign variation of discontinuous functions within their continuum response factor spaces. However in the discrete factor spaces, they are described as the NP-complete algorithms. For solving real optimization problems, it has been common to apply methods marked "heuristics". These methods are, according to the authors, the most perspective to obtain solutions for the multiextremal problems [5][6][7][8][9][10][11].

A. *Formulation of the problem*

As mentioned above, the motivation is to research the most common heuristic SO methods in an environment of a more typical, universal and complex ME problem. The performed research revealed the possibility of finding, some or all, extremes by applying each of the chosen methods. Along with this qualitative evaluation, it is necessary to numerically assess the accuracy of determining the extremes values, as well as their coordinates. Therefore, in the first stage of this research, we suggest to choose the ME test function that might provide a common environment for all the methods when solving ME tasks. In the second stage of this research, the exact heuristic approaches are chosen, which determine both, the well-known methods of solving ME tasks, and their implementation algorithms.

B. *Choosing multiextremal test function and a preliminary analysis of its properties*

The most common and effective test functions for developing and analyzing the SO methods are the Rosenbrock, Himmelblau and Rastrigin functions. The Rastrigin function (RF) is the most applied ME function between all of them. This universal function is not convex, and already proposed in 1974 by Rastrigin [12]. The equation of N function arguments is:

$$f(x) = A \cdot n + \sum_{i=1}^{n} \left[x_i^2 - A \cdot \cos(2 \cdot \pi \cdot x_i) \right], \quad (1)$$

where: $x=(x_1,\ldots,x_n)^T$ – vector; A=10.

The global minimum of this function is at the point (0,0)=0. It is difficult to find a local minimum of this function, because it has many local minimums. The isolation and evaluation of extremais a complex task.

In Section 2, the 3 most popular approaches of finding the set of extremaproblem are discussed for the 2-dimensional Rastrigin function. Section 3 describes the related work. In Section 4, the conclusion of the conducted research is given.

II. SELECTING A GROUP OF HEURISTIC METHODS

In this article, the authors settled on 3 most relevant tasks that are common in practice, when solving various search optimization tasks.

A. RF using swarming particles method

The essence and reasons in using the method of swarming particles (MSP) in SO tasks are well known [13][14][15][16][17]. The classic MSP algorithm simulates the real behavior patterns of insects, birds, fishes, many protozoa, etc. However, ME objects require to know some specific properties of this algorithm.

The authors [18][19][20] and other students of R. Neudorf [7][8][9][10][11] have significantly reworked the canonical MSP version. In particular, a new modified version of this algorithm was developed for solving the ME tasks, which is based on a model of the mechanical principles of the particle movement, and complemented by the mechanisms borrowed from the biological laws, as well as, the method of adaptation mechanisms, as property of the ME task.

The Mechanical Movement Model (MMM) of particles [20] in MSP was significantly modified and refined:

$$X_{ti} = X_{(t-\Delta t)i} + \vec{V}_{(t-\Delta t)i} \cdot \Delta t, \quad (2)$$

$$\vec{V}_{ti} = \vec{V}_{(t-\Delta t)i} + \vec{A}_{(t-\Delta t)i} \cdot \Delta t, \quad (3)$$

$$\vec{A}_i = \vec{A}_{pi} + \vec{A}_{tri}, \quad (4)$$

where: $X_{(t\text{-}\Delta t)i}$ – i-th particle previous position; X_{ti} – i-th particle current position; V_{ti} – i-th particle velocity at the current time; $V_{(t\text{-}\Delta t)i}$ – i-th particle current velocity; $A_{(t\text{-}\Delta t)i}$ – particle previous acceleration in previous time; Δt – integration interval; A_{pi} – acceleration caused by the particles biologically action attractive forces; A_{tri} – slowing under the action of friction forces.

To improve the searching properties, the stochastic blur parameter was introduced:

$$\lambda^{\xi}(\varepsilon) = \lambda \cdot (1 + 2 \cdot \varepsilon(rnd(1) - 0.5)), \quad (5)$$

where: $\lambda^{\xi}(\varepsilon)$ – fluctuating parameter value by tact; ε – distorted relative deviation parameter from nominal value; $rnd(1)$ – random number in the range [0, 1].

For particles, the natural clustering mechanisms were proposed and tested:

- gradient, based on particles sensitivity to change the velocity changing sign [9][10][11];
- potential, based on the introduction in MMM attractive forces at all local extrema, which detected by swarming and scanning the search space:

$$\vec{A}_{pi} = \vec{A}^{G}_{pi} + \vec{A}^{L}_{pi} + \vec{A}^{C}_{pi}, \quad (6)$$

where: A^{G}_{pi} - particles attraction to global extremum; A^{L}_{pi} - particles attraction to the local extremum; A^{C}_{pi} - particles attraction to the cluster center.

The ME MSP algorithm showed good selectivity by localization extremaareas, but the clustering and clusters localization of mechanisms (finding values of extremaand their coordinates) require substantial structural and parametric improvements.

This mechanism does not break the swarm into multiple clusters. It only saves the particles position that entered into the cluster. This allows the particles to be attracted, at all times to the global, local and cluster extrema, and does not stop them within their cluster.

In this research, we have introduced and verified the following modifications:

- mechanism for dropping out "bad" clusters was introduced by certain criteria (the worst for a given number of iterations);
- mechanism for combining similar clusters was introduced at each step;
- parametrical settings were introduced for conditional attraction to the nearest cluster center;
- clusters areas localization mechanism and a mechanism finding local extremaparameters in them were added.

The modification of the dynamic clustering mechanism allows reducing the time and increasing the search accuracy. However, in the follow up studies the authors suggest a modification, which might reduce the processing time to drop out the "bad" cluster's members and to combine the clusters by several criteria.

The testing modifications effectiveness was carried out for RF in coordinate range $(x,y) \in [-1.5, 1.5]$. In this area, RF has 9 local minimums, including one global. Fig. 1(a), 1(b) and 1(c) show extremaareas localization process and creation corresponding clusters.

Fig. 1(a), 1(b) and 1(c) show that the particles are initially attracted to the resulting cluster, which is located in the global extremum area. This is due to the overall prevalence of the global attraction power over the local forces of attraction. Some peripheral particles might find the

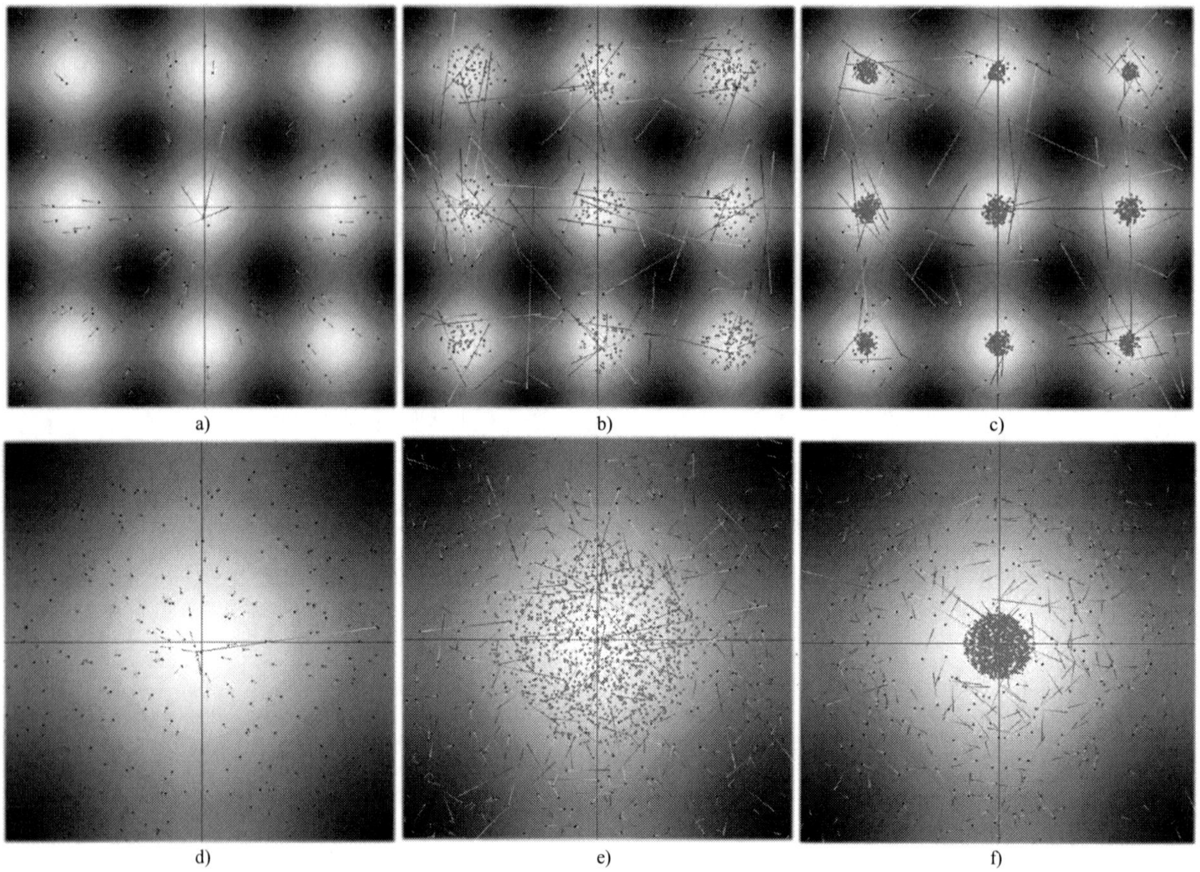

Figure 1. Extremaareas localization of (a – the 1st iteration, b – the 15th iteration, c – the 50th iteration). Local identification of one local extremum of (d – the 1st iteration, e – the 33rd iteration, f – the 50th iteration)

local extrema, which are attracted to them, and gathered in clusters. In strict clusters areas, the ME MSP algorithm (in case of having less isolated and significant extrema) is repeated. This process is iteratively repeated until the desired accuracy of the local and global extremaparameters is achieved.

Within an unlimited time for fulfilling the algorithm of each cluster, a quite stable dynamic equilibrium of particles is set. The calculations, for the modelling activity, make obvious, that the average number of the particles is correlated with the value of the extremum. The degree of correlation depends on the ME MSP algorithm settings.

In order to improve the accuracy of any extremum parameters estimation, the repetition of ME MSP algorithm, for the contracted areas of the defined clusters, is applied. This process can be iteratively repeated until the desired accuracy is achieved in respect to all the local and global extrema.

The examples in Fig. 1(d), 1(e) and 1(f) demonstrate the fragments of the iterative identification of the local extremum, which is located at the point [-1, 1]. TABLE I shows the results obtained by the localization in all areas. The table presents the coordinates $x=x_1$ and $y=x_2$, and the RF values obtained by applying the equation (2). The increase of number of iterations (and the search time) increases the estimation accuracy.

TABLE I. RESULTS OF THE EXPERIMENT

Standard			**Extremum evaluation item**		
x	*y*	*f (x, y)*	*Coordinates*		*Value*
			x	*y*	*f (x, y)*
-1	1	2	-0,9957	0,9953	1,9901
-1	0	1	-0,9949	0,0001	0,995
-1	-1	2	-0,9951	-0,9947	1,9899
0	1	1	$-3{,}20*10^{-5}$	0,9948	0,995
0	0	0	$9{,}85*10^{-5}$	$-6{,}49*10^{-6}$	$1{,}94*10^{-6}$
0	-1	1	0,00017	-0,995	0,995
1	1	2	0,9949	0,995	1,9899
1	0	1	0,995	0,00011	0,995
1	-1	2	0,9952	-0,9951	1,9899

Thus, we can conclude that ME MSP is an effective tool for solving the ME tasks.

B. RF using evolutionary-genetic algorithm

The Evolutionary-Genetic Algorithm (EGA) is one of the most popular tools for solving optimization tasks [21][22][23][24]. The structure and basic operators of EGA are well known, and the specific parametric features depend on the application. In particular, the use of EGA for solving ME tasks [25][26][27][28] requires the addition of the classic EGA with the tools of extremaselection by type (max or min), by the value and by the object's coordinates in the factor space. This paper develops the approach for the extremaselection, based on the use of one sample Student's t-test [27][28][29]. Its essence lies in the consistent use of EGA with further clustering values, which are obtained in its generations of the final results. Latter on, they are separated, as coordinate groups, in order to test the null hypothesis for each of them.

The arithmetic model of the present clustering method involves the consistent comparison of vectors with the middle value of vectors group $v=\{\Delta v_i=v_i-v_0 \mid i \in\{1;n\}\}$, where n – quantity of vectors. Regarding the specified probability, the decision on the set membership of vector v is taken into account. To clarify, for the set membership, it is necessary to calculate the average value of the group vectors lengths, used for their comparison:

$$\Delta v = \sum_{i=1}^{n} \Delta v / n . \quad (7)$$

Then, we calculate the standard deviation of the vectors lengths of already identified cluster:

$$S_{\{\Delta v\}} = \sqrt{\sum_{i=1}^{n} (\Delta \bar{v} - v)^2 / (n-1)} , \quad (8)$$

$$S_{\{\Delta v\}} = S_{\{\Delta v\}} / \sqrt{n} . \quad (9)$$

Using the calculated values, the experimental values of one-sample Student's t-test are counted:

$$t_0 = |\Delta \bar{v} - \Delta v| / S_{\{\Delta v\}} . \quad (10)$$

If the determined experimental t_0 value does not exceed the table t_r value [30] at n freedom degrees and a chosen level of confidence probability P, we can assume that t_0 belongs to this group of objects.

This method has proven to be well adapted to study the ME dependencies [27][28][29][30][31].

By following this approach, the algorithm and respective software tool (ST) were developed. By using ST, we studied RF in the same range, as we described in the previous section of this paper, while investigating RF by the algorithm of the swarming particles.

The structure of the EGA parameters input, which was used in the RF investigation, includes the generations of EGA individuals = 10, in each generation = 1000, the probability of crossover = 95% and probability of mutation = 30%. It should be noted that the search area parameter is the same, as in the previous section, and the accuracy of the research in this area = 7 digits, after the decimal point. Consequently, it becomes possible to allocate 9 clusters, whose minimums can correlate with those that came into the study area.

Fig. 2 shows the graphs of sequential detection of RF values and their different coordinates (X and Y), as well as the corresponding values of the objective function ($F(X, Y) \approx 2$), which are in descending order (for clusters formed around minimums with (-1,1), (1,-1), (1,1), (-1,-1) values).

Eight peripheral clusters characterize local minimums, and the central cluster contains the results approaching the global minimum of the function (see Fig. 3(a). It clearly shows, that close (and in some cases equal) to the value of the function objectives, which contain significant differences in the coordinate parameters (i.e., parameters of the objective function, that provide values close to the minimum are unlike). The ME of the studied object confirms this fact.

The results of the function study in terms of global and local minimums are shown in TABLE II. Their actual values are written down under the data in the table. The values of the objective function, adjusted for the second iteration, as well as their corresponding coordinates are shown in TABLE III.

Based on the data presented in TABLE II, it can be mentioned that extremavalues and their coordinates are not very accurate.

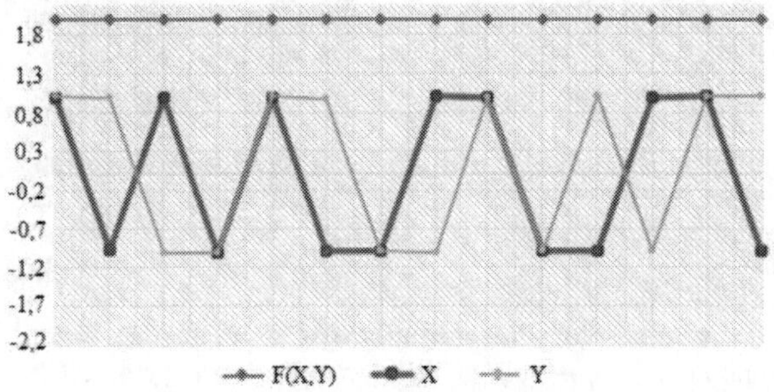

Figure 2. Clusters allocation in the experiment.

TABLE II. FOUNDED PARAMETERS OF THE OBJECTIVE FUNCTION AT THE FIRST ITERATION (IN CLUSTERS)

Standard			**Extremum evaluation item**		
			Coordinates		*Value*
x	*y*	*f(x,y)*	*x*	*y*	*f(x,y)*
0	0	0	0,00188	0,00015	0,00071
-1	0	1	-0,98932	0,00073	1,00137
0	-1	1	0,00824	-1,00043	1,01436
1	0	1	0,99948	-0,01328	1,03398
0	1	1	0,01403	1,00665	1,0611
1	-1	2	0,99146	-0,99314	1,993
1	1	2	0,99702	1,00467	2,00947
-1	-1	2	-0,9897	-1,01397	2,06707
-1	1	2	-1,00528	1,00077	2,01775

TABLE III. FOUNDED PARAMETERS VALUES OF THE OBJECTIVE FUNCTION AT THE SECOND ITERATION

Values	**2nd cluster**	**4th cluster**	**8th cluster**
x	-0,999996	0,999992	-0,999996
y	0,000005	-0,000008	-1,000005
f(x,y)	0,999997	0,999989	1,999991

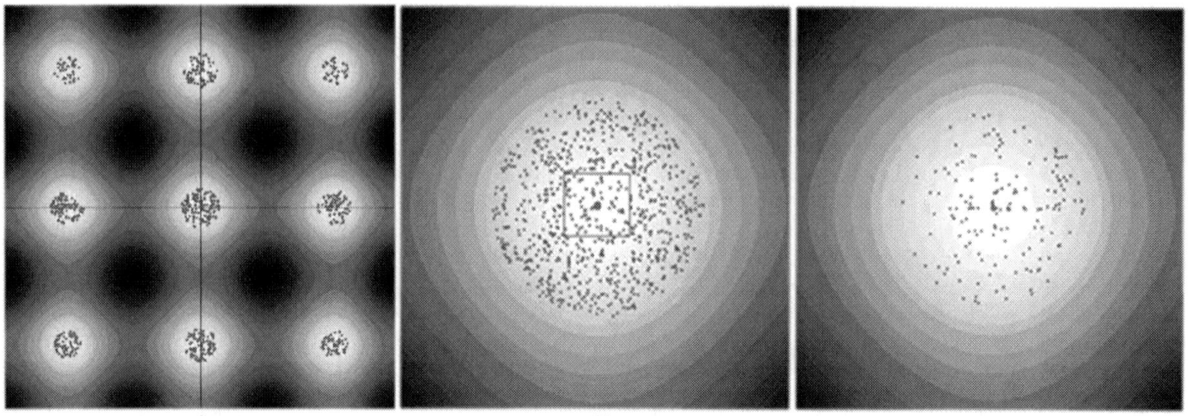

a) b) c)

Figure 3. Extremalocalization areas of (a - the selected RF clusters). Forming clusters in the localized region of (b - the 100th generation, c - the 110th generation).

If the obtained values are not satisfying the required accuracy, we can find a value that is more accurate in the next RF minimum, and which is found within each cluster. The evidence of this, as example is presented in the research of 2nd, 4th and 8th cluster, according to Table II. The authors have developed the approach to localize search in the extreme areas [29]. This approach is based on EGA using [27][28], where close minimum values of second cluster can be observed in Fig. 3(b)), with the best extreme estimation highlighted by a red circle. By using the localized search, another search was carried out in the area around the highlighted extreme (see Fig. 3(c)).

C. RF using ant colony optimization

The Ant Colony Optimization (ACO) is another group of methods used in solving different optimization tasks. The ACO distinctive feature is that the key behavioral characteristics of real ants are simulated [32]. Commonly, ACO is mostly applied to minimize the path in graph tasks [33], but the given algorithms also show good results in other domains [34][35]. In this paper, the classical ACO is applied to optimize ME RF benchmark task [12].

The described method, based on the classic ACO realization, is applied for solving graph problems [35], however with some additions.

Similar to the classic ACO, in this modification, we can distinguish such steps as "initialization and arrangement", "moving of ants", "updating of pheromone" and "breakpoint checking".

For example, a RF fragment for the range $(x,y) \in [-1.5, 1.5]$ was examined. It is divided into nxn fragments, each of them associated with function value in the center and some pheromone level. The specified amount of ants is placed on each fragment. As all the fragments are equal, the size of the fragment can be calculated by the following formula:

$$m = (X_{\max} - X_{\min}) / n . \qquad (11)$$

Thus, the set of fragments is defined by the matrix $B=(I_{i,j})^{n,n}_{i=q,j=1}$.

When an ant is moving from fragment $I_{i,j}$, it is calculating the moving probabilities towards the adjacent fragments, by using the following formula:

$$P_{ij,k}(t) = $$

$$= \begin{cases} \forall f(x_{i,j}, y_{i,j}) > f(x_{i+1,j+1}, y_{i+1,j+1}) \rightarrow Q^*, \\ \forall f(x_{i,j}, y_{i,j}) \leq f(x_{i+1,j+1}, y_{i+1,j+1}) \rightarrow 0. \end{cases} \qquad (12)$$

where: $Q^*=Q(\tau_{i+1,j+1}, \tau_{ij}, \eta_{i+1,j+1}, \eta_{ij}, \alpha, \beta, t)$ - dependence function of pheromone number in fragments $\tau_{i+1,j+1}$, τ_{ij} on the algorithm parameters within the task. In the quality of the function algorithm, we consider: $\eta_{i+1,j+1}$, $\eta_{ij} = |f(x_{ij}, y_{ij}) - f(x_{i+1,j+1}, y_{i+1,j+1})|^{-1}$ - weight (virtual distance) between 2 fragments; α - pheromone influence changeable coefficient; β - weight influence changeable coefficient; t - iteration number.

On the basis of the described algorithm and the model (see (11) and (12)) a software tool (ST) that implements the search of local and global extremawas developed. As an example, Fig. 4(a), 4(b) and 4(c) show the search results of RF global and local minimums. To solve the task, RF search area borders similar to the ones accepted in the previous sections were selected. The selected area was initially divided with a step of 0.25, and 2 ants were placed on each fragment. Coefficients are α=1, β=0.5, ρ=0.5, K=1 and τ=1. Fig. 4(a), 4(b) and 4(c) shows separate stages of work for ST.

For example, let us consider the higher area of subdivisions with the smaller fragments. This algorithm is iteratively applied to the localized fragments until the required accuracy is achieved. The operation results of ACO are presented by Fig. 5(a), which shows the obtained results of localization and two clarifications of global extremum with division into 100x100 fragments situated at point (0, 0).

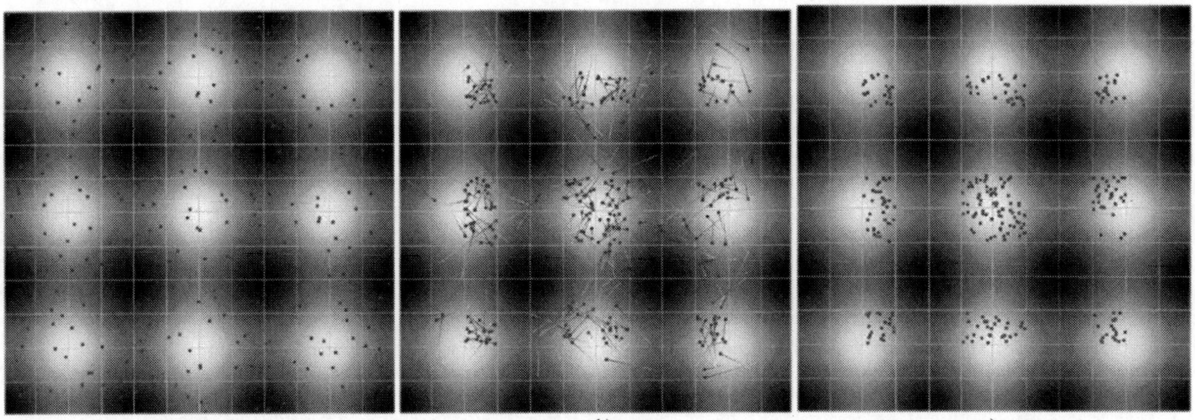

a) b) c)

Figure 4. Visualization of software work stages of (a – initialization, b – the 3rd iteration, c - the final result).

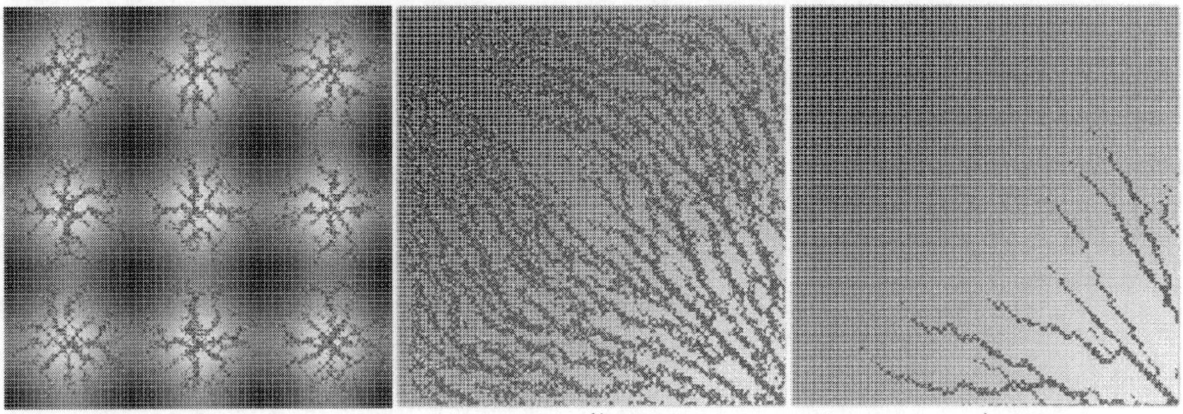

a) b) c)

Figure 5. The results of the location and clarification in the 100x100 division area of (a - selection of all local extrema, b - the selection of the best local extremum, c - clarification of the global extremum).

The localization resulted in 4 extremain 4 central fragments (see Fig. 5(a)). In their centers, distant 0.015 apart from the point (0,0), the value of the function is equal to 0.089210707938399. This enables to suggest that the extremum is located at the joining point of these fragments. For more accurate solutions ACO is applied for one of the fragments $x \in [-0.03, 0]$, $y \in [0, 0.03]$. Fig. 5(b) shows that the ants tend to move to the lower right corner and accumulate in the fragment $x \in [-0.0003, 0]$, with assessed value $8{,}92764330373552*10^{-6}$. The ACO application (see Fig. 5(c)) specifies the value of the extremum to be $8{,}92761420345778*10^{-10}$, and its coordinates to be $1{,}5*10^{-6}$.

D. Computational resources and performance

Searching the extremaby swarming particles, evolutionary-genetic and ant colony algorithms on 2-dimensional Rastrigin function is carried out on a PC with processor AMD Phenom II P960 with 6 GB of RAM.

To achieve the accuracy 10^{-3}, the time was in range 20-100 sec. Additional search within each area was required in range 20-110 sec. for one area.

III. RELATED WORK

In the design optimization process, we are often confronted with problems facing the multiextremal conditions. Such situation requires decisions, which take into consideration several identical or close extrema, and the best choice in-between them has to be made. The classical theory of schedules gives examples, where several identical optimums and identical suboptimums, close to them exist [2][3][4][7][8][36]. The majority of discrete, integer and combinatory programming problems differs in such property [37][38][39], in particular, when finding solution for graphs [40][41][42][43]. The finite number (though very big) of admissible decisions requires considering the multiextremal solutions for the discrete environment optimization. It is important to have a complete solution of the multiextremal task, because the criterion is usually a numerical expression related to the optimized object. However, there are many additional conditions, which can help to choose the extrema, equivalent or close in size, and satisfy both, the numerical criteria estimates and the heuristic ideas. Therefore, the choice, of the most effective methods and algorithms, is an extremely important step to find such solution of the multiextremal task.

However, not all the search methods provide the successful solution for the multiextremal task. It is well known that the determinate methods are sensitive to the sign-variable, so-called "gullied" surfaces, which define the real variables in the factor space. The solution of discrete tasks by such methods leads to the nondeterministic polynomial, in order to define for the complete problem in time. The methods of the accidental search are poorly predictable, since it is impossible to control the time expenditure, and even the basic decision, which heuristic method to apply, when having a real search optimization problem. In particular, in Russia, in the last years, the quite intensive research is conducted, to find appropriate solutions for the many optimization problems. Among these methods, it is important to mention the swarming particles algorithm [13][14][15][16][17][18][19][20] the ant colony algorithm [31][32][33][34][35] and the evolutionarily genetic algorithm [21][22][23][24][25][26][27][28]. These algorithms were investigated, as the traditional optimization tasks, and in relation to find the solution of the multiextremal tasks. For the last case, they have been significantly modified, by experimenting with different heuristic methods, which research was conducted earlier by the authors [9][10][11]. Therefore, the presented work brings forward a peculiar theoretical result, and trace the roadmap for the future research in this direction.

IV. CONCLUSION

The analysis of the application of the 3 heuristic algorithms for solving the ME tasks showed that these methods are efficient, effective, and bring some essential features to the described solutions.

The specific approaches to solve the task for each of these particular cases is determined through the analysis of the algorithms features; the detection and identification of local extrema, clustering methods and subsequent operations for the results analysis. However, in all these cases the modifications of algorithms is connected with the data clustering necessity, which was proved to be essential. Also, all the methods showed adequate performance.

To conclude, all the 3 methods, studied in this paper, are considered to be relevant and promising for future applications. The specific choice of the algorithm tool for solving ME tasks depends on the experience and personal researcher preferences, as well as on the special features of the subject research area.

In this paper, the task of finding the set of extremafor 2-dimensional Rastrigin test function was examined. In future research, it is advisable to study the problem of higher dimension (3 or more) in order to assess the impact of algorithms' parameters on time and search accuracy, and to enable algorithms modifications for the mathematical models of any problem dimension.

REFERENCES

[1] S. Boettcher and A. G. Percus, "Extremal optimization: methods derived from co-evolution", Proceedings of the 1999 Genetic and Evolutionary Computation Conference (GECCO '99), pp.825-832, 1999.

[2] C. A. Floudas and P. M. Pardalos, "Encyclopedia of optimization, 2nd Edition", Springer, New York: Springer Scince+Dusiness Media, LCC, 2009.

[3] K. B. Jones, "Search engine optimization, 2nd edition", Indianapolis: Wiley Publishing, 2010.

[4] R. Shreves, "Drupal search engine optimization", Birmingham: Packt Publishing LTD, 2012.

[5] I. M. Vinogradov, "Mathematical encyclopedia", Soviet Encyclopedia, vol.4, 1977-1985, pp.135-140.

[6] R. G. Strongin, "Algorithms for multi-extremal mathematical programming problems", pp.357-378, 1992.

[7] R. A. Neydorf, A. V. Filippov, and Z. H. Yagubov, "Commute algorithm of biextreme solutions of the homogeneous distribution problem", Herald of DSTU, №5(56), vol.11, pp.655-666, 2011.

[8] R. A. Neydorf and A. A. Zhikulin, "Research of properties solutions of multi distribution problems", System analysis, management and information processing: Proceedings of the 2nd International Scientific Seminar, Rostov-on-Don: IC DSTU, pp.377-380, 2011.

[9] R. A. Neydorf and A. A. Dereviankina, "The methodology of solving problems of the modified method of multi swarming particles", Innovation, ecology and resource-saving technologies at the enterprises of mechanical engineering, aviation, transport and agriculture, Proceedings of the IX International Scientific and Technical Conference, Rostov-on-Don: IC DSTU, pp.328-330, 2010.

[10] R. A. Neydorf and A. A. Dereviankina, "Decision of multi tasks by dividing swarms", Herald of DSTU, №4(47), vol.10, pp.492-499, 2010.

[11] R. A. Neydorf and A. A. Dereviankina, "The solution of problems of recognition by swarming particle swarm division", News of SFU. Technical science. Special Issue "Intellectual CAD", Taganrog: Publisher TTI SFU, №7(108), pp. 21-28, 2010.

[12] L. A. Rastrigin, "Systems of extremal control", Nauka, Moscow (in Russian), 1974.

[13] R. C. Eberhart and J. Kennedy, "New optimizer, using particle swarm theory", Proceedings of the Sixth International Symposium on Micromachine and Human Science, Nagoya, Japan, pp.39-43, 1995.

[14] J. Kennedy and R. Eberhart, "Particle swarm optimization", Proceedings of IEEE International Conference on Neural Networks IV, pp. 1942-1948, 1995.

[15] Y. Shi and R. C. Eberhart, "A modified particle swarm optimizer", Proceedings of the IEEE Congress on Evolutionary Computation, Piscataway, New Jersey, pp.69-73, 1998.

[16] M. Clerc and J. Kennedy, "The particle swarm-explosion, stability, and convergence in a multi-dimensional complex space", IEEE Transactions on Evolutionary Computation, pp.58-73, 2002.

[17] Mendes, J. Kennedy, and J. Neves, "The fully informed particle swarm: simpler, maybe better", Evolutionary Computation, IEEE Transactions on 8(3), pp.204-210, 2004.

[18] R. A. Neydorf and I. V. Chernogorov, "Parametric configuration of the algorithm of searching optimization by swarming particles using experimental planning", International Institute of Science "Educatio", №2(9), vol.4, pp.44-49, 2015.

[19] R. A. Neydorf and I. V. Chernogorov, "Increased functionality of the method of swarming particles by kinematic and dynamic modification of the algorithm of its realization", LTD "Aeterna", International Journal "Innovative science", №6, vol. 1, pp. 24-28, 2015.

[20] R. A. Neydorf and I. V. Chernogorov, "A parametric research of the algorithm of swarming particles in the problem of finding the global extremum", Mathematical methods in technique and technologies – MMTT-28: Proceedings XXVIII International Scientific Conference, YA.6, Saratov: SSTU, pp.75-80, 2015.

[21] A. Fraser, "Computer models in genetics", New York: McGraw-Hill, 1970.

[22] D. Goldberg, "Genetic algorithms in search, optimization and machine learning", Addison Wesley, 1989.

[23] H. Mühlenbein, D. Schomisch, and J. Born, "The parallel genetic algorithm as function optimizer", Parallel Computing, vol. 17, pp.619-632, 1991.

[24] N. A. Barricelli, "Esempi numerici di processi di evoluzione", Methodos, pp.45–68, 1954.

[25] S. Boettcher, "Extremal optimization - heuristics via co-evolutionary avalanches", Computing in Science & Engineering 2, pp.75–82, 2000.

[26] S. Boettcher, "Extremal optimization of graph partitioning at the percolation threshold", pp.5201–5211, 1999.

[27] R. A. Neydorf and V. V. Polyakh, "Method of multisearch using evolutionary genetic algorithm and sample t-test", LTD "Aeterna", International Journal "Innovative science", №3, vol.1, pp.135-140, 2015.

[28] R. A. Neydorf and V. V. Polyakh, "Study of multi dependencies using an evolutionary genetic method and one sample Student's t-test", Mathematical methods in technique and technologies – MMTT-28: Proceedings XXVIII International Scientific Conference, YA.6, Saratov: SSTU, pp. 83-87, 2015.

[29] R. A. Neydorf and V. V. Polyakh, "Localization search scopes evolutionary genetic algorithm for solving problems of multi nature", Science.Technology.Production, №6, vol.2, pp.18-22, 2015.

[30] M. Lovric, "International encyclopedia of statistical science", Springer-Verlag Berlin Heidelberg, 2011.

[31] A. Kazharov and V. Kureichik, "Ant colony optimization algorithms for solving transportation problems", Journal of Computer and Systems Sciences International, №1, vol.49, pp.30–43, 2010.

[32] M. Dorigo and L. M. Gambardella, "Ant colony system: a cooperative learning approach to the traveling salesman problem", IEEE Transactions on Evolutionary Computation, №1, vol.1, pp.53-66, 1997.

[33] X. Liu and H. Fu, "An effective clustering algorithm with ant colony", Journal of Computers, №4, vol.5, pp.598-605, 2010.

[34] M. D. Toksari, "Ant colony optimization for finding the global minimum", Applied Mathematics and Computation 176, pp.308–316, 2006.

[35] R. A. Neydorf and O. T. Yarakhmedov, "Development, optimization and analysis of parameters of classic ant colony algorithm in solving travelling salesman problem on graph", Science. Technologies. Production, №3, vol.2, pp.18-22, 2015.

[36] Michael L. Pinedo Scheduling Theory, Algorithms, and Systems Fourth Edition ISBN 978-1-4614-1986-0 e-ISBN 978-1-4614-2361-4 DOI 10.1007/978-1-4614-2361-4 Springer New York Dordrecht Heidelberg London Mathematics Subject Classification (2010): Library of Congress Control Number: 68Mxx, 68M20, 90Bxx, 90B35.

[37] https://www.encyclopediaofmath.org/index.php/Discrete_programming (September 29, 2016).

[38] Donald E. Knuth - The Art of Computer Programming. Volume 4, Fascicle 0: Introduction to Combinatorial Algorithms and Boolean Functions (vi+240pp, ISBN 0-321-53496-4).

[39] http://www.cs.utsa.edu/~wagner/knuth/ (September 29, 2016).

[40] GRhttp://diestel-graph-theory.com/index.html (September 29, 2016).

[41] Keijo Ruohonen. Graph theory (Translation by Janne Tamminen, Kung-Chung Lee and Robert Piché) 2013.

[42] Christopher Griffin, Graph Theory: Penn State Math 485 Lecture Notes Version 1.4.2.1 2011-2012.

[43] Paul Van Dooren Graph Theory and Applications Université catholique de Louvain Louvain-la-Neuve, Belgium Dublin, August 2009.

Prototype Design of Computationally Efficient Digital Down Converter for 3G Applications

Rajesh Mehra
Electronics & Communication Engineering Department
National Institute of Technical Teachers Training & Research
Chandigarh, UT, India
Email: rajeshmehra@yahoo.com

***Abstract*— This paper presents Digital Down Converter (DDC) design for Software Defined Radio (SDR) base stations using reconfigurable logic. A computationally efficient multistage design technique is used to achieve an efficient solution for third generation (3G) mobile communication. The proposed design is developed in three stages and each stage has been optimized using Park McClellan algorithm to minimize the filter order. This was further supplemented with computationally efficient polyphase decomposition technique. The Partially Serial Pipelined MAC algorithm is used to optimize both speed and area simultaneously. The embedded multipliers of target Field Programmable Gate Array (FPGA) are optimally utilized and efficiently mapped to enhance the system performance. The proposed DDC has shown an improvement of 19 % in speed with improved resource utilization to provide a computationally efficient and cost effective solution for SDR based wireless applications.**

Keywords-3G Mobile Communication; Base Stations; Radio Transceivers; Reconfigurable Logic; Software Radio.

I. INTRODUCTION

Digital Signal Processors (DSPs) are specialized devices designed to implement digital signal processing algorithms on a stream of digitized signals. The highly competitive nature of the wireless communications market and constantly evolving communication standards have resulted in short design cycles and product lifetimes. This environment has led to the emergence of a new class of configurable DSPs, which can leverage hardware flexibility, programmability, and reusability, to provide highly customizable DSP solutions [1]. In the recent past, telecommunications techniques have achieved a wide popularity, mainly due to the huge diffusion of cellular phones and wireless devices. The request for more complex and complete services, such as high speed data transmission and multimedia content streaming, has moved many research groups in the electronic field towards the study of new and efficient algorithms, codes and modulations. In Software Defined Radios, most radio receiver processing functions are to be run on a general purpose programmable processor rather than being implemented strictly on non-programmable hardware. The functionality of SDR receiver processor can be changed via "software reprogramming." The concept of SDR is now an IEEE Standard, i.e., IEEE P1900 [2]. These radios are reconfigurable through software updates. For high end digital signal processing where the highest possible performance is needed at low power consumption, Application Specific Integrated Circuits (ASICs) are still the processors of choice. However, ASICs require very long design and development times and are very expensive to design and manufacture. Moreover, ASICs are inherently rigid and are not very well suited to applications that are constantly evolving. For these reasons, Programmable Logic Device like Field Programmable Gate Arrays have emerged as an alternative to ASICs in wireless communication systems.

FPGAs are mainly used for the flexibility they provide. Like programmable DSPs, FPGAs are programmed and configured in software. This makes it very easy to upgrade or add functionality to an FPGA, even if it is already deployed in the field. Like ASICs, FPGAs achieve high levels of performance by implementing complex algorithms in hardware. FPGAs are particularly well suited for accelerating algorithms that exhibit a high degree of data flow parallelism. The FPGAs suffer from the drawbacks of inefficient resource utilization, high cost and power consumption [3]. The cost factor can be improved by using less expensive FPGAs for system design and by efficient utilization of FPGA resources. The power factor can be improved by optimal usage of SRAM based programming interconnections. With increasing demand of battery dependent devices, methods for reduction of the power consumption of the memory blocks have received significant interest. Six transistor SRAM cells are preferred for many applications because of its high speed and robustness. The rest of the paper is structured as follows. Section II presents the design specifications of Wideband Code Division Multiple Access (WCDMA) DDC and related state of the art design approaches. Section III shows design simulations and structures. Hardware implementation with area and speed comparison is in Section IV and we conclude in Section V.

II. DIGITAL DOWN CONVERTER

The SDR system can change its radio functions by swapping software instead of replacing hardware, which seems to be the best solution given that mobile standards are springing up like mushrooms [5]. SDR thereby makes it possible to reprogram cell phones to operate on different radio interface standards. But that's not all. Putting much of a radio's functionality in software opens up other benefits. A mobile SDR device can cope with the unpredictable dynamic characteristics of highly variable wireless links [6]. SDRs use a single hardware front end but can change their frequency of operation, occupied bandwidth, and adherence to various wireless standards by calling various software algorithms. Such a solution allows inexpensive, efficient interoperability between the available standards and frequency bands [7]. Fig. 1 illustrates SDR Base Station (BS) receiver that consists of two sections – a front-end high-data rate processing section and a back-end symbol rate or chip-rate processing section.

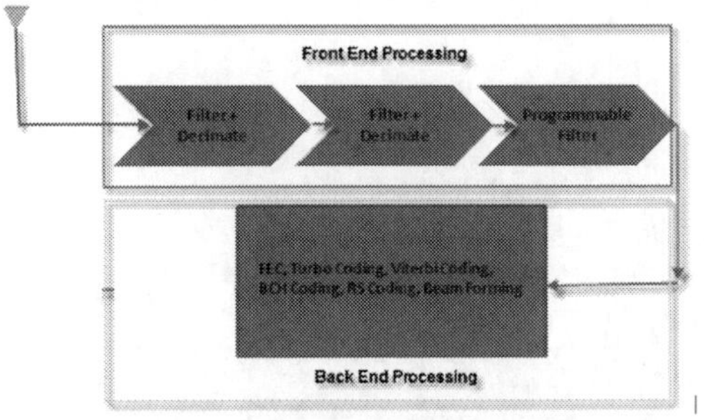

Figure 1. Reconfigurable SDR BS Receiver

Reconfigurable architectures provide flexible and integrated system-on-chip solutions that accommodate smooth migration from archaic to innovative designs, allowing recycling of hardware resources across multiple generations of the standards [8]. SDR technology enables such functionality in wireless devices by using a reconfigurable hardware platform across multiple standards. Sampling rate converters play important role in SDR systems [9]. Digital up-converters (DUCs) and digital down-converters (DDCs) are important components of every modern wireless base station design. DUCs are typically used in digital transmitters to filter up-sample and modulate signals from baseband to the carrier frequency [10]-[12]. DDCs, on the other hand, reside in the digital receivers to demodulate, filter, and down-sample the signal to baseband so that further processing on the received signal can be done at lower sampling frequencies. They are more popular than their analogue counterparts because of small size, low power consumption and accurate performance [13]-[17].

DDC performs decimation and matched filtering to remove adjacent channels and maximize the received signal-to-noise ratio (SNR) [18]. For the reference WCDMA DDC design, the carrier bandwidth is equal to 5.0 MHz, the number of carriers is 1, intermediate frequency (IF) sample rate is equal to 61.44 MSPS, the DDC output rate is 7.68 MSPS, the input precision equals 14 bits, the output precision equals 16 bits and the mixer resolution is 0.25 Hz approximately and SFDR up to 115 dB is required.

The DDC input is assumed to be real, directly coming from the Analog to Digital Converter (ADC). The mixer translates the real band pass input signal from intermediate frequency to a complex baseband signal centered at 0 Hz. Mathematically, the real input signal is multiplied by a complex exponential to produce a complex output signal with real and imaginary components. The sinusoidal waveforms required to perform the mixing process are obtained by using the Direct Digital Synthesizer (DDS). The decimators in the DDC need to down sample the IF data from 61.44 MHz back to 2x chip rate. The factor of 61.44/7.68 = 8 can be partitioned using different possible configurations. The down sampling by eight at once will result in an extremely long filter length and result in an inefficient hardware implementation. The use of shaping filter with decimation factor of 2 allows the remaining stages to be implemented as either one half band filter with decimation factor of 4 or two half band filters with decimation factor of 2 each. The second configuration is more suitable for hardware implementation because of less hardware consumption [19]-[21]. The existing designs suffer from the limitations that their implementation is based on Xilinx FIR compiler blocks and DDS compiler blocks which are based on DSP 48E/A slices. The DSP 48 E/A slice based FPGAs are costly as compared to multiplier based FPGAs and results in costly design implementation. So there is great necessity to implement DDC design on multiplier based low cost FPGA to provide an economically optimized solution in terms of area and speed, which is presented in following sections.

III. PROPOSED DDC

An efficient DDC is designed for WCDMA applications. The proposed DDC design is using three decimator stages. The input sample rate of first decimator is 61.44 MSPS, and the output sample rate is 30.72 MSPS. The pass band frequency is 2.34 MHz and the pass band ripple is 0.002 dB. It results in a digital filter of order 10 whose response is shown in Fig. 2.

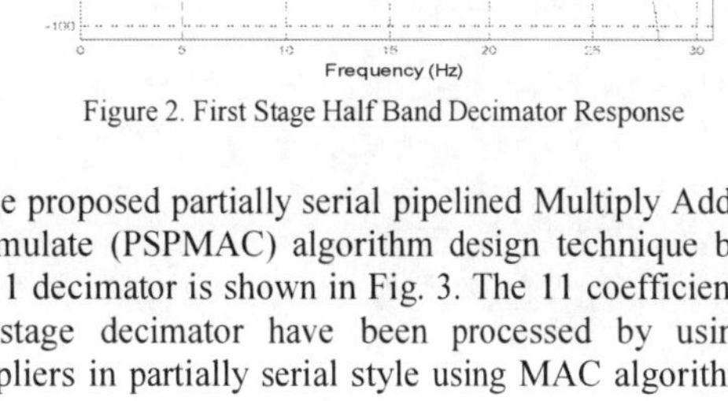

Figure 2. First Stage Half Band Decimator Response

The proposed partially serial pipelined Multiply Add and Accumulate (PSPMAC) algorithm design technique based stage 1 decimator is shown in Fig. 3. The 11 coefficients of first stage decimator have been processed by using 3 multipliers in partially serial style using MAC algorithm to optimize both speed and area factor simultaneously. The input pipeline registers are used to store the new coefficient values required for processing in the next cycle to further enhance the speed. The Cascade Enable (CE) delays are used to synchronize between stage 1 and stage 2. The pass band edge of second decimator is 2.34 MHz and pass band ripple is 0.0001 dB. It results in a digital filter of order 18, whose response is shown in Fig. 4.

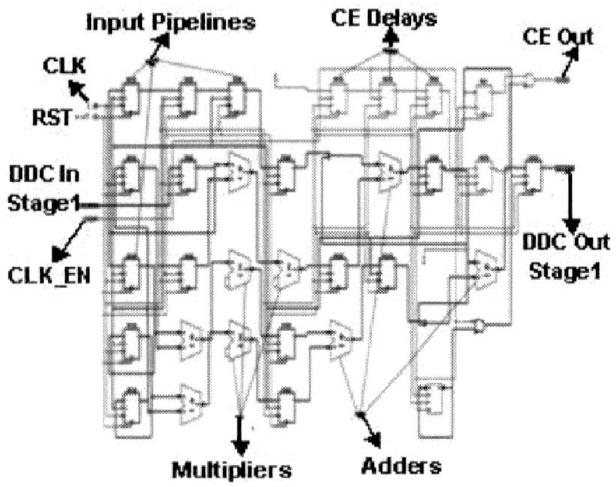

Figure 3. Stage 1 PSPMAC Based Decimator

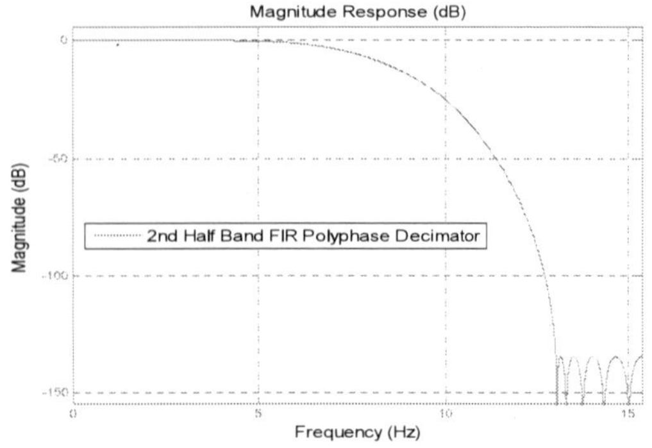

Figure 4. Second Stage Half Band Decimator Response

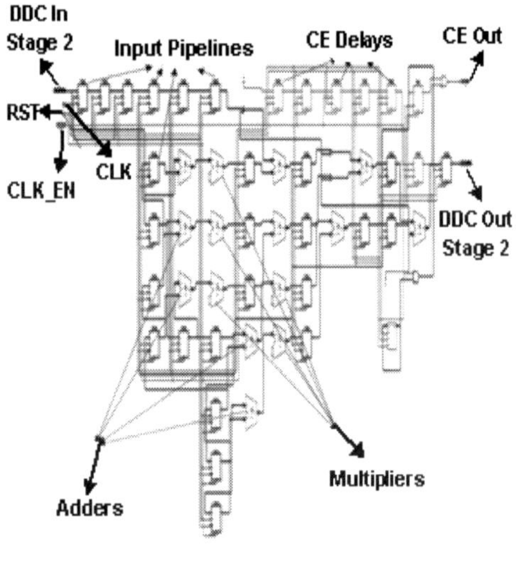

Figure 5. Stage 2 PSPMAC Based Decimator

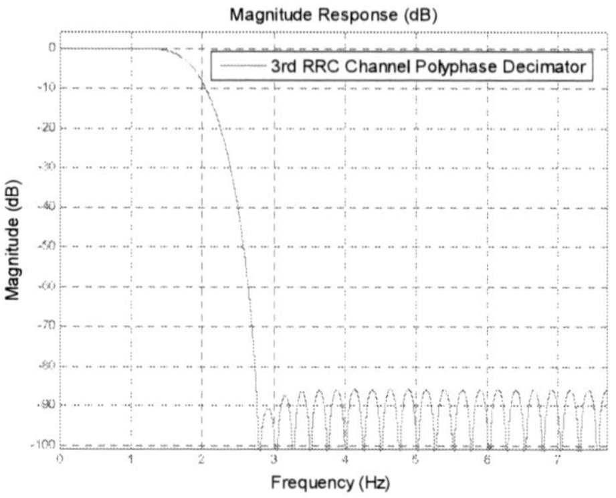

Figure 6. RRC Channel Filter

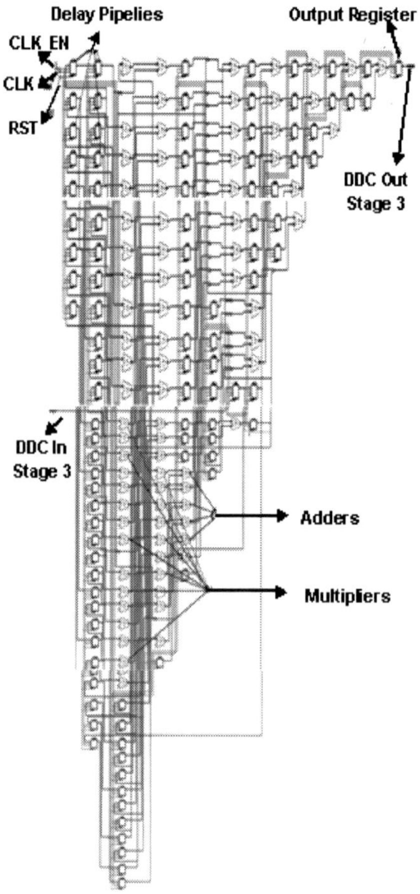

Figure 7. Stage 3 PSPMAC Based RRC Decimator

The second stage decimator requires 27 coefficients for its hardware implementation. To design the required decimator in PSPMAC style, 5 multipliers have been used as shown in Fig. 5. The input pipeline registers are used to store the new coefficient values required for processing in the next cycle to enhance the speed further. The CE delays are used to make synchronization between stage 2 and stage 3. The next stage RRC filter is used for sampling rate conversion from 15.36 MSPS to 7.68 MSPS. This 2x over-sampling rate is needed in the timing recovery process to avoid the signal loss due to the sampling point misalignment. Root Raised Cosine (RRC) filter is designed with 1.92 MHz cut off frequency, 0.22 MHz roll-off factor and 50 dB side lobe attenuation using Chebyshev window [20] whose filter response is shown in Fig. 6. The third stage RRC decimator has also been designed using partially serial architecture as shown in Fig. 7.

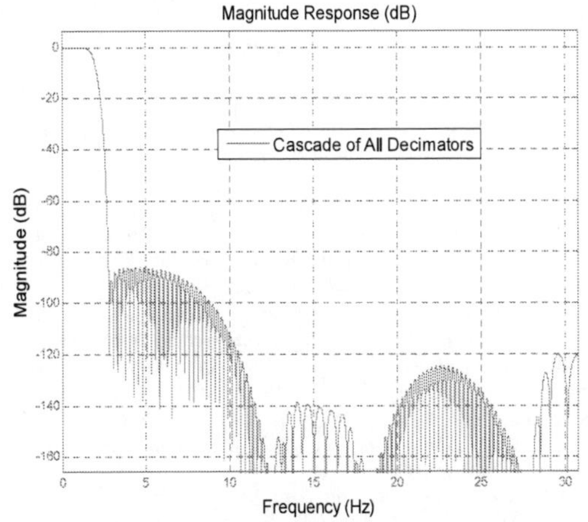

Figure 8. WCDMA DDC Output Response

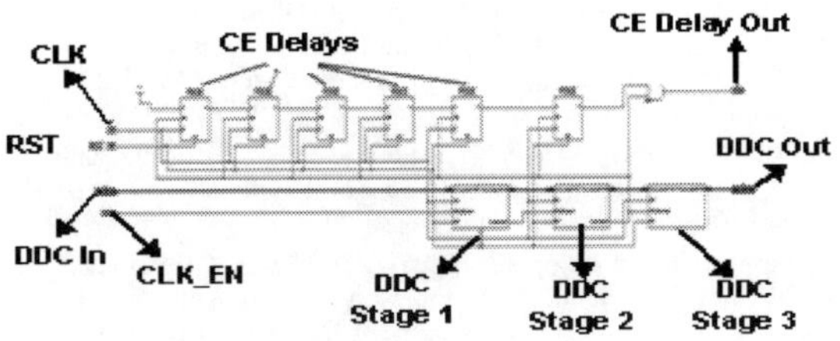

Figure 9. Proposed WCDMA DDC

The 61 coefficients required to design this RRC filter have been processed using 38 multipliers to improve both area and speed. The delay pipelining and output registers are used for synchronization. Finally, DDC is designed by cascading these three stages as shown in Figure 8 with 16 bit coefficients. The cascade of all optimized stages is shown in Fig. 9.

IV. H/W SYNTHESIS & SIMULATION

In the proposed DDC designs CORDIC algorithm based optimized DDS design is used in place of DDS compiler block to generate sinusoidal waveform needed for frequency translation [22]. The FIR Compiler blocks of existing designs are replaced by Equiripple techniques based decimators for optimal filter length to reduce the hardware requirement. It is further supported by the half band filter concept to improve the computational complexity for enhanced speed. Finally, the poly-phase decomposition technique is utilized in the hardware implementation of the proposed design to optimize both speed and area together by introducing the partially serial pipelined MAC architecture. The third stage of decimation has been developed using efficient RRC filter [23] design. All the decimators are implemented using MAC Algorithm with optimal number of embedded multipliers of target FPGA along with pipelined registers to enhance the speed performance and resource utilization. The Virtex-II Pro FPGA device is used for implementation that contains 136 embedded multipliers [24].

Two designs have been developed using different input output precisions. DDC is implemented using input precision of 14 bits and output precision of 16 bit and DDC 2 is implemented using input and output precision of 12 bits. The developed DDCs are simulated using Modelsim Simulator. The output response of DDC1 is shown in Fig. 10 and output response of DDC 2 is shown in Fig. 11. It can be observed from the simulated waveforms that the output response of both the designs is similar but speed performance of DDC2 is better as compared to DDC1.

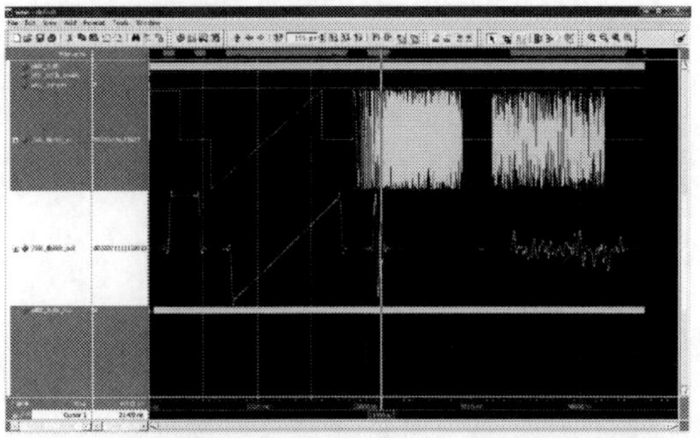

Figure 10. Optimized WCDMA DDC 1 Response

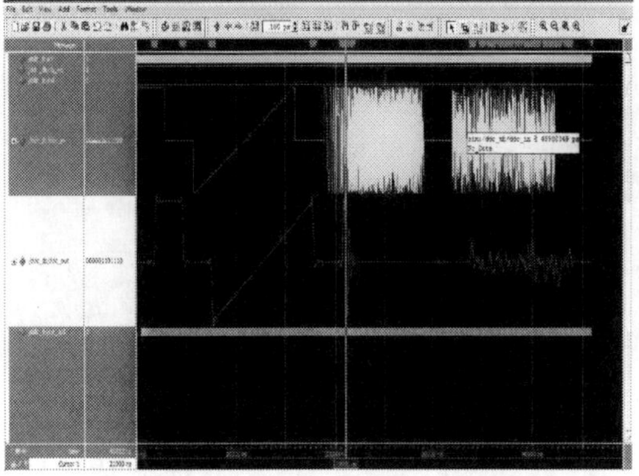

Figure 11. Optimized WCDMA DDC 2 Response

The optimized DDC designs are finally mapped for hardware implementation and synthesised on Virtex-II Pro based xc2vp30-7ff896 target device. The resource consumption of the proposed design on specified target device is shown in Table I.

TABLE I. RESOURCE UTILIZATION

Logic Utilization	DDC Design 1	DDC Design 2
Number of Slices	1477	1462
Number of Flip Flops	2535	2533
Number of LUTs	1429	1366
Number of I/Os	34	28
Number of MULT	46	46

The proposed optimized DDC 2 can operate at a maximum frequency of 146.36 MHz and DDC 1 can operate at 119 MHz as compared to 122.88 MHz in case of [20]. So the proposed DDC 2 provides an improvement of 19% in speed and DDC 1 provides almost the same speed as that of the existing DDC design. The developed DDC designs have shown better resource utilization as compared to DDC design of [21] which is shown in Table II.

TABLE II. RESOURCE UTILIZATION COMPARISON

Logic Utilization	DDC Design [21]	Proposed DDC Designs
Number of Flip Flops	4.93%	9%
Number of Slices	7.9%	10%
Number of MULT	3.8%	33%

V. CONCLUSION

This paper presents an efficient and cost effective DDC design for software defined radios. The existing DDC designs suffer from the drawback of cost effectiveness because their implementation includes DSP 48E slice based Virtex 4 and Virtex 5 FPGAs. The proposed DDC designs are developed and implemented on multiplier based Virtex II Pro target FPGA using optimized MAC algorithm. Three decimator stages are optimized separately and then cascaded together. The optimized DDC has been developed using partially serial pipelined MAC algorithm for area and speed optimization. The DDC designs are efficiently floor planned and routed to achieve the desired timing constraints. The developed DUCs have shown improved speed performance and resource utilization to provide cost effective solution for software radios.

ACKNOWLEDGMENT

The author would like to thank Dr. M. P. Poonia, Director National Institute of Technical Teachers' Training & Research, Chandigarh, India for constant motivation and support throughout this research work.

REFERENCES

[1] B. B. Carvalho, A. J. N. Batista, F. Patrício, M. Correia, H. Fernandes, J. Sousa, and C. A. F. Varandas, "Multi-Rate DSP/FPGA-Based Real-Time Acquisition and Control on the ISTTOK Tokamak" IEEE Transactions on Nuclear Science, VOL. 55, NO. 1, pp. 54-58, February 2008.

[2] Veerendra Bhargav Alluri, J. Robert Heath, Michael Lhamon "A New Multichannel, Coherent Amplitude Modulated, Time-Division Multiplexed, Software-Defined Radio Receiver Architecture, and Field-Programmable-Gate-Array Technology Implementation" IEEE Transactions on Signal Processing, Vol. 58, No. 10, pp. 5369-5384, October 2010.

[3] Amir Beygi, Ali Mohammadi, Adib Abrishamifar. "An FPGA-Based Irrational Decimator for Digital Receivers" IEEE International Symposium on Signal Processing and its Applications (ISSPA), pp. 1-4, 2007.

[4] Prashant Upadhyay, Rajesh Mehra, Nivedita Thakur "Low Power Design of an SRAM cell for Portable Devices", IEEE International conference on Computer and Communication Technology (ICCCT), pp.255-259, 2010.

[5] Takashi Shono, Yushi Shirato, Hiroyuki Shiba, Kazuhiro Uehara, Katsuhiko Araki, Masahiro Umehira, "IEEE 802.11 Wireless LAN Implemented on Software Defined Radio With Hybrid Programmable Architecture" IEEE Transactions on Wireless Communications, Vol. 4, No. 5, pp. 2299-2308, September 2005.

[6] Francois Rivet, Yann Deval, Jean-Baptiste Begueret, Dominique Dallet, Philippe Cathelin, Didier Belot, "A Disruptive Receiver Architecture Dedicated to Software-Defined Radio" IEEE Transaction on Circuits and Systems-II: Express Briefs, Vol.55, No. 4, pp. 344-348, April 2008.

[7] Pedro Cruz, Nuno Borges Carvalho, Kate A. Remley "Designing and Testing Software Defined Radios" IEEE Microwave magazine, pp. 83-94, June 2010.

[8] Navid Lashkarian, Ed Hemphill, Helen Tarn, Hemang Parekh, and Chris Dick "Reconfigurable Digital Front-End Hardware for Wireless Base-Station Transmitters: Analysis, Design and FPGA Implementation" IEEE Transactions on Circuits and Systems-I: Regular Papers, Vol. 54, No. 8, pp. 1666-1677, August 2007.

[9] Vandita Singh, Rajesh Mehra "Rational Rate Converter Design Analysis using Symmetric Technique", International Journal of Computer Trends and Technology, Vol. 27, No. 2, pp. 116-120, September 2015.

[10] G. Swathi, M. Revathy, "Design of a Multi-Standard DUC Based FIR Filter using VLSI Architecture", International Journal of Scientific Engineering and Research, Vol.3, Issue 11, pp. 41-44, November 2015.

[11] Renuka Verma, Rajesh Mehra, "FPGA Implementation of FIR Interpolator for IEEE 802.11n WLAN", International Journal of Engineering Science and Technology, Vol.8, Issue 7, pp. 121-127, July 2016.

[12] Renuka Verma, Rajesh Mehra, "Design of Low Pass FIR Interpolator for Wireless Communication Applications", International Journal of Advanced Research in Computer and Communication Engineering, Vol.6, Issue 7, pp. 355-362, July 2016.

[13] Fei Wang. "Digital Up and Down Converter in IEEE 802.16d", 8th international Conference on Signal Processing, pp. 16-20, 2006.

[14] Rajesh Mehra, Rashmi Arora "FPGA-Based Design of High-Speed CIC Decimator for Wireless Applications" International Journal of

Advanced Computer Science and Applications (IJACSA), USA, Vol. 2, No. 5, pp. 59-62, May-2011.

[15] Rajesh Mehra, Dr. Swapna Devi' "Efficient Hardware Co-Simulation of down Convertor for Wireless Communication Systems" International Journal of VLSI design & Communication Systems (VLSICS), pp. 13-21, Vol.1, No.2, AIRCC, June 2010.

[16] Xiaoxiao Xu, Xianzhong Xie, Fei Wang, "Digital Up and Down Converter in IEEE 802.16d" IEEE International Conference on Signal Processing (ICSP), Vol. 1, pp. 17-20, 2006.

[17] Saad Mahboob, "FPGA Implementation of Digital Up/Down Convertor for WCDMA System" IEEE International Conference on Advanced Communication Technologies (ICACT), pp. 757-760, 2010.

[18] Kong Chunli, Fan Xiangning, Xu Zhiyuan, Zheng Hao "Design and Simulation of Two-channel DDC in Satellite Cellular Integrated System" IEEE International Conference on Wireless Communication networking and Mobile Computing (WiCoM), pp. 1-4, 2010.

[19] Rajesh Mehra, "Reconfigurable Optimized WCDMA DDC for Software Defined Radios" Journal of Selected Areas in Telecommunications (JSAT), Cyber Journals: Multidisciplinary Journals in Science and Technology, Ontario, Canada, pp. 1-6, December Edition, 2010.

[20] Helen Tarn, Kevin Neilson, Ramon Uribe, David Hawke, "Designing Efficient Wireless Digital Up and Down Converters Leveraging CORE Generator and System Generator" Application Note on Virtex-5, Spartan-DSP FPGAs, XAPP1018 (v1.0), pp. 8-44, October 2007.

[21] LIN Fei-yu, QIAO Wei-ming, WANG Yan-yu, LIU Tai-lian, FAN Jin, ZHANG Jian-chuan, "Efficient WCDMA Digital Down Converter Design Using System Generator" IEEE International Conference on Space Science and Communication, pp. 89-92, 2009.

[22] Bindiya Kamboj, Rajesh Mehra "Efficient FPGA Implementation of Direct Digital Frequency Synthesizer for Software Radios" International Journal of Computer Applications, New York, USA, Volume 37, No.10, pp. 25-29, January 2012.

[23] Rajesh Mehra, Dr. Swapna Devi, "FPGA Implementation of High Speed Pulse Shaping Filter for SDR Applications" Springer International Conference on Recent Trends in Networks and Communications, Communication in Computer and Information Science (CCIS), Volume 90, Part 1, pp. 214-222, 2010.

[24] Xilinx User Guide "Virtex-II Pro and Virtex-II Pro X FPGA User Guide" UG012 (v4.2), pp. 178-185, November 2007.

A 3D Model Skeleton Correcting Algorithm using Templates of Inspecting Voxel Disconnection

Xun Jin
Dept. of Copyright Protection,
Sangmyung University
Seoul, Korea
email: jinxun@cclabs.kr

Jongweon Kim
Dept. of Contents and Copyright,
Sangmyung University
Seoul, Korea
email: jwkim@smu.ac.kr

***Abstract*—A 3D model skeleton is an abstraction of a 3D model, which is useful for feature description, 3D model identification and many other applications. However, the skeleton may be disconnected when thinning the 3D model after voxelization. In this paper, a 3D model skeleton correcting algorithm is proposed. It uses 3 pre-defined correcting templates to inspect disconnections and correct them. The templates inspect 26-adjacent voxels of each target voxel after it is removed. After a target voxel is removed, the templates inspect the distances among the rest of 26-adjacent voxels of the target voxel whether any of the distances are greater than or equal to 2. The proposed algorithm is simple and practical. The experimental results show some comparisons between before and after correcting skeletons. The skeleton generated by the proposed method has less noises than that of conventional method and maintains connectivity.**

Keywords-3D model; voxelization; thinning; skeletonization; correcting.

I. Introduction

In recent years, the development of 3D printing technology has led to the explosive growth of 3D models. Hence, the 3D printing services are increasing rapidly [1][2]. However, copyright infringement of 3D models has become an issue for the 3D printing ecosystem of product distribution websites, design-sharing and 3D scanning [3][4]. To prevent unauthorized use of copyrighted 3D models, the identification of 3D models remains.

Many researchers have proposed various methods for 3D model feature extraction and retrieval [5][6][7][8][9]. Because of the high discriminative property of 3D skeleton-based features for 3D model representation, 3D skeleton-based approaches have attracted much attention [5][6][7]. A 3D model skeleton is not only an abstraction of the model at the center-line of the model but also a fundamental shape feature, which is used for shape description, 3D model identification, and many other applications.

However, the conventional methods of generating skeleton have some weaknesses. In [10], authors used as input a subvoxel precise distance field and employed a number of fast marching method propagations to extract the skeleton at subvoxel precision. The algorithm can't generate the skeleton of each branch of a 3D model. In [11][12], authors used a thinning algorithm to generate skeleton and rechecked eight subvoxels with non-overlapping neighborhoods in parallel. However, the generated skeleton included some noises. In [13], authors modified and improved a fully parallel 3D thinning algorithm described in [14]. The parallel thinning algorithm is based on several pre-defined removing templates (class A, B, C and D). The target voxel will be removed, if the neighborhoods of the voxel match one of the templates. The modified algorithm generates the skeleton of each branch of a 3D model and has very few noises, but the skeleton may be disconnected when thinning the 3D model.

In this paper, we present a 3D model skeleton correcting algorithm using some templates of inspecting voxel disconnection. It uses 3 pre-defined correcting templates to inspect disconnections and correct them. The templates inspect 26-adjacent voxels of each target voxel after it is removed. The templates inspect the distances between the rest of 26-adjacent voxels of the removed voxel, whether they are greater than or equal to 2. The proposed algorithm is simple and practical. Some comparisons between before and after correcting the skeletons are shown in the section of experimental results.

The remainder of this paper is organized as follows. A brief overview of the basic theory of the adjacencies in a 3D binary array is given in Section 2. The methodology of the 3D parallel thinning algorithm is reviewed in Section 3. In Section 4, the proposed 3D skeleton correcting algorithm is introduced. The experimental results of skeletons generated by the proposed method and the other methods are shown in Section 5. Finally, we conclude the proposed method in Section 6.

II. Basic Theory

First of all, a voxelization process is performed to a 3D mesh model as in [15]. The 3D space of voxels is transformed to a 3D binary array. Each voxel is denoted by 1 in the 3D binary array. A binary value 0 means that there is no voxel.

Suppose there are two voxels p_1 and p_2 with coordinates (x_1, y_1, z_1) and (x_2, y_2, z_2) in the 3D binary array. The Euclidean distance between p_1 and p_2 is defined as (1) [13].

$$d = \sqrt{(x_1 - x_2)^2 + (y_1 - y_2)^2 + (z_1 - z_2)^2} \quad (1)$$

If $d = 1$, p_1 and p_2 are 6-adjacent. If $d \leq \sqrt{2}$, p_1 and p_2 are 18-adjacent. If $d \leq \sqrt{3}$, p_1 and p_2 are 26-adjacent. Fig. 1 shows the adjacencies of a voxel p.

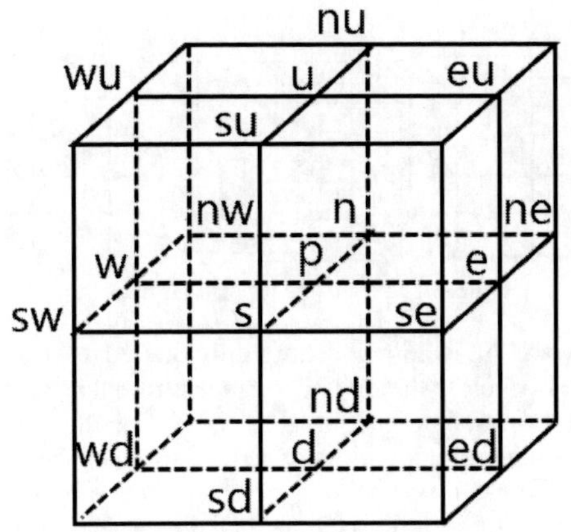

Figure 1. The adjacencies in a 3D binary array.

The n(p), e(p), s(p), w(p), u(p) and d(p) are 6 adjacent voxels of p, where the n, e, s, w, u and d denote north, east, south, west, up and down. The 18-adjacent voxels of p (not include 6-adjacent voxels) are nu(p), ne(p), nd(p), nw(p), eu(p), ed(p), su(p), se(p), sd(p), sw(p), wu(p) and wd(p), and so on.

III. 3D PARALLEL THINNING ALGORITHM

The parallel thinning algorithm is based on several pre-defined removing templates (class A, B, C and D) [13][14]. The target voxel will be removed, if the voxel is a non-tail voxel and the neighborhoods of the voxel match one of the templates.

Fig. 2, 3, 4 and 5 show the templates of four classes. There are 6 templates in class A, 12 templates in class B, 8 templates in class C and 36 templates in class D. A solid black circle denotes a binary value 1, a white circle denotes a binary value 0. The voxels in the unmarked positions are "don't care" voxels, which means the binary values can be either 1 or 0. The white squares mean that at least one of them is 1. The two white triangles in Fig. 5 mean that both of them can't be 1 simultaneously, which means at most one of them is 1 or both of them are 0.

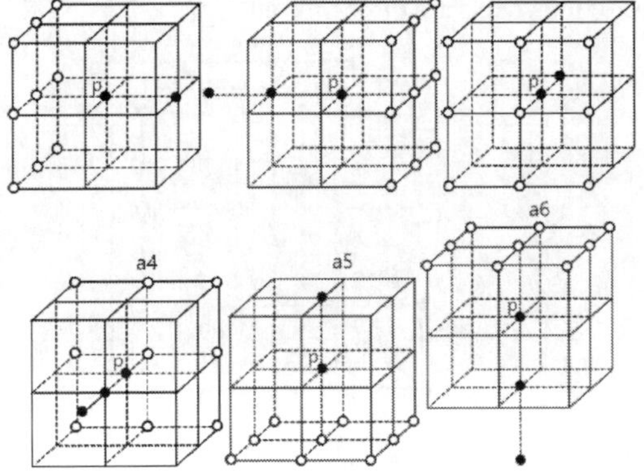

Figure 2. 6 removing templates in class A.

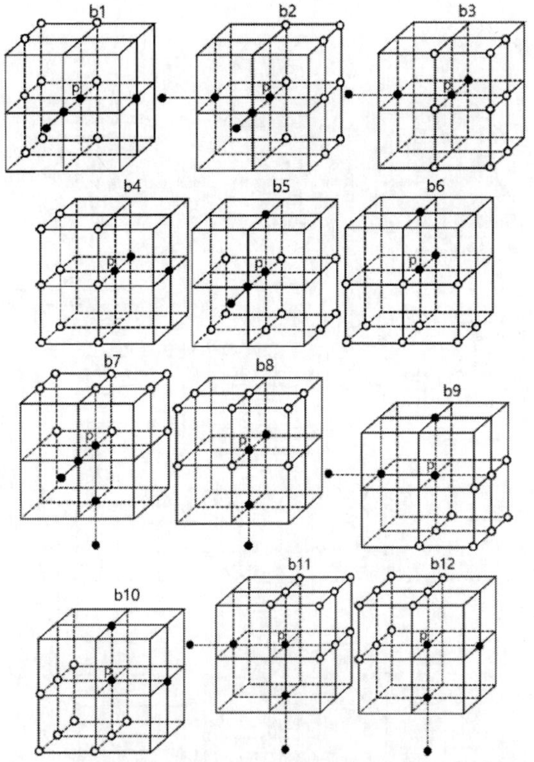

Figure 3. 12 removing templates in class B.

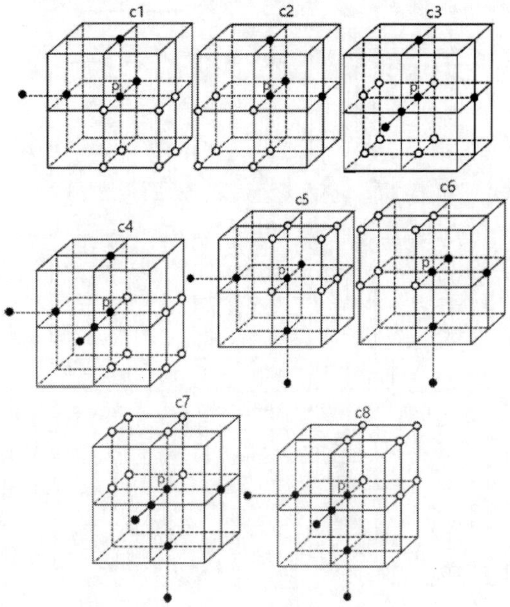

Figure 4. 8 removing templates in class C.

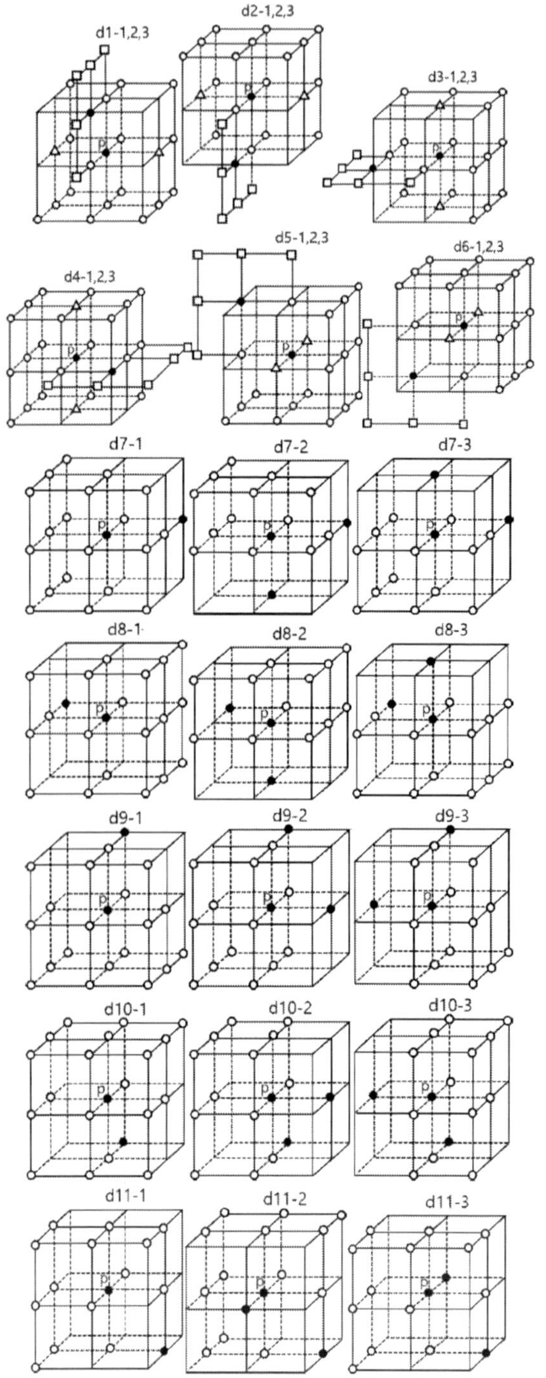

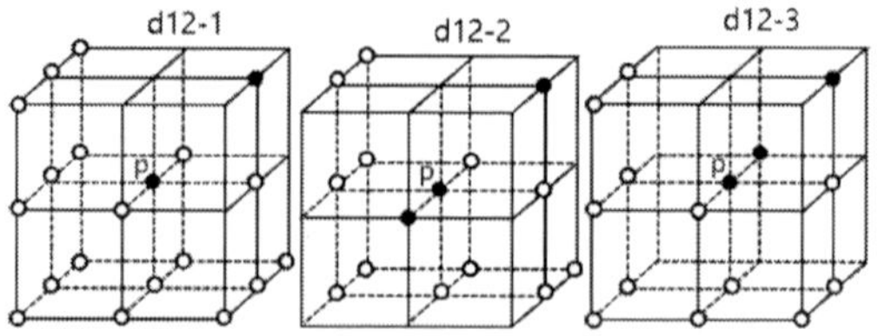

Figure 5. 36 removing templates in class D.

If a voxel p is 26-adjacent to only one voxel, it is called a line-end voxel. If the p is 26-adjacent to only two voxels, it is called a near-line-end voxel. If the p is either a line-end or a near-line-end voxel, it is called a tail voxel, otherwise it is called a non-tail voxel. Analyze each voxel of a 3D model whether it is a non-tail voxel and satisfies at least one of the removing templates of any classes. After analyzing and marking the whole voxels, the voxels which satisfy both conditions will be removed simultaneously. Repeat the process until no voxel can be removed. The authors in [13] found that the 12 conventional templates of class D in [14] may disconnect the skeleton. Therefore, they modified and expanded each template of class D to 3 templates. Each of the templates from d1 to d6 in Fig. 5 is expanded to 3 templates according to the binary values of the two triangles. Thus, there are 36 templates in class D.

IV. The Proposed 3D Skeleton Correcting Algorithm

A 3D model thinning algorithm should keep the generated skeleton connected. However, we found that the modified algorithm failed to preserve connectivity. Fig. 6 shows an example about how the algorithm disconnects the skeleton. The voxel p1 is a non-tail voxel, because it is 26-adjacent to 6 voxels: p2, p3, q1, q2, q3 and q4. It also satisfies the template d7-2 in class D. Thus, it will be removed. The voxel p2 is a non-tail voxel, because it is 26-adjacent to 5 voxels: p1, p3, q2, q3 and q4. It also satisfies the template a5 in class A. Therefore, it will be also removed. The voxel p3 is a non-tail voxel, because it is 26-adjacent to 4 voxels: p1, p2, q2 and q3. It also satisfies the template d9-3 in class D. Therefore, it will be also removed. When the voxels p1, p2 and p3 are removed, the rest of the voxels are disconnected.

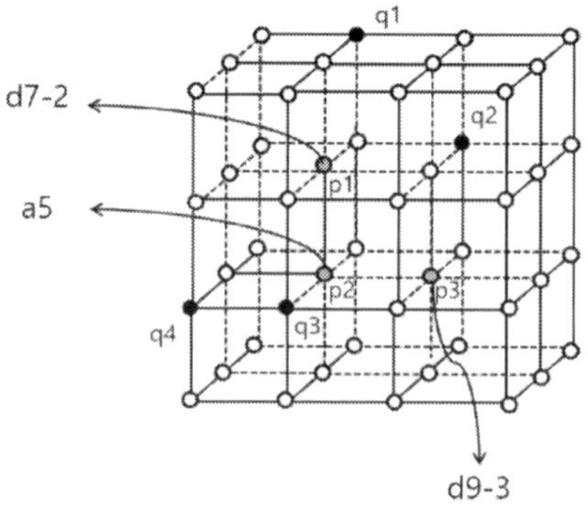

Figure 6. An example of disconnection.

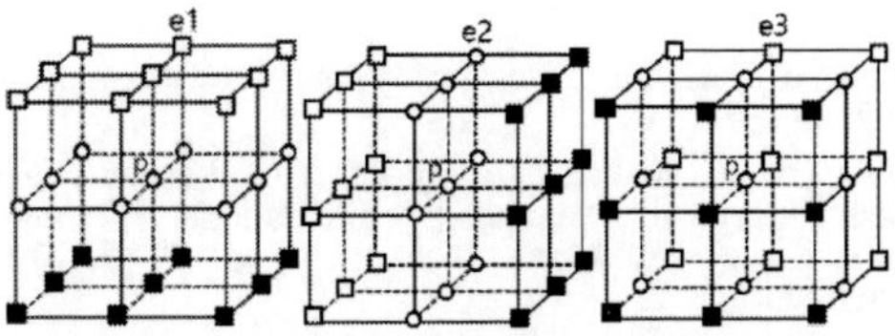

Figure 7. Correcting templates of class E.

To solve this problem, we present a 3D skeleton correcting algorithm with 3 templates of inspecting voxel disconnection. These templates are assigned to class E as shown in Fig. 7. The black squares mean that at least one of them is 1. The templates inspect the connectivity of the voxels by checking the distance between the voxels, whether it is greater than or equal to 2. Thus, after the target voxel p is removed, to satisfy the templates, there are at least two voxels left, one of them is black square and the other one is white square. If the 26-adjacent voxels of the removed voxel satisfy the templates of class E, the removed voxel p can be recovered. With the templates in class E, we can inspect that the voxel q2 and q3 satisfy the template e3 after the last voxel of p1, p2 and p3 is removed. Thus, we can recover the last removed voxel to correct the disconnection of the skeleton and preserve connectivity.

V. EXPERIMENTAL RESULTS

In this section, we show some experimental results of comparisons between before and after correcting the skeletons with Matlab. The proposed algorithm is compared with 3 other skeletonization algorithms. First one is described in [10], which used fast marching methods (FMM). Second one is proposed in [11][12], which built skeleton via 3D medial surface and axis (MSA). Last one is proposed in [13][14], which used a fully parallel thinning algorithm (FPT). The performances of the algorithms are evaluated with two 3D models in SHREC 2015 benchmark. Fig. 8 shows the two 3D models: bird and armadillo.

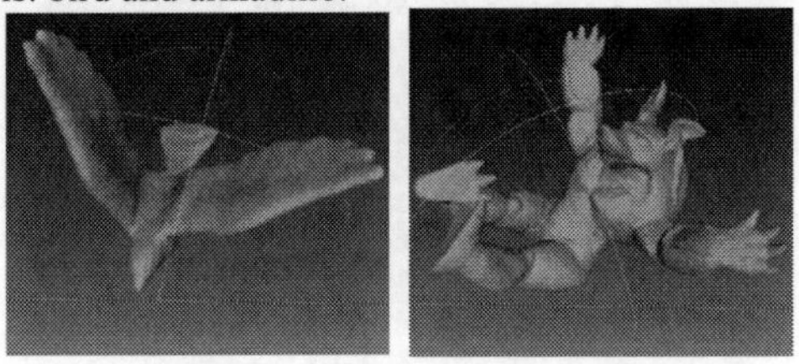

Figure 8. Bird and armadillo models.

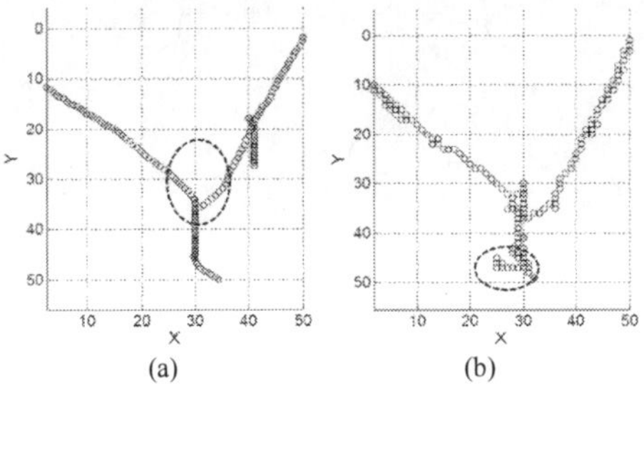

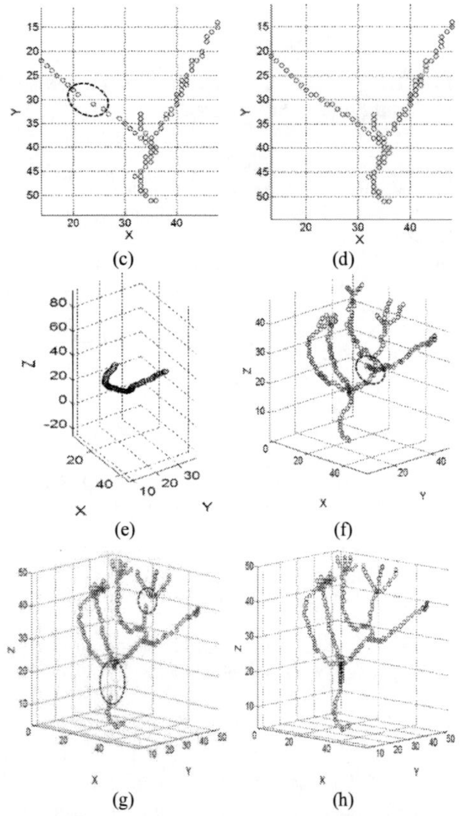

Figure 9. Skeletons generated by the four algorithms.

The skeletons generated by the four algorithms are shown in Fig. 9. Fig.9 (a) and (e) show the skeletons generated by FMM. The skeletons of the bird's head and the armadillo's two arms and one leg are not generated. Fig. 9 (b) and (f) show the skeletons generated by MSA. The skeletons of the bird's tail and armadillo's chest contain many noises. Fig. 9 (c) and (g) show the skeletons generated by FPT. The skeletons of bird's left wing and armadillo's tail and head are disconnected. Fig. 9 (d) and (h) show the skeletons generated by the proposed correcting algorithm. The skeleton of the bird's head is generated and that of bird's tail doesn't have many noises. The connectivity of the left wing is also preserved. The skeletons of armadillo's arms and legs are generated. They don't have many noises and maintain connectivity.

VI. CONCLUSION AND FUTURE WORK

In this paper, we present a 3D model skeleton correcting algorithm using templates of inspecting voxel disconnection. Three pre-defined correcting templates are used to inspect disconnections and recover them. The templates inspect the connectivity of 26-adjacent voxels of each removed voxel. The proposed algorithm is simple and practical. The experimental results show that the proposed algorithm can repair the disconnection and provide corrected skeletons. In the future work, we will apply the algorithm to the identification of 3D models.

ACKNOWLEDGMENT

This research project was supported by the Ministry of Science, ICT and Future Planning in 2015.

REFERENCES

[1] F. R. Ishengoma and A. B. Mtaho, "3D Printing Developing Countries Perspectives," International Journal of Computer Applications, vol. 104, pp. 30–34, 2014.

[2] A. Harris, "The Effects of In-home 3D Printing on Product Liability Law," Journal of Science Policy and Governance, vol. 6, pp. 1-11, 2015.

[3] D. Gupta and M. Tarlock, "3D Printing, Copyright Challenges, and the DMCA," New Matter, vol. 38, pp. 1-16, 2013.

[4] S. H. Lee et al., "Watermarking scheme for copyright protection of 3d animated model," IEEE Consumer Communications and Networking Conference (CCNC), Las Vegas, NV, USA, pp. 1-4, 2012.

[5] R. Shen, T. Wang, L. Shi, X. D. Yang, and I. Cheng, "3D Model Retrieval Using Semantically Rich Skeleton: A Review," IEEE MMTC E-letter, vol. 6, pp. 22-26, 2011.

[6] N. D. Cornea et al , "3D Object Retrieval using Many-to-many Matching of Curve Skeletons," International Conference on Shape Modeling and Applications, Washington, DC, USA, pp. 368-373, 2005.

[7] H. Lei et al , "A novel sketch-based 3 model retrieval method by integrating skeleton graph and contour feature," Journal of Advanced Mechanical Design, Systems, and Manufacturing, vol. 9, pp. 1-16, 2015.

[8] S. Jain and S. Mishra, "Survey Paper on Various 3D View Based Retrieval Methods," International Journal of Engineering Research and Technology, vol. 3, pp. 470-473, 2014.

[9] L. Y. Jie, B. Feng, L. Z. Min, and L. Hua, "3D Model Retrieval Based on 3D Fractional Fourier Transform," The International Arab Journal of Information Technology, vol. 10, pp. 421-427, 2013.

[10] R. V. Uitert and I. Bitter, "Subvoxel precise skeletons of volumetric data based on fast marching methods," Medical Physics, vol. 34, pp. 627-638, 2007,.

[11] T. C. Lee, R. L. Kashyap, and C. N. Chu, "Building Skeleton Models via 3-D Medial Surface/Axis Thinning Algorithms," Graphical Models and Image Processing, vol. 56, pp. 462-478, 1994.

[12] M. Kerschnitzki et al , "Architecture of the osteocyte network correlates with bone material quality," Journal of bone and mineral research, vol. 28, pp. 1837-1845, 2013.

[13] T. Wang and A. Basu, "A note on 'A fully parallel 3D thinning algorithm and its applications'," Pattern Recognition Letters, vol. 28, pp. 501-506, 2007.

[14] C. M. Ma and M. Sonka, "A Fully Parallel 3D Thinning Algorithm and Its Applications," Computer Vision and Image Understanding, vol. 64, pp. 420-433, 1996.

[15] S. Patil and B. Ravi, "Voxel-based representation, display and thickness analysis of intricate shapes," International Conference on CAD and CG, Hong Kong, pp. 415-422, 2005.

Non-Rigid 3D Model Retrieval Based on Topological Structure and Shape Diameter Function

Yiyu Hong
Dept. of Copyright Protection
Sangmyung University
Seoul, Korea
e-mail: hongyiyu@cclabs.kr

Jongweon Kim
Dept. of Contents and Copyright
Sangmyung University
Seoul, Korea
e-mail: jwkim@smu.ac.kr

***Abstract*—With the increasing popularity of 3D technology like 3D printing, 3D modeling, etc., there is a growing need for searching similar models on the Internet. Subsequently, matching non-rigid shapes has become an active research field in computer graphics. In this paper, we present an efficient and effective non-rigid model retrieval method based on topological structure and Shape Diameter function (SDF). The integral geodesic distances are first calculated for each vertex on a mesh to construct the topological structure. Next, each node on the topological structure is assigned a local volume, which is calculated using the Shape Diameter function. Finally, we utilize the Hungarian algorithm to measure similarity between two non-rigid models. Experimental results on the latest benchmark (*SHREC' 15 Non-rigid 3D Shape Retrieval*) demonstrate that our method works well compared to the state-of-the-art.**

Keywords-non-rigid model retrieval; integral geodesic distance; shape diameter function; the Hungarian algorithm;

I. Introduction

The rapid development of 3D technology (3D printing, 3D scanning, 3D modeling, etc.) and computer networks have naturally led to more and more 3D models being widely used in many fields. Considering that designing and creating a 3D model is not that simple, retrieving 3D accurately and quickly from a huge database is becoming more and more necessary.

In the beginning of 3D shape retrieval, most efforts were focused on retrieval methods for rigid 3D models. However, in recent years, retrieval methods for non-rigid 3D models, which may require more shape analysis, have been an active research area in computer graphics. As shown in Fig. 1, non-rigid 3D models indicate that, with different poses or articulations, the human and hand models in each row are in the same category.

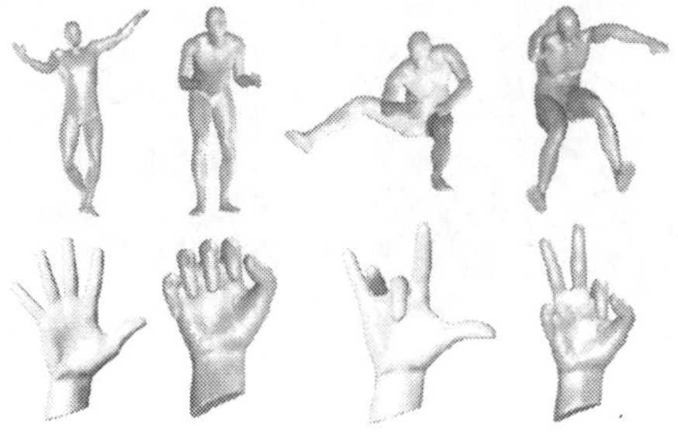

Figure 1. Non-rigid models

For the purpose of comparing two non-rigid models appropriately, shape descriptors are required to be invariant to non-rigid bending and articulations. In this paper, we utilize two characteristics on non-rigid models to measure dissimilarity between two non-rigid models. The first characteristic is geodesic distance and path, which means shortest distance and path between two vertices on the mesh surface. As we can see in Fig. 2 (a), the distance and path on the mesh between two pose-deformed models are nearly unchanged. The second characteristic is local volume on the corresponding position between two non-rigid models. In Fig. 2 (b), the color on the models indicates local volume which we calculated by SDF [1]. We can see the local volume on the corresponding positions are very similar.

II. Related Work

During the past few years, many algorithms [2-7] have been proposed for 3D shapes retrieval. Generally, existing methods can be divided into mainly two types: retrieval methods for rigid and non-rigid 3D models. For rigid model retrieval, there were algorithms based on 2D views, spectral transformation, topology and statistic, etc. For more details about these algorithms, we refer readers to [9]. The second type is retrieve approaches for non-rigid models that can be seen as an extension of algorithms for rigid model retrieval.

Figure 2. (a) Geodesic path (b) Local volume

The extension requires extracted features from models to be isometry-invariant. For example, Lian et al. in [4] extended a 2D-view based rigid model retrieval method [3], which they had proposed before, to work on non-rigid model retrieval by first utilizing Multidimensional Scaling on the 3D model to get its bending invariant representation. Readers can refer to [10] for a good comparison of methods for non-rigid 3D shape retrieval.

One intuitive approach for non-rigid 3D model retrieval is to compare the topological structure and the corresponding geometric features between two non-rigid 3D models. Hilaga et al. [2] presented Multi-resolution Reeb Graph which is a topology construction method based on geodesic distance and reed graph theory. The topology matching used coarse-to-fine strategy to search the node pairs that give the maximum similarity. However, these kind of topology construction and similarity measure algorithms need to satisfy many conditions which cannot achieve good performance. Sfikas et al. [5] proposed a conformal factor guided topological structure construction algorithm. Nevertheless, conformal factor is mainly based on curvature, which can be easily affected by geometric noise.

Gal [6] proposed a 2D histogram based pose-oblivious shape signature which combines two scalar functions defined on the surface of a 3D model. The first function called as local-diameter function can measure local volume of a 3D model. In the following study [1], they did a little modification on this function and renamed it as SDF used in consistent mesh partitioning and skeletonisation. The second function is called centricity function, which measures the integral geodesic distances for the whole 3D model.

Inspired by the papers mentioned above, we propose here an efficient and effective approach for non-rigid 3D model retrieval, which is largely based on two pose invariant features: geodesic distance and SDF.

III. Method Description

A. Construction of Topological Structure

Our algorithm for construction of topological structure needs four steps. First, integral geodesic distances are calculated for every vertex on the mesh. Second, we extract vertices that reside on tips of protrusions and vertex on the center of surface using integral geodesic distances. Third, the protrusion tips and vertex on the surface center are connected by finding shortest geodesic paths. Finally, we sample points on the geodesic paths to extract topological nodes. Fig. 3 illustrates the overall topology construction process. We will discuss the process in detail below.

Integral geodesic distances were first proposed by Hilaga et al. [2] and their discrete case can be defined as following:

$$IGD(p) = \sum_{q \in S} g(p,q) \quad (1)$$

where $g(p,q)$ denotes the shortest geodesic distance between vertex p and q. So $IGD(p)$ means integral of all geodesic distances from p to all vertices q on a surface S. In our approach, all geodesic distances and paths are computed by fast marching method [8]. Fig. 3 (b) shows color-coding of integral geodesic distances of the model. Generally, the vertex which has minimum integral geodesic distance would reside on the center of surface, and the vertices that farther from the center of surface would have larger scalar value of integral geodesic distance. Using this property of integral geodesic, we could extract vertices on the tips of protrusions by measuring whether the scalar value of integral geodesic distance of a vertex is the local maxima within a radius of geodesic neighborhood [7]. In our implementation, the radius of geodesic neighborhood is set as $\sqrt{0.08 * area(S)}$. In Fig. 3 (c), the blue point and the red points represent the surface center and extracted protrusion tips respectively.

To construct the topological structure simply and effectively, we found that connecting protrusion tips and surface center on the mesh surface can approximately represents the topology of a model without any complex process (Fig. 3 (c)). The connection can be easily done by finding the shortest paths from each protrusion tip to the surface center using fast marching method [8]. In Fig. 3 (c), the black line represents the shortest paths. For better presentation, we show the topological structure alone in Fig 3 (d). Every path from protrusion tip to surface center, we call *topological path* in this paper.

Figure 3. Overall topology construction process (a) Original model (b) Color-coding of integral geodesic distance of the model (c) Shortest paths from each protrusion tip to surface center (d) Topological structure (e) Selected topological nodes.

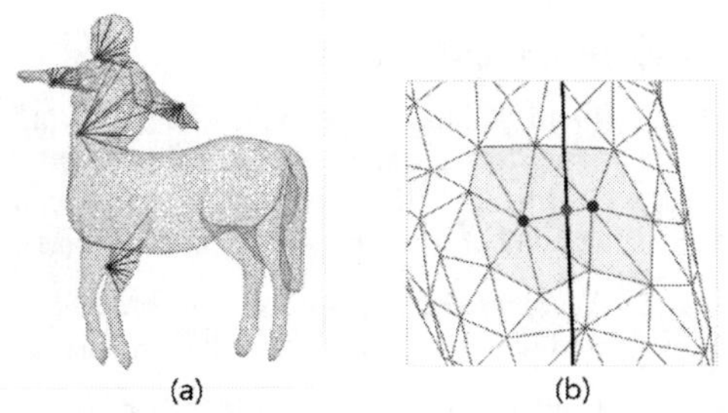

Figure 4. (a) Cone-shaped rays sent to the inside of the mesh (b) Faces related to SDF values assignment.

After constructing the topological structure, we select the topological nodes which can represents corresponding sub-part of the 3D model. On every topological path, we choose points from protrusion tip to surface center in a certain geodesic distance interval T_n, and regard it as topological nodes. In Fig. 3 (e), the points with the same color represent selected topological nodes on the same topological path. We define the topological nodes on the same topological path with order from the protrusion tip to surface center as a *topological string*.

B. SDF values Assignment

Shapira et al. in [1] have introduced the SDF, which is a scalar function defined on the mesh surface to measure the local shape's volume of a 3D mesh. For a given face on a mesh, the SDF send cone-shaped rays (Fig. 4 (a)) from the centroid of a face to its normal-opposite side (inward direction to the mesh). The length of the rays can be calculated by checking the ray-mesh intersections. Finally, the scalar value of the SDF for the face is the weighted average of all ray's lengths.

In our implementation, SDF is computed using a cone of angle 120° with 30 rays. We do not calculate SDF values for every face on the mesh, we only need to care about faces which are nearby the topological nodes. As shown in Fig. 4 (b), assume that the red point is a topological node which we selected on a topological path (thick black line), and then we find the one vertex-ring faces (yellow faces) of the two blue points which construct the edge where the topological node resides on. Subsequently, the topological node is assigned the average SDF values of these faces.

After calculating all SDF values for topological nodes, in order to be compatible with 3D meshes in different scales and resolution, the SDF values are normalized as follows:

$$nsdf(TN) = \frac{sdf(TN)}{\sqrt{area(S)}} \tag{2}$$

where $sdf(TN)$ and $nsdf(TN)$ denote the original SDF value and normalized SDF value for topological node respectively, and S denotes surface of the mesh. Instead of using the logarithmized version [1], we normalize the SDF values by dividing them by the root area of the mesh. Because we do not calculate SDF values for every face on the mesh, as mentioned before, to reduce computation time, it may be that the max SDF value and the min SDF value could be different between two non-rigid models in the same class.

C. Matching Approach

For matching approach, we first calculate all dissimilarity distance among topological strings with node-by-node SDF values between two 3D models. Next, the Hungarian algorithm is utilized to find a "minimum matching". The Hungarian algorithm is a combinatorial optimization algorithm that solves the assignment problem. Our matching approach is similar to [5], but different in penalizing method.

For calculating the dissimilarity between two topological strings, if two topological strings have the same number of topological nodes, the dissimilarity can be simply calculated by averaging the difference between the corresponding SDF scalar values. If two topological strings have different lengths, we first append the shorter topological string with its last topological node to have same length as the longer one. Then we penalizing these appended values by putting weights. Let p and q be two topological strings, and let $p[i].sdf$ denotes the SDF value of the ith topological node start from protrusion tip on p. Assuming that p has more topological nodes than q, the dissimilarity between two topological strings is defined as:

$$Dis(p,q) = \frac{\left(\begin{array}{c} \sum_{k=1}^{len(q)} |p[k].sdf - q[k].sdf| + \\ \sum_{l=len(q)+1}^{len(p)} |p[l].sdf - q[len(q)].sdf| \\ \times w_{l-len(q)} \end{array} \right)}{len(q)} \tag{3}$$

$$w_t = 1 + t \times \alpha, \quad t = 1, \dots, len(p) - len(q) \tag{4}$$

where len denotes the number of topological nodes in a topological string. w denotes the penalizing weights. Fig. 5 illustrates the comparison between two topological strings. In our experiments, $\alpha = 0.2$ yields good retrieval result.

Let M and N be two 3D models. Assuming they have m and n topological strings respectively, after comparing each topological string in M with each in N, we can get a $m \times n$ matrix filled with the dissimilarity values, which are calculated using equation (3). To apply the Hungarian algorithm, the dissimilarity matrix is required to be a square

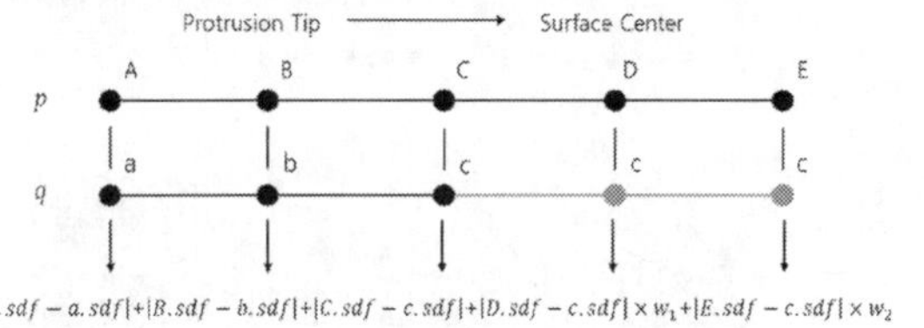

Figure 5. Comparison between two topological strings (p, q) with SDF values, where $len(p) > len(q)$

matrix. In the case of $m = n$, the Hungarian algorithm can be directly applied. And if $m \neq n$ we pad the rows (or columns) of the dissimilarity matrix with mean of existing values of the columns (or rows). Assuming that $m > n$, we can define a $m \times m$ dissimilarity matrix as $Dism(i,j)$, where $1 \leq i \leq m$, $j \leq n$ have the dissimilarity values of topological strings. The padding procedure is mathematically formulated as follows:

$$Dism(i,j) = \sum_{u=1}^{n} Dism(i,u)/n, \quad (5)$$
$$1 \leq i \leq m, n < j < m, m > n$$

After applying the Hungarian algorithm, it will return the "minimum matching" indexes. The final dissimilarity value between the two models is the average of the indexed value of the dissimilarity matrix.

IV. EXPERIMENTAL RESULTS

In this section, we evaluate the retrieval performance of the proposed algorithm and compare it with other state-of-the-art methods. We carry out experiments on the datasets of the *SHREC' 15 Non-rigid 3D Shape Retrieval* [11]. The datasets contain 1200 deformable models, classified into 50 classes, each with 24 models. The retrieval accuracy is evaluated by the following five quantitative measures [9]:

- Nearest Neighbor (NN): The percentage of best matches that belong to the query's class.
- First Tier (FT) and Second Tier (ST): The percentage of models belonging to the query's class that appear within the top $(K-1)$ and $2(K-1)$ matches respectively, where K is the number of models in the query's class.
- E-measure: A composite measure of the precision and recall for a fixed number (32) of retrieved models.
- Discounted Cumulative Gain (DCG): A statistic that weights correct results near the front of the list more than correct results later in the ranked list.

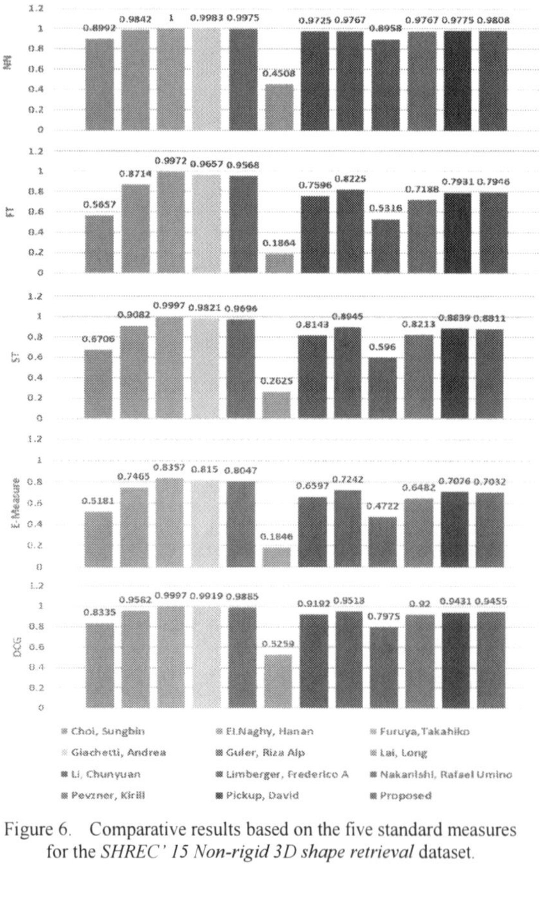

Figure 6. Comparative results based on the five standard measures for the *SHREC' 15 Non-rigid 3D shape retrieval* dataset.

All metrics above are in the range [0,1] and higher values indicate better retrieval results. For more details about the metrics, we refer readers to [9].

We implemented the proposed algorithm in Matlab on a personal computer with a 3.60 GHz i7-4790 CPU, 8GB DDR3 memory. As the calculation of geodesic distances is computationally expensive, we first use QSlim [12] to simplify mesh with 1500 faces and it takes only around 3 seconds for topological structure construction and corresponding SDF values calculation of a mesh by adopting parallel computation with 4 cores. For mesh matching which uses the Hungarian algorithm, it takes around 2 milliseconds for comparing between two meshes. The proposed algorithm was evaluated on the datasets with parameters: $T_n = \sqrt{0.0025 * area(S)}$, $\alpha = 0.2$

As we can see from Fig. 6, our method obtains competitive results among the 11 contestants. There are only two contestants writing about their running time, Giachetti's HAPT algorithm needs 3 min on average for extracting feature map of the tested dataset, and Limberger's algorithm needs 18 seconds to compute three local descriptors on a model. Moreover, our topological structure and SDF value based descriptor is compact, which only need less than 2000 bytes.

V. CONCLUSION

In this paper, we developed an efficient and effective method for the retrieval of non-rigid 3D models mainly based on geodesic distance and Shape Diameter function, which are two pose-invariant features on the mesh surface. The experiment on the *SHREC' 15 Non-rigid 3D Shape Retrieval* shows that our method is competitive against state-of-the-art. Furthermore, our method has the advantage of low complexity to implement, fast running time and small data storage space for descriptors.

ACKNOWLEDGMENT

This research was supported by Institute for Information & communications Technology Promotion (IITP) funded by the Ministry of Science, ICT and Future Planning (No. R0126-15-1024).

REFERENCES

[1] L. Shapira, A. Shamir, and D. Cohen-Or, "Consistent mesh partitioning and skeletonisation using the shape diameter function," The Visual Computer, vol. 24, pp. 249-259, 2008.

[2] M. Hilaga, Y. Shinagawa, T. Kohmura, and T. Kunii, “Topology Matching for Fully Automatic Similarity Estimation of 3D Shapes,” Proc. ACM SIGGRAPH ’01, pp. 203-212, 2001.

[3] Z. Lian, A. Godil, and X. Sun, “Visual similarity based 3D shape retrieval using bag-of-features,” Proc. SMI’10, pages 25–36, 2010.

[4] Z. Lian, A. Godil, X. Sun, and H. Zhang, “Non-rigid 3D shape retrieval using multidimensional scaling and bag-of-features,” Proc. ICIP 2010, pages 3181–3184, 2010.

[5] K. Sfikas, T. Theoharis, and I. Pratikakis, “Non-rigid 3D object retrieval using topological information guided by conformal factors,” The visual Computer, vol. 28, pp. 943-955, 2012.

[6] R. Gal, A. Shamir, and D. Cohen-Or, “Pose-Oblivious Shape Signature,” IEEE Trans. Visualization and Computer Graphics, vol. 13, no. 2, pp. 261-271, 2007.

[7] A. Agathos et al., “3D articulated object retrieval using a graph-based representation,” The Visual Computer, vol 26, pp. 1301–1319, 2010.

[8] J. Sethian and R. Kimmel, “Computing geodesic paths on manifolds”, Proc. of Natl. Acad. Sci. vol. 95, no. 15, pp. 8431–8435, 1998.

[9] P. Shilane, P. Min, M. Kazhdan and T. Funkhouser, “The Princeton Shape Benchmark,” Proc. SMI’04, pages 167-178, 2004.

[10] Z. Lian et al., “A comparison of methods for non-rigid 3D shape retrieval”, Patten Recognition, vol. 46, no. 1, pp. 449-461, 2013.

[11] Z. Lian et al., “SHREC’15 Track: Non-rigid 3D Shape Retrieval,” Proc. Eurographics Workshop on 3D Object Retrieval, pp. 107-120, 2015.

[12] M. Garland, Qslim Simplification Software, Available from: http://www.cs.cmu.edu/~./garland/quadrics/qslim.html [retrieved: July, 2016].

Robust Digital Image Watermarking Algorithm against RST Attacks using Self-patch Correlation

Ruichen Jin
Dept. of Copyright Protection,
Sangmyung University
Seoul, Korea
Email: jinruichen@cclabs.kr

Jongweon Kim
Dept. of Contents and Copyright,
Sangmyung University
Seoul, Korea
Email: jwkim@smu.ac.kr

Abstract— **In this paper, we propose an effective watermarking scheme using self-patch correlation based on Radon transform for image. The robustness against Rotation, Scaling, and Translation (RST) attacks is achieved using the translation property of the Radon transform and self-patch correlation. The Radon transform emphasizes and detects the linear characteristic to calculate the angle of image rotation. We insert random number blocks in the frequency domain to determine whether the image is scaled and predict the scale degree. The watermark is a hologram generated by quantization based on the cover image. We used hologram quantization to spread the watermark information and analyze the cover image in detail. The hologram is transformed by a discrete fractional random transform (DFRNT) with a random seed β. It makes the watermark security. We detect the watermark after restoring the image. The proposed method uses discrete wavelet transform (DWT) domain. DWT domain watermarking is robust against signal processing attacks. We have performed an intensive simulation to show the robustness in geometrical attacks.**

Keywords-image watermakring; radon transform; self-patch corrilation; digital wavelte transfotm; robust.

I. INTRODUCTION

As more and more people are interested in the intellectual property rights, extensive research has been done on copyright protection technology. With the improvement of science and copyright protection technology, many high-performance multimedia devices are produced, as well as high definition multimedia products. Thus, we have to develop and improve a corresponding technique for copyright protection.

Digital watermarking is an efficient solution for copyright protection, which inserts copyright information such as author name or ID into the contents [1]-[4]. The watermarking methods should be robust against various attacks. Geometric attack is known as one of the most difficult attacks to resist. It includes rotation, scaling and translation (RST). There are many research works dealing with geometric attacks, such as non-blind scheme [5], invariant domain embedding [6][7], template based synchronization [8][9] and feature-based synchronization [10]-[18].

We propose an algorithm to predict the geometrical attacks and automatically restore and then detect the watermark from the restored image.

First, we predict whether or not the image is rotated and calculate the degree of angle of rotation using image normalization [19]. Second, we predict whether or not the image is scaled and translated, and we calculate the degree of scaling and distance of translation. After this pre-processing, we extract the watermark.

II. RELATED WORKS

A. Image normalization

We use image normalization resistant against rotation attack. Figure 1. shows the process of image normalization. Through the image normalization, a rotated image can be corrected.

Step 1: Detect the edge of the original image using canny detect operator.

Step 2: Link the edge with thickening operation.

Step 3: Calculate the rotation angle and normalize image.

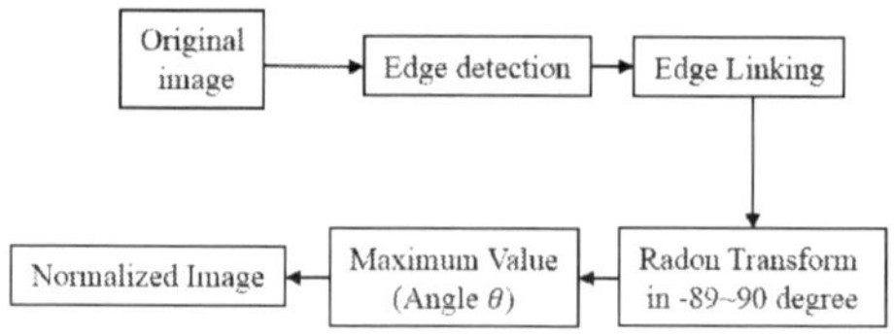

Figure 1. The process of Image Normalization.

B. Radon transform

The Radon transform is the integral transform consisting of the integral of a function over straight lines. The transform was introduced in 1917 by Radon [20]. The Radon transform of image function f (x, y) is denoted by R (θ, r), which is defined as follows:

$$R(\theta, r) = \iint f(x,y)\delta(r - x\cos\theta - y\sin\theta)dxdy \quad (1)$$

where δ is the Dirac function. $\theta \in [0, \pi)$ denotes the angle between the beam and x-axis. $r \in (-\infty, \infty)$ is the perpendicular distance from the beam crossing the origin.

III. SELF-PATCH CORRILATION

For predicting whether or not the image is scaled and translated, and for calculating the degree of scaling and distance of translation, we used the self-patch correlation. It consists of the following steps:

Step 1: Transform the original image in frequency domain.

Step 2: Generate the n×n pseudo random number block. Arrange the random number blocks as same size of image transformed.

Step 3: Add the transformed image and random number blocks.

Step 4: After scaling and translating the image, transform the attacked image in frequency domain

Step 5: Split the block (n*n) as patch, and add with generate a blank block which size as same as attacked image.

Step 6: Based on the peaks position and inserted random number block size, we can calculate the scale proportion and the distance of translation.

Figure 2. shows the process of predicting the scale degree using self-patch correlation

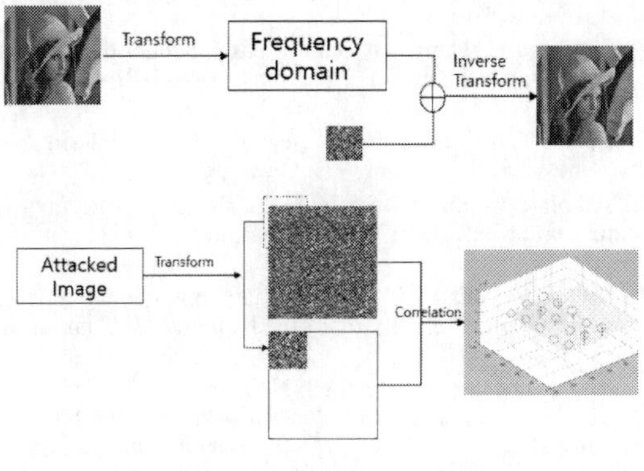

Figure 2. The process of predicting the scale degree using self-patch correlation.

IV. PROPOSED ALGORITHM

A. *Embedding Scheme*

Step 1: Insert the random number blocks into the transformed image on frequency domain.

Step 2: Encode the watermark message by quick response (QR) code encoder.

Step 3: Transform the QR code using a discrete fractional random transform (DFRNT) with seed β, and generate the hologram.

Step 4: Normalize the original image and get angle value by radon transform.

Step 5: Rotate the hologram by angle θ and get the new matrix.

Step 6: Transform them by two-depth, two- dimension Inverse DWT.

Step 6: Add the matrixes that gained in Step1 and Step 6.

B. *Eslimate attatcks and restore*

First, we predict whether or not the image is rotated and calculate the degree of angle of rotation using image normalization. Next, we predict whether or not the image is scaled and translated, calculate the degree of scaling and distance of translation.

Through the normalization algorithm and self-patch correlation, we can get the degree of rotation angle and the scale proportion. Based on these values, we restore the image and execute subsequent processing.

C. *Extraction Scheme*

The extraction process is the reverse of the embedding process, as follows:

Step 1: Transform the matrix using a two-depth, two-dimension discrete wavelet transform (DWT), and select the subbands.

Step 2: Add the subbands and transform them by DFRNT with seed β.

Step 3: Restore them with ReHologram and decode with QR decoder.

Step 4: If the QR decoder cannot decode the message, then distort the image. Loop from Step 1 to Step 4 until the decoder can read the QR code.

V. EXPERIMENTAL RESULTS

In this paper, we used a QR code for the watermark message. QR codes consisted of black modules arranged in a square pattern on a white background. The size of the QR code was 21×21 and its payload was from 72 to 152bits. It used Reed–Solomon error correction algorithm with four error correction levels. The higher the error correction level, the lower the storage capacity. According to the level, from 7% to 30% damaged QR Code can be restored.

Each 0.23% means that the QR code has the 1pixcel point error in 21×21. According to the QR code attribution that can be restored from 7 to 30%, the results with the values of BER are enough to restore the watermark information. In rotation attack 0~20 degree scale 0.8~1.4, we detect the watermark with 0.7~4.3% BER. We used the QR code as watermark which can restore the damaged QR code.

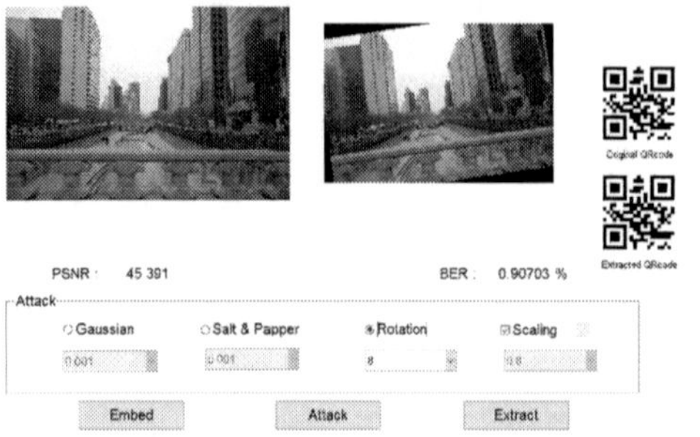

Figure 3. The performace of the expriment.

VI. Conclusion and Future Work

In this paper, we propose a watermarking scheme using self-patch correlation based on Radon transform for image. The robustness against geometrical attacks is achieved using the translation property of the Radon transform and self-patch correlation. To evaluate the performance of the proposed method, watermark information was embedded in the wavelet-transformed domain. The experimental results showed that the proposed method gives robustness under RST attacks. In rotation attack 0~20 degree scale 0.8~1.4, we detect the watermark with 0.7~4.3% BER. We proposed an algorithm is robust to limited scale and angle degree. In many previous watermarking technology researches, they extract the watermark after rotation attack means that it is robust to the interpolation between rotate the image and re-rotate the image. In this paper, we predict the rotate the degree of rotating attack and restore. In the future work, we need more research to overcome the limitations.

Acknowledgment

This research is supported by Ministry of Culture, Sports and Tourism (MCST) and Korea Creative Content Agency (KOCCA) in the Culture Technology (CT) Research & Development Program 2016.

References

[1] J. Kim, N. Kim, D. Lee, S. Park, and S. Lee, "Watermarking two dimensional data object identifier for authenticated distribution of digital multimedia contents," Signal Processing: Image Communication 25, pp. 559–576 (2010)

[2] Y. Lee and J. Kim, "Robust Blind Watermarking scheme for Digital Images Based on Discrete Fractional Random Transform," Communications in Computer and Information Science 263, pp. 139-145 (2011)

[3] R. Jin and J. Kim, "Rotation-Invariant Image Watermarking Scheme Based on Radon Transform", Advanced Science and Technology Letters, vol. 120(DCA2015), pp753-758, 2015

[4] J. Nah, J. Kim, and J. Kim, "Video Forensic Marking Algorithm Using Peak Position Modulation," Applied Mathematics & Information Sciences (AMIS) 6(6S) , pp. 2391-2396, 2012

[5] J. Seo and C. Yoo, "Localized image watermarking based on feature points of scale-space representation," Pattern Recognition ,Volume 37, Issue 7, July 2004, pp.1365–1375, 2004

[6] F. A. P. Petitcolas, R. J. Anderson, and M. G. Kuhn, "Attacks on copyright marking systems," in Proc. Int. Workshop on Information Hiding, pp. 218–238, Springer-Verlag, 1998.

[7] M. Kutter, "Watermarking resisting to translation, rotation and scaling," Proc. SPIE 3528, pp. 423–431, 1998.

[8] S. Pereira and T. Pun, "Robust template matching for affine resistant image watermark," IEEE Trans. Image Process. 9(6), pp. 1123–1129, 2000.

[9] C. Lin and I. Cox, "Rotation, scale and translation resilient watermarking for images," IEEE Trans. Image Process. 10(5), pp. 767– 782, 2001.

[10] J. Ruanaidh and T. Pun, "Rotation, scale and translation invariant spread spectrum digital image watermarking," Signal Process. 66(3), pp. 303–317, 1998.

[11] P. Bas, J. Chassery, and B. Macq, "Geometrically invariant watermarking using feature points," IEEE Trans. Image Process. 11(9), pp. 1014–1028, 2002.

[12] M. Kutter, S. K. Bhattacharjee, and T. Ebrahimi, "Toward second generation watermarking schemes," in IEEE Int. Conf. on Image Processing,Vol. 1, pp. 320–323 , 1999.

[13] A. Nikolaidis and I. Pitas, "Region-based image watermarking," IEEE Trans. Image Process. 10(11), pp. 1726–1740, 2001.

[14] C. Tang and H. Hang, "A feature-based robust digital image watermarking scheme," IEEE Trans. Signal·Process. 51(4), pp. 950–959, 2003.

[15] D. Lowe, "Distinctive image features from scale-invariant keypoints," Int. J. Comput. Vis. 60(2), pp. 91–110, 2004.

[16] K. Mikolajczyk and C. Schmid, "Scale and affine invariant interest point detectors," Int. J. Comput. Vis. 60(1), pp. 63–86, 2004.

[17] T. Tuytelaars and L. V. Gool, "Matching widely separated views based on affine invariant regions," Int. J. Comput. Vis. 59(1), pp. 61–85, 2004.

[18] S. Voloshynovskiy, A. Herrigel, N. Baumgartner, and T. Pun, "A stochastic approach to content adaptive digital image watermarking," in Proc. Int. Workshop on Information Hiding, pp. 212–236, Springer-Verlag, 1999.

[19] J. Kim and J. Jin, "A Robust Watermarking Scheme for City Image," International Journal of Security and Its Applications, Vol. 10, No. 1 (2016), pp.303-314, 2016

[20] A. Paplinski, "Rotation invariant categorization of visual objects using Radon transform and self-organizing modules," in Lect. Notes in Comp. Sci. vol. 6444. Springer, pp. 360–366, 2010.

Learning Method by Sharing Activity Logs in Multiagent Environment

Keinosuke Matsumoto, Takuya Gohara, and Naoki Mori
Department of Computer Science and Intelligent Systems
Graduate School of Engineering, Osaka Prefecture University
Sakai, Osaka, Japan
email: {matsu, gohara, mori}@cs.osakafu-u.ac.jp

***Abstract*—Applications of multiagent systems are expected from the point of view of the parallel and distributed processing. Reinforcement learning is used as an implementation method for learning agents' actions. However, the problem is that, the higher the number of agents to deal with, the slower the speed of learning becomes. To solve this problem, this paper proposes a new reinforcement learning method that can learn quickly by using past actions of its own and of other agents. Agents can learn good actions in the early stage of learning by this method. However, if agents keep learning, learning efficiency will deteriorate. The method controls to reduce effects of other agents' actions in the later stage of learning. In experiments, agents learned good actions in various environments. Thus, the success of the proposed method was verified.**

Keywords- machine learning; Q-learning; sharing of activity history; agents; hunter game

I. INTRODUCTION

In recent years, information has distributed and grown by the rapid development of the Internet and multimedia. Systems also become large and complicated. It is difficult for centralized systems, that make decisions by bringing information in one place, to deal with a lot of information and to process it. From the viewpoint of the parallel and distributed processing, the application of multiagent systems [1] that exchange information between agents [2] is expected.

It is difficult to follow environmental changes that humans could not forecast and do not carry out suitable actions. The most important thing for each agent in a multiagent system is to learn by itself. Each agent needs to learn a suitable judgment standard from one's experience and information collected from other agents. Reinforcement learning [3][4] attracts attention as an implementation method of multiagent systems. It can be very effective means, because it autonomously learns by setting only a reward, if a goal has been given.

In this study, reinforcement learning is applied to a multiagent problem, a hunter game [5]. It is widely used as a cooperative problem solving [6][7] under multiagent environment as a benchmark. If a hunter game becomes complicated and the number of agents increases, the number of states increases exponentially. The problem is that the speed of learning slows down. Ono et al. proposed Modular Q-Learning (MQL) [8] to solve this problem, but it had a disadvantage of using much memory. With respect to memory, another method that reduced memory [9] was proposed. In this method, each agent has only one Q-value table by not distinguishing each agent with the same purpose. On the basis of these methods, this study proposes a method that increases learning efficiency by using each agent's activity log [10][11] of hunter agents.

This method does not need to prepare any special communication algorithms between agents, strategies to exchange information [12][13], special exploration agents [14][15][16] etc., according to various situations. This method saves only activity history and updates the Q-value using its own or other hunters' activity history. In this way, the method shares experiences between agents by simple way of adding other hunters' activity history to Q-value table, and picks up learning speed. It makes collective intelligence efficient.

The rest of the paper is structured as follows. In Section II, the explosion of the number of states in reinforcement learning is explained. In Section III, conventional methods are described. In Section IV, the proposed method is explained. In Section V, the results of application experiments to confirm the validity of the proposed method are given. Finally, in Section VI the conclusion and future work are presented.

II. HUNTER GAME

This section describes a hunter game and the explosion of the number of states.

A. Definition of hunter game

A hunter game is one of the standard problems in multiagent systems. It is a game in which multiple hunters catch a prey (runaway) chasing in on a two-dimensional field. The definition of hunter game in this study is shown below.

-A field is a two-dimensional lattice and torus space as shown in Fig. 1.

-It is possible for multiple agents to take one lattice space.

-Each agent can take five actions of moving right, left, up, down or stop.

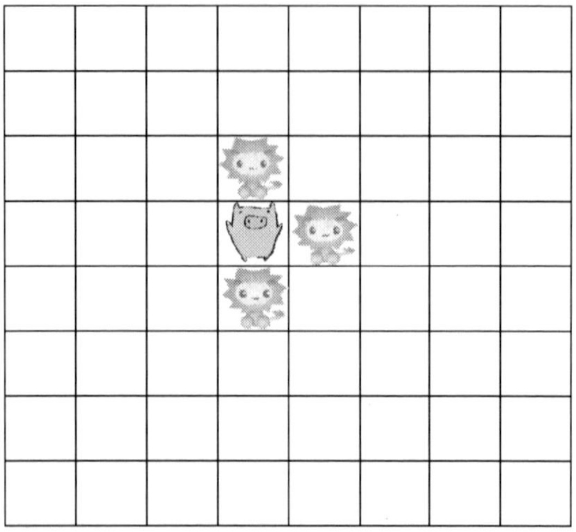

Figure 1. Hunter game.

-A hunter has perfect perception, and it recognizes a prey and other hunters in relative coordinates from itself.

-A unit time during which each agent takes one action is called a time step, and a period of time from an initial state to a goal (i.e., hunters catch a prey) is called an episode.

B. Explosion of the number of states

Q-Learning [17] is one of bootstrap type reinforcement learning. In Markov decision process, like Q-Learning, if a learning rate is appropriately adjusted, convergence to an optimal solution in infinite time has been proven [18].

In Q-Learning of the hunter game, an action is evaluated on pair (*s*, *a*) considering all observable states *s* and each possible action *a*. The evaluated value is utilized for the same pair of state and action. It requires a lot of information on (*s*, *a*) to make Q-Learning effective. For example, if the size of field is $m \times m$ and the number of hunters is *n*, one hunter can see m^{2n} identifiable states (positional combinations of other hunters and the prey). Because each state has five kinds of actions, state and action pair is $5m^{2n}$. In the hunter game with multiple hunters, state explosion cannot be avoided because the exponent includes *n*.

By the explosion of the number of states, the learning speed will become slow. Therefore, in Q-Learning in multiagent environment, it becomes an important subject to figure out how the number of states can be reduced.

III. CONVENTIONAL METHODS

This section describes related work of this study.

A. Modular Q-Learning

Ono et al. proposed MQL [8] to solve the state explosion in hunter games. Completely Perceptual Q-Learning (CPQL) [19] is perfect perception learning, and it uses relative coordinates of all hunters in order to define states. On the other hand, MQL uses a partial state that consists of a hunter and another one. The number of states of field size $m \times m$ and *n* hunters is m^4. Since the exponent is a constant and it is not influenced by the number of hunters, it can prevent the state explosion.

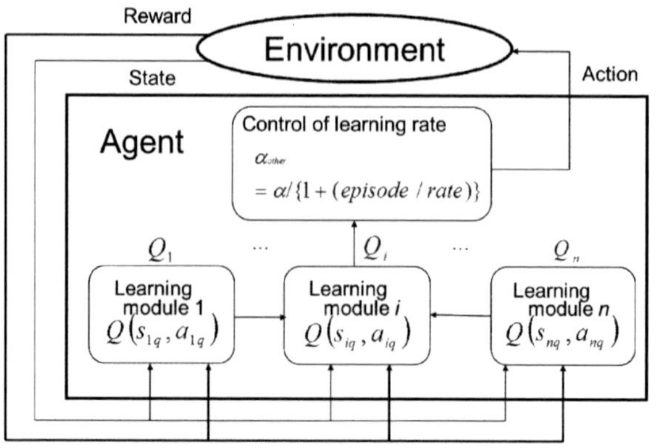

Figure 2. Architecture of the proposed method.

The learning accuracy of MQL deteriorates because of imperfect perception by observing partial states. In addition, if *n* hunters exist, the number of partial states becomes *n*-1, and *n*-1 learning machines are prepared per hunter. A total of *n*(*n*-1) learning machines are needed. The size of Q-value tables tends to become large and the amount of memory will increase.

B. Centralized Modular Q-Learning

Matsumoto et al. proposed Centralized Modular Q-Learning (CMQL) [9] to solve the memory problem that is one of the problems of MQL. In a hunter game, hunters should just surround a prey. It is not necessary to recognize the kind of hunters that surround the pray. Therefore, CMQL does not distinguish the characteristics of each hunter and *n*-1 learning machines that the hunter has in MQL can be reduced to one learning machine. In CMQL, a hunter has only one Q-value table of the partial state. Since the number of Q-value tables becomes one per hunter, only *n* Q-value tables are required in all if *n* hunters exist.

IV. PROPOSED METHOD

In this section, a method that raises learning efficiency is described on the basis of MQL and CMQL. Fig. 2 shows the basic concept of the proposed method.

A. Learning method by sharing activity logs

In the hunter game, all hunters have the common purpose of catching a prey. In such environment, it is useful to use learned actions of other hunters to catch the prey. Appropriate actions can be learned with fewer number of trial times by learning actions of other hunters. In this study, a method of updating Q-value on the basis of other hunters' activity logs is proposed. The number of times of updating for every episode increases, but the method raises the learning efficiency for every episode. The algorithm of the proposed method is shown below.

The number of hunters is n and a prey is captured at q steps. Each hunter is observing states s_1, s_2, ---, s_n and actions are a_1, a_2, ---, a_n.

(1) In each episode, save hunters' coordinates and actions for every step, and for up to t steps. These are activity logs.

(2) Give awards to all hunters' Q-value Q (s_1, a_1), Q (s_2, a_2), ---, Q(s_n, a_n) if the prey is captured.

(3) $i = q$

(4) $Q(s_{i-1}, a_{i-1}) \leftarrow (1-\alpha)\, Q(s_{i-1}, a_{i-1}) + \alpha\, [r+\gamma \max_a Q(s_i, a_i)]$

(5) Replace i by i-1 and repeat (4) until $i \leq q-t$ or $i \leq 1$.

In the above-mentioned algorithm, t is t=1000. Combining this algorithm with CMQL makes a more efficient learning method.

Although learning has become early in the proposed method, final learning results tend to deteriorate compared with the conventional methods without sharing activity logs. The learning accuracy of the proposed method becomes bad by learning actions of other hunters at the final learning stage. For this reason, the learning rate using other hunters' actions is decreased according to the number of episodes. An influence on learning by other hunters' actions is lessened as learning progresses. This will be an approach that utilizes other hunters' activity logs at the early learning stages and uses only each hunter's log at the final learning stage.

B. *Control of learning rate*

It is difficult to find an optimal action if a hunter learns other hunters' actions in the final stage of learning. Learning rate of learning other hunters' activity logs should be decreased in proportion to the number of episodes. If other hunters' activity logs are used at the last stage of learning, learning accuracy will reduce a little. It does not become bad by learning only for one's own log, and the learning rate at the time of updating for other hunters' activity logs should be gradually made small.

The influence of other hunters' activity logs on learning was reduced with the number of times of learning. This method (hereinafter referred to as Turned Experience CMQL (TECMQL)) is a learning approach that utilizes other hunters' activity logs in the early stage of learning and only its own log in the final stage.

The following formula defines the learning rate at learning other hunters' activity logs.

$$\alpha_{other} = \frac{\alpha}{1 + (episode \;/ \; rate\,)} \tag{1}$$

where, α_{other} is a learning rate updating Q-value using other hunters' activity logs and *rate* is a constant that determines reduction rate of the learning rate. The learning rate at learning using other hunters' actions should be decreased according to the number of episodes. The value of learning rate is determined to eliminate the effect of other hunters' actions in proportion to the number of episodes.

V. EXPERIMENTS

In this section, the proposed method was applied to hunter games to confirm its validity.

A. *The outline of experiments*

The experiments compare the learning efficiency of the following three methods.

- Proposed method: CMQL using other hunters' activity logs (referred to as Sharing Experience CMQL (SECMQL)).
- Comparison method: CMQL using only each hunter's log (referred to as Own Experience CMQL (OECMQL)).
- Conventional method: CMQL that does not use activity logs.

These three methods were applied to a hunter game in a maze environment and two-prey hunter game.

B. *Experiment 1: Hunter games in maze environment*

The performances of the above-mentioned three methods were compared in the hunter game in a maze environment. In this case, hunters learn ways of bypassing walls in the maze and leading a prey to the place where is easy to catch it using the walls. The positions of walls do not change from the beginning of this experiment. Walls are grasped by absolute coordinate system. In this experiment, a partial state of CMQL consists of a relative coordinate from a hunter to any other one hunter, a relative coordinate from the hunter to a prey, and an absolute coordinate of the hunter. By this means, actions can be learned considering the positions of walls in each partial state.

Experimental conditions were as follows:

- Size of field: 8 x 8
- Number of walls in the mazy field: 21
- Number of hunters: n =3
- Action selection strategy: ε-greedy (ε = 0.01)
- Prey's action: It escapes from hunters.
- Capture state: Four lattices in left, right, top and bottom of a prey's position are surrounded by hunters or walls.
- Cost per one time step: 0.05
- Learning rate: α=0.2
- Discount rate: γ=0.8
- Maximum number of learning episodes: 300000 episodes
- Reward of hunter that caught a prey directly: 5
- Reward of hunter that did not caught the prey directly: 4

In this experiment, only three hunters cannot catch a prey without making use of walls. Hunters will learn actions that guide a prey near walls and catch a prey using the walls. At least two or less hunters can catch a prey if they make use of walls. In this case, one hunter could guide a prey for other two hunters to catch it. A reward reduced a little bit was given to the hunter that did not catch a prey directly since it contributed to the catch.

The results are shown in Fig. 3. The horizontal axis indicates the number of episodes and the vertical axis indicates the time steps to catch a prey from an initial state. Every plot shows average time steps to catch a prey of every 100 episodes. The fewer the time steps are, the better action patterns can be learned.

The learning of SECMQL became earlier until near episode no. 5000 than other methods, but the final learning result was bad compared with other methods. On the other

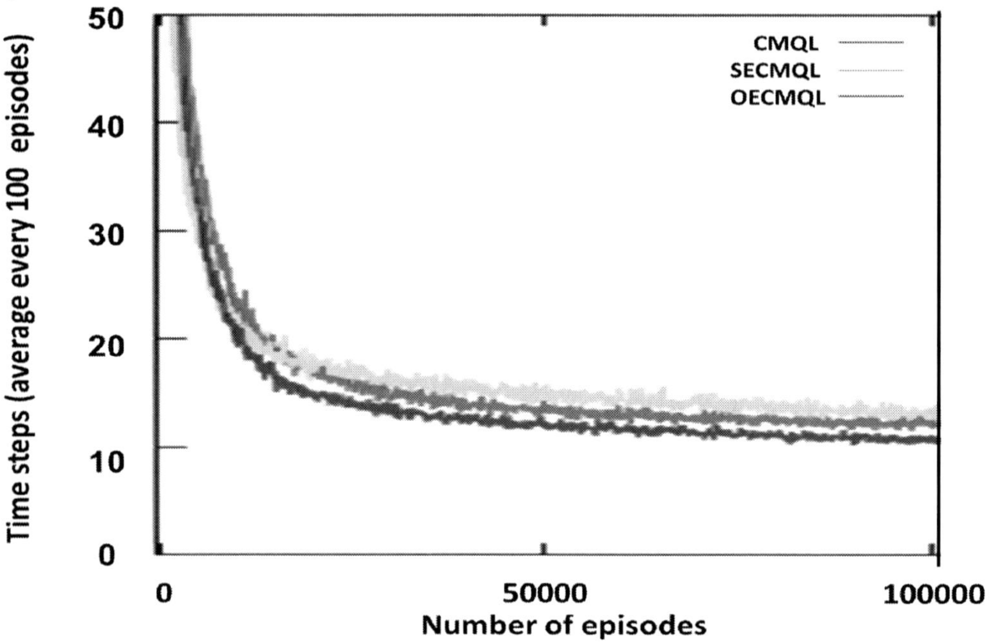

Figure 3. Results of the proposed method for maze task.

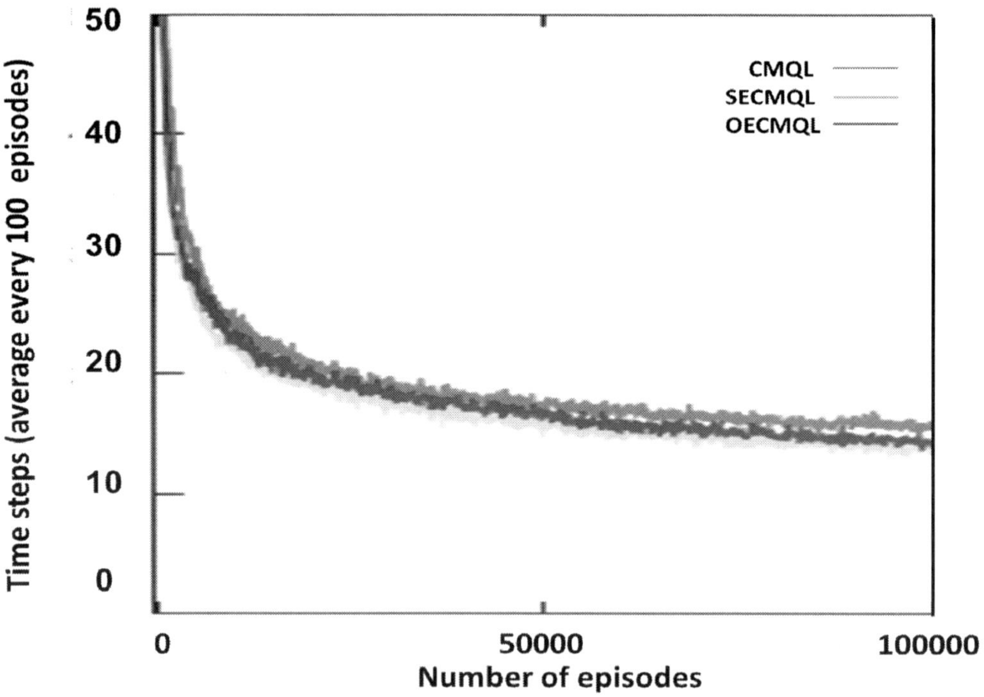

Figure 4. Results of the proposed method for two-prey game.

hand, OECMQL could catch with fewer number of steps compared with CMQL. SECMQL's learning accuracy was deteriorated by learning other hunters' actions in the final stage of learning.

C. *Experiment 2: Two-prey hunter games*

Performances of the above-mentioned three methods were compared in a hunter game that has two preys. In this game, hunters' purpose is to catch one of two preys. Since the candidate actions of a hunter increase in number, learning becomes difficult compared with the problem of one prey. In this experiment, a partial state of CMQL consists of a relative coordinate from a hunter to any other one hunter and two relative coordinates from the hunter to two preys. Since the positions of both preys can be seen, actions can be learned considering two preys.

Experimental conditions were as follows:

- Size of field: 8 x 8
- Number of hunters: n =3
- Action selection strategy: ε-greedy ($\varepsilon = 0.01$)
- Prey's action: They escape from hunters.
- Capture state: At least two hunters exist in left, right, top and bottom of one prey.
- Cost per one time step: 0.05
- Learning rate: α=0.2
- Discount rate: γ=0.8
- Maximum number of learning episodes: 300000 episodes
- Reward of hunter that caught a prey directly: 5
- Reward of hunter that did not caught the prey directly: 4

In this experiment, preys observe all hunters' positions and they escape from hunters on the basis of hunters' coordinates. A reward reduced a little bit was given to the hunter that did not catch a prey directly since it contributed to catch.

The results are shown in Fig. 4. In this experiment, the learning efficiency of SECMQL is the best in the early stages of learning. Since action patterns that lead to catch in early stages of learning by only one hunter are insufficient, it is useful to use other hunters' activity logs for learning. However, OECMQL found good action strategies over 100000 episode. The way a hunter individually learned in the final stage is better to get good action strategies.

D. *Experiment 3: Hunter games in maze environment after control of learning rate*

Performance was compared with the cases where they are with or without reducing learning rate of hunter games in a maze environment. TECMQL was added to the three methods of experiments 1 and 2 as a compared method. Experimental conditions were the same as experiment 1, and *rate* of TECMQL was 500.

Results are shown in Fig. 5. In this experiment, OECMQL shows the best learning result. TECMQL also showed equivalent learning result to OECMQL, while TECMQL maintained good efficiency in the early stage of learning.

E. *Experiment 4:Two-prey hunter games after control of learning rate*

Performance was compared with the cases where they are with or without reducing learning rate of hunter games that have two preys. The compared method was the same as experiment 3. Experimental conditions were the same as experiment 2, and *rate* of TECMQL was 10000.

Results are shown in Fig.6. In this experiment, TECMQL discovered the policy that could catch a prey with fewer steps than other methods. From these results, it seems to be effective to assemble a rough action strategy using actions of other hunters in early stages of learning, and then to learn the action strategy that is suitable for each hunter by individual learning.

In addition to experiment 3, TECMQL found actions that were easy to catch a prey rather than the conventional methods in various environments. However, it is necessary to adjust learning rate according to the environments.

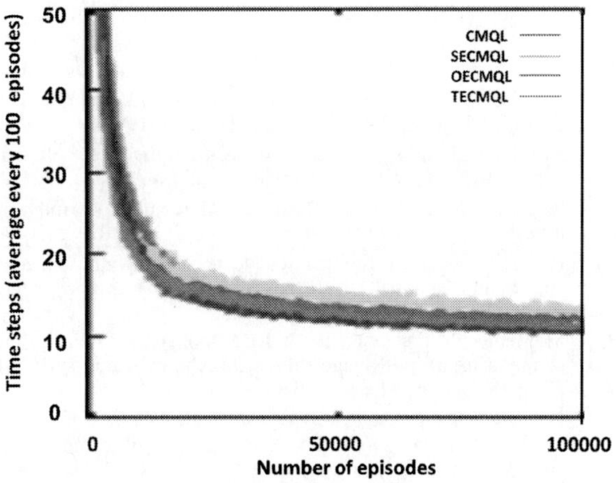

Figure 5. Results of the proposed method for maze task after control of learning rate.

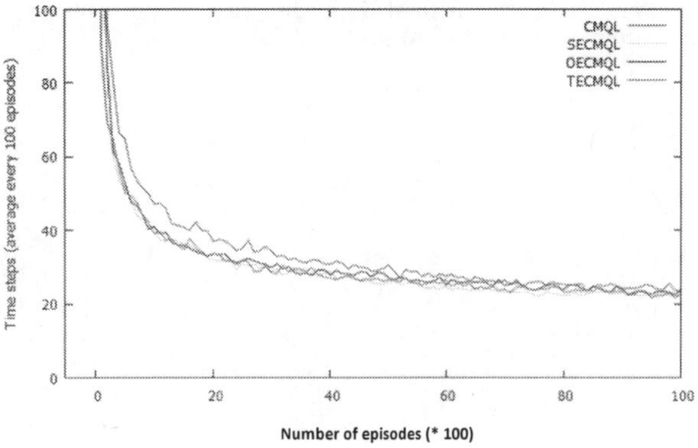

Figure 6. Results of the proposed method for two-prey game after control of learning rate.

VI. CONCLUSION

In this paper, a method, which can learn in fewer trials by sharing activity logs among hunters, was proposed. The method is based on MQL and CMQL that are methods to prevent explosion of the number of states. The performance of the proposed method was compared with CMQL. To solve the problem that the learning performance of the proposed method deteriorates in the later stage of learning when using other hunters' activity logs, it makes learning rate decrease according to the number of episodes. At the present method, the control of learning rate is dependent on the number of episodes, but it is not controlled by the contents of learning. As a future task, an index should be established to control the learning rate according to Q-value during learning.

ACKNOWLEDGMENT

This work was supported in part by JSPS KAKENHI Grant Number JP16K06424.

REFERENCES

[1] G. Weiss, Multiagent Systems: a modern approach to distributed artificial intelligence, MIT Press, 1999.

[2] S. J. Russell and P. Norving, Artificial intelligence: a modern approach, Prentice-Hall, Englewood Cliffs, 1995.

[3] R. S. Sutton and A. G. Barto, Reinforcement learning: an introduction, MIT Press, 1998.

[4] H. Van Hasselt, "Reinforcement learning in continuous state and action spaces," in Reinforcement Learning, Springer Berlin Heidelberg, pp. 207-251, 2012.

[5] M. Benda, V. Jagannathan, and R. Dodhiawalla, On optimal cooperation of knowledge sources, Technical Report, BCS-G 2010-28, Boeing AI Center, 1985.

[6] I. Nahum-Shani, M. Qian, D. Almirall, W. E. Pelham, B. Gnagy, G. A. Fabiano, and S. A. Murphy, "Q-learning: A data analysis method for constructing adaptive interventions," Psychological methods, vol. 17, no. 4, p. 478, 2012.

[7] S. Shamshirband, A. Patel, N. B. Anuar, M. L. M. Kiah, and A. Abraham, "Cooperative game theoretic approach using fuzzy Q-learning for detecting and preventing intrusions in wireless sensor networks," Engineering Applications of Artificial Intelligence, vol. 32, pp. 228-241, 2014.

[8] N. Ono and K. Fukumoto, "Multi-agent reinforcement learning: a modular approach," Proc. of AAAI ICMAS-96, pp.252-258, 1996.

[9] K. Matsumoto, T. Ikimi, and N. Mori, "A switching Q-learning approach focusing on partial states," Proc. of the 7th IFAC Conference on Manufacturing Modelling, Management, and Control (MIM 2013) IFAC, pp. 982-986, ISBN: 978-3-902823-35-9, June 2013.

[10] M.Tan, "Multi-agent reinforcement learning : independent vs. cooperative agents," Proc. of the 10th International Conference on Machine Learning, pp.330-337, 1993.

[11] R. M. Kretchmar, "Parallel reinforcement learning," Proc. of the 6th World Conference on Systemics, Cybernetics, and Informatics, vol.6, pp.114-118, 2002.

[12] H. Iima and Y. Kuroe, "Swarm reinforcement learning algorithm based on exchanging information among agents," Transactions of the Society of Instrument and Control Engineers, vol. 42, no. 11, pp. 1244-1251, 2006 (in Japanese).

[13] S. Yamawaki, Y. Kuroe, and H. Iima, "Swarm reinforcement learning method for multi-agent tasks," Transactions of the Society of Instrument and Control Engineers vol. 49, no. 3, pp. 370-377, 2013 (in Japanese).

[14] T. Tateyama, S. Kawata, and Y. Shimomura, "Parallel reinforcement learning systems using exploration agents," Transactions of the Japan Society of Mechanical Engineers Series C vol. 74, no. 739, pp. 692-701, 2008 (in Japanese).

[15] Y. M. De Hauwere, P. Vrancx, and A. Nowe, "Future Sparse Interactions: A MARL approach," Proc. of the 9th European Workshop on Reinforcement Learning, pp. 1-3, 2011.

[16] H. Igarashi, M. Handa, S. Ishihara, and I. Sasano, "Agent control in multiagent systems– Reinforcement learning of weight parameters in particle swarm optimization," The Research Reports of Shibaura Institute of Technology, Natural Sciences and Engineering vol. 56, pp. 1-8, 2012 (in Japanese).

[17] C. J. C. H. Watkins and P. Dayan, "Technical note Q-learning," Machine Learning, vol. 8, no. 3, pp. 279-292, 1992.

[18] S. J. Bradtke and M. O. Duff, "Reinforcement learning method for continuous-time Markov decision problems," Advances in Neural Information Processing Systems, vol. 7, pp. 393-400, 1994.

[19] A. Ito and M. Kanabuchi, "Speeding up multi-agent reinforcement learning by coarse-graining of perception — hunter game as an example—," IEICE Trans. Information and Systems D-I, vol. J84-D-I, no. 3, pp. 285-293, 2001 (in Japanese)

Higher Education Cloud Computing in Zimbabwe: Towards Understanding Trends of Adoption

Maxmillan Giyane
School of Computing, College of Science and Engineering
University of South Africa
Florida Campus, South Africa
E-mail: giyanem@msu.ac.zw

Sheryl Buckley
Postnet Suite #35, P. Bag X1, Florida Hills, 1716
Florida, South Africa
E-mail: sherbuck@gmail.com

Abstract – **Cloud computing has gained attention in the field of Information Technology (IT). The technology has created new opportunities for many organisations worldwide. Organisations have adopted cloud computing due to its enormous economic benefits. Cloud computing can be used by the education sector as a computing solution required to deliver improved services to stakeholders. The majority of studies carried out are more biased towards business organisations. The educational sector has received little attention with regards to cloud computing technology. Therefore this study investigates the trends of adoption of cloud computing by Zimbabwe state universities. A sample of 5 IT directors was selected from 5 universities under study. In-depth interviews were used to uncover the trends of adoption of this cutting-edge technology. Literature was used to corroborate the findings. The encouraging factors and challenges confronting the extensive adoption and utilization of cloud services were also investigated. The results indicated that all the universities under study adopted cloud computing to a certain extent. The library services and anti-plagiarism systems were the major services adopted. The universities were though not fully enjoying the benefits of the technology due to bandwidth, security and privacy issues. The paper concludes by recommending strategies to mitigate the challenges being faced by universities.**

Keywords - Cloud computing; Cloud adoption; Zimbabwe state universities; Higher education.

I. INTRODUCTION

Universities in developing countries face problems in acquiring the right type of technologies in order to execute tasks in an efficient and effective way. Distance learning is often affected by software and hardware which is limited and sometimes non-existent. State owned universities also suffer from inadequate funding by the Government. To reduce technology-driven overheads, while at the same time improving end-user productivity, a subscription-based model that provides computing utilities is adopted by many institutions. Computing solutions that do not involve huge initial capital investments and that have minimal difficulties in maintaining complex IT infrastructure are being opted for by a number of organizations.

In order for universities to overcome their IT-related problems, cloud computing [1] is the solution they can implement. Cloud computing can help students communicate with lecturers within and outside universities [1]. Services, such as learning management systems, library management systems and document creation can be adopted at affordable costs [2][3]. According to Ding et al. [4], cloud computing technology can give support in online learning, virtual learning, distance learning and the assessment system in universities. Collaboration is facilitated and hardware, software and maintenance costs are reduced [5][6]. Virtual laboratories can be developed to improve students' academic performance through cloud computing.

The majority of research done in the field of cloud computing concentrated on business organisations and few studies have been done in the education sector [7][8][9]. Previous studies focused on the factors that influence the adoption of cloud computing in the education sector [5][10][11][12]. More empirical studies were called upon in the education sector by Hashin et al. [13]. Some state universities might have adopted cloud computing services in Zimbabwe, and there is need to investigate and understand cloud computing adoption trends, the reasons for adoption and the challenges faced by Zimbabwe state universities in the adoption and utilization process.

In Section II, the specific objectives of the paper will be presented, Section III will shade light on the actual data gathering techniques that were used for the study. Section IV will describe related work and justify the reasons for undertaking this study so as to contribute more to the knowledge in the field of cloud computing. Section V presents a discussion of the findings obtained. In Section VI, a summary of the findings is explained. Section VII gives an overall conclusion and recommendations for future research in the education sector in relation to cloud computing in Zimbabwe.

II. STUDY OBJECTIVES

The aim of this study is to investigate cloud computing adoption trends in the higher education sector in Zimbabwe. The study concentrates on the 5 selected state universities. To achieve the main goal, the following are the specific objectives of the study:

1. To determine the adopted cloud computing service by each university under study.

2. To identify the delivery and deployment models that are currently adopted by the universities.
3. To understand the major reasons for the adoption of cloud computing and challenges which hinder the utilization of this technology.
4. To assess the technological readiness of each university.
5. To recommend strategies to mitigate challenges faced by universities.

III. METHODOLOGY

The case study approach was used to understand the adoption trends in Zimbabwe state universities. Having a total of 10 provinces in Zimbabwe, 5 provinces were conveniently chosen for the study and 1 university was purposively chosen from each province. An IT director from each university was interviewed and literature was used to corroborate the findings. The inquiry was qualitative and a relatively small sample was purposefully selected [14]. The identity of the chosen IT directors who participated in the study was made anonymous so as to get more information pertaining to the adoption trends in state owned universities of Zimbabwe [15]. Appointments were made with the directors and, due to their tight schedules, face-to-face interviews were conducted with only 1 IT director and the rest were telephone interviews. Semi-structured questions were used in the interviewing process and also follow up interviews were conducted for clarity sake. All interviews were recorded with the consent of the interviewee and later on transcribed into a document.

IV. LITERATURE REVIEW

A. Cloud Computing

Cloud computing has received different definitive definitions from different researchers. No definition of cloud computing has been universally accepted, though the National Institute of Standards Technology (NIST) [16] definition is widely used since it offers a more detailed definition. In its broader sense, cloud computing is a model that offers IT services as computing utilities that are paid for per-use, and accessed through the Internet. The cloud has 5 essential characteristics, 3 service/ delivery models and 4 deployment models [16]. Fig. 1 depicts the essential characteristics of cloud computing.

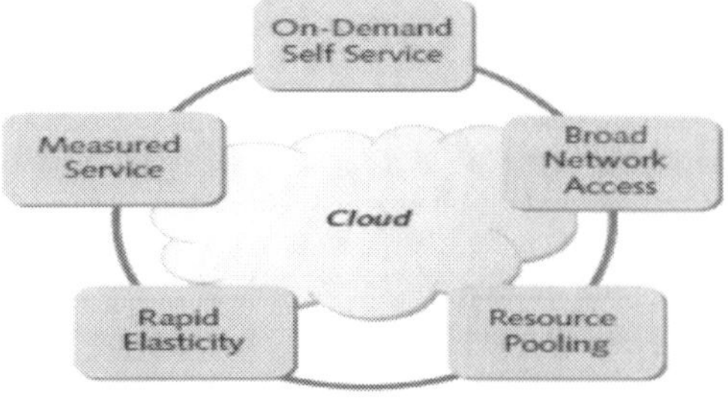

Fig. 1. Essential characteristics of cloud computing [16]

A consumer can access cloud services without support from the service provider (*on-demand self-service*), various devices with Internet capabilities can access the cloud services worldwide (*broad network access*), multiple users can access shared resources concurrently (*resource pooling*), services are flexible, they can expand or contract depending on the user's demands (*rapid elasticity*) and lastly consumers pay for the services they would have used (*measured service*) [16][17][18].

Cloud computing can be delivered using Software-as-a-Service (SaaS), Infrastructure-as-a-Service (IaaS) and Platform-as-a-Service [16][17][19]. Software packages that can be accessed through the web browser yet they reside on someone's infrastructure fall under SaaS [18], computing power and hardware resources are delivered as a service to consumers under IaaS delivery model. In PaaS, a platform for designing, testing, debugging, deployment and implementation is offered to developers over the Internet [20].

B. Cloud computing in education

Universities provide the necessary education that allows the economy of every nation to grow, decrease disparities among citizens and greatly reduce poverty. For universities to carry out their educational activities, they need resources. The appropriate hardware and software required is scarce or sometimes non-existent and cloud computing can be the right computing solution to alleviate the IT-related problems [10]. Cloud computing therefore can be used in teaching and learning activities [21]. Distance learning, online learning and formative assessment systems in universities can be supported by this cutting-edge technology. Students can communicate with lecturers or their peers regarding educational issues through communication tools such as Google hosted students and academic staff electronic mails (emails) [1][4][22]. Students in rural areas can be engaged in the learning process as long as they have an Internet connection and a gadget with the capability to access the "mother" of all networks, thereby bridging the digital divide. Cloud computing can then be used as a tool that supports collaboration in the education sector. Learning management systems, library management systems and anti-plagiarism systems can also be supported by this technology [3][23][24]. The costs of acquiring appropriate software and hardware are therefore reduced, even the maintenance costs are minimised since a third party will be responsible for maintaining the outsourced hardware and software [5]. Students in the IT sector can develop, test, debug and deploy their applications over the Internet through the PaaS delivery model [20].

Previous studies indicate that the educational sector has few studies in cloud computing especially in resource constrained environments. In Zimbabwe, cloud computing has received few studies. The studies conducted concentrate on business organisations such as Small and Medium

Enterprises (SMEs). Very little has been done in the education sector, yet education is the pillar of every nation.

V. RESULTS AND DISCUSSION

A. *University A*

Results show that university A adopted cloud computing. The services adopted include Domain Name System (DNS) server, Google hosted students and staff electronic mails, electronic mail routing, anti-plagiarism system and library services (library management system, institutional repository and library management system backup). The IT director mentioned that the services were adopted due to the fact that the technology offers the service at any time and can be accessed through thick and thin clients over the Internet, the services open doors for advanced research and support offline usage. It can be noted that the delivery models that were adopted are SaaS and IaaS. The aforementioned library services, anti-plagiarism system and Google hosted staff and student electronic mails fall under SaaS. The library virtual server and the DNS server fall under IaaS. The university uses a hybrid deployment model, thus both the private and public model are used. The private model is used onsite and is used to service multi campuses of the university. Sensitive data of the university such as student records, registration details and student grades resides on an onsite server.

Since the cloud services are accessed through the Internet, it was rendered imperative to assess the technological readiness of the university. Stakeholders of the university that use cloud services were noted to have adequate Information and Communication Technology (ICT) equipment which included desktops, laptops, tablets and smart phones among other gadgets with Internet capabilities. Internet connectivity and its transmission speed was regarded as acceptable. A bandwidth of 750Mbps was found to be sufficient. The university uses optic fiber as a transmission medium and networking nodes are connected using a star topology, which is used as a backbone of the wireless network within the institution. It was also noted that the IT support staff was experienced and supported the users in an acceptable way. In terms of compatibility and complexity, the IT director highlighted that the technology is compatible with the technological infrastructure currently in place, the culture, work style and performance. The users of the services within the institution were said not to be aware that some services they are using are offsite.

Though the technology was adopted there were some challenges that hindered the extensive adoption and utilization of this technology. The issue of limited bandwidth, sanctions and Internet services were mentioned as some of the challenges. If the issue of bandwidth is not addressed then utilization of the technology will be impossible. Some services are not offered in Zimbabwe due to sanctions imposed on the country and lastly cloud services depend on the Internet and if there is no connection then it will be difficult, if not impossible, to access the services. Economic sanctions limited trade and financial relations which crippled the Zimbabwean economy. The economic status of the country affected adversely the operations of the state owned universities. The monetary resources needed to support the innovation are scarce and some cloud services cannot be afforded by the state universities.

B. *University B*

University B adopted cloud computing technology; though not as many services as adopted by university A, the university managed to adopt the following services offered by the technological innovation: anti-plagiarism system and learning management system. The IT director vowed that though few services were adopted they were planning to adopt more cloud services but of interest the IT director did not have the knowledge on whether they had adopted cloud computing or not. The term cloud computing was still cloudy to the IT director. After in-depth interviews it was uncovered that the aforementioned services were actually adopted by the institution. It was noted that the delivery model adopted by university B was SaaS as evident by the anti-plagiarism and learning management system adopted. The hybrid deployment model was adopted by this institution, with the private cloud being used to store sensitive data while the public cloud being used to store less sensitive data. The major reasons for adopting the cloud services were reduced costs, infrastructure maintenance and reduced mobility.

It was noted that the ICT equipment with Internet capabilities existed in the institution. The Internet connectivity was deemed reliable and a bandwidth of 71Mbps was regarded sufficient since the institution has few users who consume the bandwidth. Optic fiber was used to connect the wired star network which works as the backbone of the wireless network. The IT director revealed that cloud computing was consistent with their culture, needs and past experience, and also users are embracing the technology without any difficulties. Limited bandwidth, security and reliable Internet connections were noted as challenges that hinder the adoption and utilization of the technological innovation fully.

C. *University C*

The library management system, institutional repository and the anti-plagiarism system are the services that the institution allowed a third party to host. The services fall under the SaaS delivery model. The institution uses the hybrid deployment model, as some services are hosted by a third party and some are hosted locally to service users in their geographically dispersed multi campuses. The adoption of the services was mainly due to reduced costs and transfer of the management to a third party. The IT director of this institution knew that some services were hosted by a third party but the term cloud computing was still confusing and cloudy.

ICT equipment that is required to access cloud services is possessed by the stakeholders, a bandwidth of 220Mbps was adjudged sufficient and IT support staff was seen to be experienced. The institution has a hybrid topology and it uses fiber optic and UTP cables as transmission media. The IT director vowed that users were using the services without any complications and also the technology was compatible with their work style and culture which in turn improved performance. Resistance from other users who fear technology, limited bandwidth and capacity were seen to be challenges that hinder the institution to fully enjoy the benefits of the technological innovation.

D. University D

The institutional repository, international databases and an anti-plagiarism system are the services that are leased from the cloud service provider. The institution once adopted a learning management system but subsequently resorted to an in-house developed e-learning platform. The reason towards resorting to an in-house e-learning system was that leasing the system from a third party was more expensive than employing a full time specialist. The institution is also planning to adopt Google hosted student e-mails. The services adopted fall under the SaaS delivery model. The deployment model currently being used is the hybrid model; a private cloud is used to service the five (5) campuses of the institution. The technology was seen to be compatible with the existing infrastructure, norms and values, work style and performance. The users of the services do not face challenges in using them which means the technology is not complex.

ICT equipment which can connect to the Internet is available within the institution, a bandwidth of 65Mbps was said to be sufficient and the institution uses fiber optic as a medium for transmission. Internet dependency, limited bandwidth and lack of foreign currency were seen as major factors negatively affecting the effective utilization of the technology.

E. University E

University E adopted the following cloud services; web hosting, library services and an anti-plagiarism system. Lack of adequate resources and low costs forced the institution to adopt the cloud services. SaaS and PaaS delivery models were adopted whereby web hosting falls under PaaS and the remaining services fall under SaaS. A hybrid deployment model is used by the university, the private cloud is used to service the institution's multi campuses and that is where more sensitive data resides. The technology was adjudged compatible with the culture and work style and users were using its services easily.

In order to use the cloud services, the stakeholders have got a variety of ICT gadgets that can connect to the Internet. The institution uses optic fiber as a transmission medium. The Internet can be accessed from both a wired and a wireless mode. The IT director revealed that the current bandwidth of 150Mbps was inadequate and the institution is planning to increase it. The issue of limited bandwidth was seen as a hindrance towards the utilization of cloud computing technology.

VI. SUMMARY OF FINDINGS

All the universities under study adopted cloud computing and the major services adopted included library services and anti-plagiarism systems. In support of this [3][23][24] state that the services that are mainly adopted by institutions of higher learning are library management systems and learning management systems. The findings of this research showed that learning management systems are not widely adopted by state owned universities in Zimbabwe. A single university adopted the learning management system but it is no longer using it. The universities under study adopted the SaaS delivery model. Organisations mainly adopt SaaS delivery model [25][26]. Organisations in Zimbabwe mainly adopted communication applications which fall under SaaS delivery model [27]. In a study conducted in Nigeria, it was found out that universities adopted IaaS, PaaS and SaaS with a proportion of 10%, 20% and 70% respectively [28]. It was realised that all universities adopted SaaS, university A added IaaS and university E also added PaaS.

The hybrid deployment model was adopted by all universities investigated in order to separate data. Business critical data and services are hosted on a private cloud and non-business critical data and applications are hosted on the public cloud. The result was supported by other scholars [17][29]. All universities were adjudged to be technologically ready, ICT equipment with Internet capabilities was seen to be available, the Internet was easily accessible through a wired and wireless mode and technical support was available to give support on the cloud service. A different view was reported by a study which realised that the accessibility and availability of the ICT infrastructure is not enough and sometimes does not exist in universities [30].

Universities adopted cloud services but they have not fully enjoyed the benefits brought by the technological innovation due to some challenges. Bandwidth is a major challenge. This was also reported in a study by [31]. Security and privacy are also issues that affect the full utilization of cloud computing. Universities lack trust of cloud services offered by the cloud as witnessed by the adoption of the hybrid deployment model. Universities also have problems with reliable Internet connections due to various problems like power shortages that affect the nation as a whole. Some applications also cannot run on the cloud and some services are not offered in Zimbabwe. Table 1 shows an overview of the key findings.

TABLE 1. OVERVIEW OF THE KEY FINDINGS

	University A	University B	University C	University D	University E
Adopted cloud computing?	YES	YES	YES	YES	YES
Services Adopted	DNS server, e-mail, e-mail routing, anti-plagiarism software, Library Management System, institutional repository, LMS backup	Learning Management System, anti-plagiarism software.	Library services, anti-plagiarism software.	Library services, institutional repository, international databases, anti-plagiarism software.	Web hosting, library services, anti-plagiarism software.
Delivery models adopted	SaaS and IaaS	SaaS	SaaS	SaaS	SaaS and PaaS
Deployments models adopted	Hybrid	Hybrid	Hybrid	Hybrid	Hybrid
Reasons for adoption	Virtual continuous operation, advanced research, offline usage.	Reduced costs, infrastructure maintenance and mobility	Affordable services, easy maintenance	Availability of services on time of need.	Lack of adequate resources, reduced costs
Gadgets available	Desktops, laptops, tablets, smart phones	Desktops, laptops mobile phones, PDAs	Laptops, desktops, smart phones, tablets	Desktops, laptops, tablets, smart phones	Desktops, laptops mobile phones, tablets
Bandwidth	750Mbps	71Mbps	220Mbps	65Mbps	150Mbps
Transmission medium used	Fiber optic	Fiber optic	Fiber optic and UTP	Fiber optic	Fiber optic
Network Topology	Star topology	Star topology	Hybrid topology	Star topology	Star and Ring topology
IT Support staff experience	Satisfactory	Satisfactory	Satisfactory	Satisfactory	Satisfactory
Relative advantage	Virtual continuous operation, Risk shifted to a third party, pay per use, increased production, access to latest version of software, sharing of limited resources.	Reduced costs, mobility, reduced workload.	Easy access to resources, easy management.	24-7 access to resources	Reduced costs, pay-per-use, sharing limited resources.
Challenges	Bandwidth, Sanctions and Technology affected by absence of Internet Services.	Bandwidth, Security, reliable Internet connections.	Resistance by staff members, lack of funds, bandwidth.	Absence of Internet services, misuse of the Internet, bandwidth, lack of funds.	Limited bandwidth , interfacing
Compatibility	Compatible	Compatible	Compatible	Compatible	Compatible
Complexity	Technology is easy to use.	Learning the technology usage is straightforward.	Technology is not complicated.	Technology is easy to use.	Technology is easy to understand and use.

VII. CONCLUSION, RECOMMENDATIONS AND FURTHER STUDY

It is evident that Zimbabwe state universities adopted cloud computing technology, but they are not fully utilizing the technology due to some challenges being faced. All universities currently adopted SaaS service model due to reduced initial investments, reduced maintenance costs, reduced licensing costs and availability of services at any given moment in time. The hybrid deployment model was adopted by the universities since they do not trust the cloud with their institutional data. It was established that the universities were technically ready since they possessed the ICT equipment which is used to access cloud computing services. It was also noted that some IT directors had little knowledge about cloud computing, they adopted the services without background information about the technology. Sometimes universities adopt cloud services without proper planning, thus adopting the technology without forecasting what the future holds. The stumbling blocks that emerged were security concerns, limited bandwidth and lack of reliable Internet connections. These challenges negatively affect the full utilization of cloud computing.

Based on the findings, it is recommended that before universities adopt cloud services, they should engage the end users of the services. The users should be aware of the impending developments so that they understand the concept and realise the importance of the technology, as well as the skills required to use the services. IT directors and decision makers should also be sent to conferences, seminars and workshops so that they gain the required knowledge of this emerging technology. Collaboration is critical among universities where knowledge about this technology can be shared. Since users login to access cloud services, they should be allocated the bandwidth to use so that they do not misuse the available bandwidth. Different fund raising projects should be undertaken by universities so that they sustain themselves to a certain level rather than relying on funds from the Government. Forming partnerships with organizations in developed countries can help in acquiring skills and raw materials for projects, IT students can build and sell computers to raise funds to sustain the university. Students can develop applications and test them using Google cloud which is a cost-effective technology that can be adopted by universities. To mitigate high bandwidth costs, universities can invest in Google University Access Program. Further study should seek to develop a cloud computing security model that would work between the universities and service providers in order to ensure a secure cloud and increase trust. A cloud computing adoption framework can also be developed so that universities follow a step by step approach in the adoption process.

ACKNOWLEDGMENT

We would like to thank all the Registrars from the universities where data was gathered for approving our requests to carry out this study. Special mention goes to the IT directors who participated in this study, the information they provided was of great value. Lastly, we thank Mr T. G. Rebanowako for language editing this paper.

REFERENCES

[1] L. S. Lee and R. D. Mautz Jr, "Using cloud computing to manage costs," Journal of Corporate Accounting & Finance", 23(3), pp. 11-15, 2012.

[2] E. Aljenaa, F. S. Al-Anzi, and M. Alshayeji, "Towards and efficient e-learning system based on cloud computing," In Proceedings of the Second Kuwait Conference on Eservices and E-Systems, pp. 13-18, 2011.

[3] Y. Han, "On the clouds: a new way of computing," Information Technology and Libraries, vol. 29, pp. 87-92, 2010.

[4] Q. Ding, X. Li, Y. Liu, and Z. Shi, "Research on remote collaborative engineering practices for Master of Software Engineering based on cloud computing environment," In Software Engineering Education and Training (CSEE&T), 2012 IEEE 25th Conference on, pp. 110-114, 2012.

[5] M. Mircea and A. I. Andreescu, "Using cloud computing in higher education: A strategy to improve agility in the current financial crisis," Communications of the IBIMA, pp. 1-15, 2011.

[6] S. Stein, J. Ware, J. Laboy, and H. E. Schaffer, "Improving K-12 pedagogy via a Cloud designed for education," International Journal of Information Management, 33(1), pp. 235-241, 2013.

[7] N. Lim, A. Gronlund, and A. Andersson, "Cloud computing: The beliefs and perceptions of Swedish school principals", Computers & Education, 84, pp. 90-100, 2015.

[8] H. Gangwar, H. Date, and R. Ramaswamy, "Understanding determinants of cloud computing adoption using an integrated TAM-TOE model", Journal of Enterprise Information Management, 28(1), pp. 107-130, 2015.

[9] C. K. Flack and P. Dembla, "Influence of Cloud-Based Computing on User Productivity", pp. 1-7, 2014.

[10] M. Giyane and S. Buckley, "Cloud Computing Adoption in Zimbabwean State Universities: An Empathetic Examination", IST-Africa 2015 Conference Proceedings, Paul Cunningham and Miriam Cunningham (Eds), IIMC International Information Management Corporation, ISBN: 978-1-905824-50-2, 2015.

[11] H. S. Hashim and Z. B. Hassan, "Factors that influence the user's adoption of cloud computing services at Iraqi universities: An Empirical Study", Australian Journal of Basic and Applied Sciences, 9(27), pp. 379-390, 2015.

[12] C. Low, Y. Chen, and M. Wu, "Understanding the determinants of cloud computing adoption", Industrial management & data systems, 111(7), pp. 1006-1023, 2011.

[13] H. S. Hashim, Z. B. Hassan, and A. S. Hashim, "Factors Influence the Adoption of Cloud Computing: A Comprehensive Review", International Journal of Education and Research 3(7), pp. 295-306, 2015.

[14] M. Q. Patton, "Qualitative evaluation and research methods," SAGE Publications, inc., 1990.

[15] H. Simons, "Case study research in practice," SAGE publications, 2009.

[16] P. Mell and T. Grance, "The NIST Definition of Cloud Computing," Gaithersburg: Computer Security Division Information Technology Laboratory National Institute of Standards and Technology, 2011.

[17] C. Harding, "Cloud Computing for Business-The Open Group Guide," Van Haren, 2011.

[18] B. Williams, "The economics of cloud computing," Cisco Press, 2012.

[19] The Defense Science Board, "Cyber Security and Reliability in a Digital Cloud", Washington, D.C.: Office of the Under Secretary of Defense for Acquisition, Technology, and Logistics, 2013.

[20] H. S. Lamba and G. Singh, "Cloud Computing Future Framework for e-management of NGO's," arXiv preprint arXiv:1107.3217. 2011.

[21] L. M. Vaquero, "EduCloud: PaaS versus IaaS cloud usage for an advanced computer science course", IEEE Transactions on Education, 54(4), pp. 590-598, 2011.

[22] Z. Guoli and L. Wanjun, "The applied research of cloud computing platform architecture in the E-Learning area", In Computer and Automation Engineering (ICCAE), 2010 The 2nd International Conference on (Vol. 3, pp. 356-359), IEEE, 2010.

[23] M. Al-Zoube, "E-learning on the cloud. International Arab Journal of E-Technology, 1(2), pp. 58-64, 2009.

[24] H. Kan, Z. Yang, Y. Wang, and N. Qi, "Research on library management system for CDs attached to books based on Cloud Computing," In Computer Supported Cooperative Work in Design (CSCWD), 2010 14th International Conference on pp. 744-747, IEEE, 2010.

[25] C. Hinde and J. P. Van Belle, "Cloud computing in South African SMMEs: Risks and rewards for playing at altitude," International Journal of Computer Science and Electrical Engineering, 1(1), pp. 1-10, 2012.

[26] A. Rath, S. Mohapatra, S. Kumar, and R. Thakurta, "Decision points for adoption cloud computing in small, medium enterprises (SMEs)," In Internet Technology and Secured Transactions, 2012 International Conference for, pp. 688-691, IEEE, 2012.

[27] T. G. Zhou, C. Gosho, and M. Giyane, "Cloud Computing Adoption and Utilization amongst Zimbabwean NGOs: A Case of Gweru NGOs," International Journal of Science and Research (IJSR) ISSN (Online): 2319-7064, 2014.

[28] C. A. Oyeleye, T. M. Fagbola, and C. Y. Daramola, "The Impact and Challenges of Cloud Computing Adoption on Public Universities in Southwestern Nigeria," International Journal of Advanced Computer Science and Applications 5(8), pp. 13-19, 2014.

[29] M. Biddick "A Walk in the Clouds. Information Week Analytics Reports," Manhassett, NY: United Business Media Limited, 2008.

[30] G. Muriithi and E. Kotze, "Cloud computing in higher education: implications for South African public universities and FET colleges," In 2012 Conference, pp. 4-24, 2012.

[31] M. J. Mohlameane and N. L. Ruxwana, "The Awareness of Cloud Computing: A Case Study of South African SMEs," International Journal of Trade, Economics and Finance, 5(1), pp. 6, 2014.

Fixed and Variable Sized Block Techniques for Sparse Matrix Vector Multiplication with General Matrix Structures

Javed Razzaq, Rudolf Berrendorf, Soenke Hack, Max Weierstall
Computer Science Department
Bonn-Rhein-Sieg University of Applied Sciences
Sankt Augustin, Germany
e-mail:{javed.razzaq, rudolf.berrendorf, soenke.hack, max.weierstall}@h-brs.de

Florian Mannuss
EXPEC Advanced Research Center
Saudi Arabian Oil Company
Dhahran, Saudi Arabia
e-mail: florian.mannuss@aramco.com

***Abstract*—In this paper, several blocking techniques are applied to matrices that do not have a strong blocked structure. The aim is to efficiently use vectorization with current CPUs, even for matrices without an explicit block structure on nonzero elements. Different approaches are known to find fixed or variable sized blocks of nonzero elements in a matrix. We present a new matrix format for 2D rectangular blocks of variable size, allowing fill-ins per block of explicit zero values up to a user definable threshold. We give a heuristic to detect such 2D blocks in a sparse matrix. The performance of a Sparse Matrix Vector Multiplication for chosen block formats is measured and compared. Results show that the benefit of blocking formats depend – as to be expected – on the structure of the matrix and that variable sized block formats can have advantages over fixed size formats.**

Keywords–Sparse Matrix Vector Multiplication; Blocking; Vector Intrinsics

I. Introduction

In many fields, such as natural or financial science, computational problems arise, in which the multiplication of a sparse matrix with a dense vector (SpMV) $Ax = y$ is an important operation that may be executed repeatedly [1]. Moreover, the SpMV may also be the most time consuming operation and consequently the bottleneck of such a computational problem. It is therefore desired to optimize the SpMV operation, to solve such a problem faster. The efficiency of the SpMV operation highly depends on the used sparse matrix format, the matrix structure and how the SpMV operation is implemented and optimized according to the format. One category of sparse matrix formats that has a good optimization potential are block formats. The fundamental idea of block formats for sparse matrices is to exploit the block structure of nonzero elements in a matrix and to store dense blocks of nonzero values. Storing nonzero values together in a block can lead to an improved data locality and, by addressing more than one nonzero value by one index entry, the overall index structure and the memory indirections are reduced [2] [3]. By using a block, the index of a value is reused for the whole block and it is expected that the value will stay in the cache of the CPU or even in a register.

Another advantage of block formats is the possibility of unrolling the SpMV operation and the use of the processor's Single Instruction Multi Data (SIMD) extension [4], i.e., the processor's vector units. This approach works for dense nonzero block structures in sparse matrices and increases the performance of the SpMV operation significantly, even if explicit zeros are used to fill the blocks [5].

There are two groups of blocking formats: fixed size blocking formats, which use the same fixed block size for the whole matrix, and variable sized block formats, which use the structure of the matrix to build variable sized blocks. The advantages of fixed sized blocking formats are the possibility of optimizing the SpMV for certain, at compile time known, block sizes and the rather simple building of blocks by storing explicit zeros. The advantages of variable blocking formats are the exploitation of the matrix structure and the ability to store different sized blocks for a matrix.

Additionally, the two types can be combined with differed other optimization-techniques, like using bitmaps [6] [7] or relative indexing [8] [9]. There are also some block formats that do not fit in either of these categories or use both techniques.

Sparse matrices with an inherent block structure (usually arising from a 2D/3D geometry) can certainly benefit from blocking techniques [10]. A question is, whether rather general matrices, without a clear block structure, can also benefit from blocking techniques.

The paper is structured as follows. In Section II, an overview on related work is given. In Section III, our own newly developed dynamic block format is described, including an algorithm for block determination, the SpMV operation and optimization. In Section IV an experimental setup is shown. In Section V experimental results, which compare and evaluate relevant blocking formats on matrices without an explicit block structure, are presented. At last, in Section VI a conclusion is given.

II. Related Work

In this Section, a comprehensive overview of block formats is given, including formats where blocks are used aside with other optimization techniques.

The Coordinate Format (COO) [1] is the most simple format to store a sparse matrix. It consists of three arrays. The nonzero values, as well as the row and column index of each value are each stored explicitly in an array. The size of each array is equal to the number of nonzeros.

The Compressed Sparse Row (CSR) [11] [1] [12] format is one of the most commonly used matrix format for sparse matrices. The index structure in CSR is, in relation to COO, reduced by replacing the row index for every nonzero value with a single index for all nonzero values in row. This row index indicates the start of a new row within the other two arrays.

The Block Compressed Sparse Row (BCSR) [12] [2] format is similar to the CSR format, but instead of storing single nonzero values, the BCSR format stores blocks, i.e., dense submatrices. Only submatrices with at least one nonzero element are stored. The matrix is partitioned into blocks of fixed size $r \times c$, where r and c represent the number of rows and columns of the blocks. The optimal block size differs for different matrices and different platforms. Advantages of the BCSR format are: possible reduction of the index structure, possible loop unrolling per block, using vector units through intrinsics [13] and many other low level optimization techniques [14]. However, it may be necessary to store explicit zero values for blocks that are not fully filled with nonzero values. In the worst-case, this could lead to the same index structure as with CSR, but with additional zeros stored for each nonzero value.

The Mapped Blocked Row (MBR) [6] format is similar to the BCSR format. Like BCSR, MBR uses blocks of a fixed size $r \times c$. In addition to BCSR, bitmaps that encode the nonzero structure for each block are stored. An advantage of this bitmap array is, that only actual nonzero values need to be stored in the `values` array, even though filled in zeros exist. In exchange for the reduced memory use, additional computation time is needed during the SpMV operation.

The Blocked Compressed Common Coordinate (BCCOO) [15] format uses fixed size blocks. It is based on the Blocked Common Coordinate (BCOO) format, which stores the matrix coordinates of a fixed sized block to address the value. BCCOO relies on a `bit_flag` to store information about the start of a new row. By using a bit array instead of an integer, a high compression rate is archived. One disadvantage of the `bit_flag` array is, that an additional array is needed to execute the SpMV operation in parallel.

The Unaligned Block Compressed Sparse Row (UBCSR) [5] [16] format removes the row alignment of the BCSR format by adding an additional array. However, this optimization appears to be only applicable to a special set of matrices where blocks occur in a recurring pattern in a row and are all shifted.

The Variable Block Row (VBR) [5] format analyses rows and columns that are next to each other. Their nonzero values are stored in blocks, if they have the identical pattern of nonzero values in a row or in a column. Hereby, only completely dense blocks are stored by VBR. It is possible to relax the analyses of rows and columns by the use of a threshold, which allows VBR to store explicit zeros to build larger blocks [16].

The Variable Block Length (VBL) [3] [17] [10] format, which is also referred as Blocked Compressed Row Storage (BCRS) format, is likewise similar to the CSR format. But, rather than storing a single value, all consecutive nonzero values in a row are stored in 1D blocks. The blocks of the VBL format do not have a fixed size and only nonzero values are stored. VBL may reduce the index structure depending on the stored matrix, but an additional loop inside the SpMV is required to proceed through a block.

The aim of the Compressed sparse eXtended (CSX) [18] format is to compress index information by exploiting (arbitrary but fixed) substructures within matrices. CSX identifies horizontal, vertical, diagonal, anti-diagonal and two-dimensional block structures in a pre-process. The data structure, which is used by CSX to store the location information, is based on the Compressed Sparse Row Delta Unit (CSR-DU) [19] format. The advantages of CSX are the index reduction by using the techniques of CSR-DU and, at the same time, the provision of a special SpMV implementation for each substructure. However, implementing CSX seems to be rather complex and determaning the substructures may cause perceptible overhead.

The Pattern-based Representation (PBR) [7] format aims to reduce the index overhead. Instead of adding fill-in or relying on dense substructures in a matrix, PBR identifies recurring block structures that are sharing the same nonzero pattern. For each pattern that covers more nonzero values than a certain threshold, PBR stores a submatrix in the BCOO format plus a bitmap, which represents the repeated nonzero pattern. For each of these patterns, an optimized SpMV kernel is provided or generated. Belgin et al. state in their work [7] that it is possible to use prefetching, vectorization and parallelization to optimize each kernel individually. Advantages of PBR are the possibility of providing special SpMV kernels for each occurring block pattern as well as low level optimisation for these SpMV kernels.

The Recursive Sparse Blocks (RSB) [20] [21] format aims to reduce the index overhead while keeping locality. By building a quadtree, which represents the sparse matrix, the matrix is recursively divided into four quadrant submatrices, until a certain termination condition is reached. The termination condition for the recursive function is defined in detail by Martone et al. in [22] [23]. The submatrix is stored in the leaf node of the quadtree in COO or CSR format. All nodes before the leaf node do not contain matrix data and are pointers, which build the quadtree.

The Compressed Sparse Block (CSB) [8] [9] format aims to reduce the storage needed to store the location of a value within a matrix by splitting the matrix into huge square blocks. Further, row and column indices of each value are stored relatively to each block. Due to the relative addressing of the values, it is possible to use smaller data types for the row and column index arrays, which leads to an index reduction per nonzero. It is possible to order the values inside the `values` array to get better performance of the SpMV operation. The authors of the original work suggest a recursive Z-Morton ordering to provide spatial locality. The parallel SpMV implementation of CSB, uses a private result vector per thread, but also provides a optimization in case the vector is not required for a block row [8].

III. Development of a 2D Variable Sized Block Format

In this section, a newly developed variable sized block format, called DynB, is described. The goal of DynB is, to find rectangular 2D blocks within a matrix, to efficiently utilize a processor's vector units for the SpMV. At first, a simple algorithm for the determination of variable sized 2D blocks is introduced. Then, the overall structure of the format is given. Afterwards, the SpMV kernel is presented and at last code optimization techniques are considered.

A. Finding Variable Sized Blocks

As described in Section II, the CSX format uses a sophisticated (and probably time consuming) algorithm to find complex nonzero substructures within the entire matrix. Although the speedup of the SpMV operation may be high, many SpMV operations may be neccessary to compensate the cost of the detection algorithm. In contrast, the VBL format uses a simple (and fast) algorithm to find just 1D blocks within a row of the matrix. However, the speedup of the SpMV may not be as high as for CSX. For DynB a simple algorithm to find rectangular 2D blocks over the entire matrix should

Input: $A[\,][\,]$, T, S_{max}
Output: $B[\,][\,]$

```
for i ← 1, nRows
    for j ← 1, nColumns
        if A[i][j] ≠ 0 ∧ A[i][j] ∉ B
            r ← 1, c ← 1, rr ← 0, cc ← 0
            added ← TRUE
            while added
                added ← FALSE
                rr ← r − 1, cc ← c − 1
                search(next column n with A[i : i+rr][n] ≠ 0)
                search(next row m with A[m][j : j+cc] ≠ 0)
                if r∗(n+1−j) ≤ S_max ∧ t(A[i : i+rr][j : n]) ≥ T
                    c ← n+1−j
                    added ← TRUE
                end if
                if (m+1−i)∗c ≤ S_max ∧ t(A[i : m][j : j+cc]) ≥ T
                    r ← m+1−i
                    added ← TRUE
                end if
            end while
            B ← B + A[i : i+rr][j : j+cc]
        end if
    end for
end for
```

Figure 1: Heuristic for Dynamic 2D Blocks.

be developed. With these 2D blocks, a reasonable runtime improvement for the SpMV operation should be achieved, by using advantages similar to BCSR, while possibly generating less fill-in.

The algorithm, we developed to find 2D block structures of nonzero elements, is a greedy heuristic. It tries to find possible block candidates that should be as large as possible, even if nonzeros are not direct neighbors, i.e, fill-ins of explicit zeros are allowed up to a certain amount per block. Consequently, a threshold T is used that indicates how dense a block candidate, which has been found by the heuristic, needs to be in order to be stored as a block. That means T is a measure for how many fill-in is allowed in a block. The nonzero density $t(block)$ of a block has to satisfy the relation $t(block) = nnz_{block}/blocksize = nnz_{block}/(nnz_{block} + zeros) = nnz_{block}/(r*c) \geq T$, where nnz_{block} represents the number of nonzero values in the block and r, c the number of rows, columns of that block.

The algorithm shown in Fig. 1 describes a simplified version of the heuristic, which is used to find the blocks in a matrix, in pseudo code. The heuristic takes a sparse matrix $A[][]$, the desired threshold T (maximum portion of nonzero values in a block) and a maximum blocksize S_{max} (according to the size of the vector units) as an input. It gives the converted blocked Matrix $B[][]$ as output. The algorithm iterates rowwise over the nonzero elements of original matrix. If a nonzero of the original matrix is not already assigned to a block, a new 1×1 block will be created. Then this block will be expanded successively with new columns and rows in each iteration of the while loop. Adding a new column or row means, adding the column/row with the next nonzero element and all fill-in columns/rows with zeros that are located between the outermost block column/row and the column/row with the next nonzero. Column/rows are only added to the block, if the nonzero density of the block after adding these columns/rows would be large enough. If not enough nonzero elements would be added, i.e., the **`if`** statements for both column and row fail, the heuristic will finish the block. After the blocks are found, the memory for the DynB data structure is allocated and filled with the actual values and index structure. This data structure is described in the following section.

$$A = \begin{pmatrix} 0 & a_{01} & a_{02} & 0 & 0 & 0 & 0 & 0 \\ 0 & a_{03} & a_{04} & 0 & 0 & 0 & 0 & 0 \\ 0 & 0 & a_{05} & 0 & 0 & 0 & a_{06} & a_{07} \\ 0 & 0 & a_{08} & 0 & 0 & 0 & a_{09} & a_{10} \\ a_{11} & 0 & 0 & a_{12} & a_{13} & a_{14} & 0 & 0 \\ a_{15} & 0 & 0 & a_{16} & 0 & a_{17} & 0 & 0 \\ a_{18} & 0 & 0 & a_{19} & a_{20} & a_{21} & 0 & 0 \\ 0 & a_{22} & 0 & 0 & 0 & 0 & 0 & 0 \end{pmatrix}$$

`values` $= \{a_{01}, a_{02}, a_{03}, a_{04}, 0, a_{05}, 0, a_{08}, a_{06}, a_{07}, a_{09}, a_{10}, a_{11}, a_{15}, a_{18}, a_{12}, a_{13}, a_{14}, a_{16}, 0, a_{17}, a_{19}, a_{20}, a_{21}, a_{22}\}$
`block_start` $= \{0, 8, 12, 15, 24\}$
`row_index` $= \{0, 2, 4, 4, 7\}$
`column_index` $= \{1, 6, 0, 3, 1\}$
`block_row` $= \{4, 2, 3, 3, 1\}$
`block_column` $= \{2, 2, 1, 3, 1\}$

Figure 2: The DynB Format storing Matrix A with a Threshold of 0.75.

B. Structure of the format

The DynB format relies on six arrays. In the `values` array the nonzero values (plus fill-in zeros) are consecutively stored in block order (rowwise within a block). The `block_start` pointer stores the starting position of each block in the `values` array. The `row_index` and the `column_index` store the location of the upper left corner of each block. This is similar to the COO format for single values, but here, fewer indices are stored explicitly, because the indices are used to address a whole block of values. Finally, the `block_row` and `block_column` arrays store the column and row size of each two dimensional block, i.e., the block size is variable. Below, the purpose of the six arrays are described as well as why certain data types were chosen and how many entries they contain:

- `values[nnz+zeros] :` **`double`** contains the values of the matrix.
- `rowIndex[blocks] :` **`int`** stores the row index in which a block starts.
- `columnIndex[blocks] :` **`int`** stores the column index in which a block starts.
- `blockStart[blocks] :` **`int`** stores the start point of each block inside the `values` array.
- `blockRow[blocks] : unsingned` **`char`** stores the number of rows a block contains. The unsigned char data type is used because the maximum block size is 64, according to the size of the vector units, which means that $blockRow \times blockColumn \leq 64$.

- `blockColumn[blocks] : unsigned char` stores the number of columns a block contains.
- `nonZeroBlocks : int` stores the quantity of blocks.
- `threshold : float` needs to be set prior conversion of a matrix into the DynB format. The thresholds needs to be positive and smaller or equal to 1.0 (e.g., $1.0 = 100\%$ nonzero values, $0.5 = 50\%$ nonzero values in a block).

Fig. 2 shows how a matrix A is stored using the format.

C. SpMV Kernel

The SpMV implementation of DynB iterates over the blocks, which have been build before. It is shown in Fig. 3 in a general and simplified version. Additionally, we implemented optimized code version for some block structures (1×1, $1 \times column$, $1 \times row$ and other block sizes).

D. Optimization

It was shown that, using vector intrinsics, to adress the vector untis of a processor, can lead to a performance gain for the SpMV operation [14]. However, with this technique the programmer needs to write code on an assembler level, which can be teadious and error prone. Another approach, which showed good results in [14], is the use of compiler optimization. With the `fast` and `Ofast` option of the Intel Compiler [13] and GNU Compiler [24], processor specific code that may also adress the vector units efficiently, using the highest available instruction set, can be generated by the compiler. For the Intel Compiler, vectorization is enabled for `O2` and higher levels [13].

IV. Experimental Setup

The experiments to evaluate block formats were run on a system with an Intel Xeon E5-2697 v3 CPU (Haswell architecture) [25] and the Intel C++ Compiler [13]. A set of 111 large test matrices from the Florida Sparse Matrix Collection [26] and SPE reference problems [27] was taken as test matrices. The chosen matrices do *not* have an overall explicit nonzero block structure. The specifications of the matrices were: real, square, more than 5,000,000 nnz, no graph or model reduction problem, no pattern format. Additionally the matrices *sherman1-5*, *nlpkkt-problems*, *bone010*, *boneS10*, *Cube_Coup_dt0*, *ML_Geer* were used. Compiler optimization and vecotor intrinsics were used, if possible. The following matrix formats were chosen to be compared in the experiments:

- DynB (variable): own implementation according to Section III, with and without intrinsics, threshold T varied from 0.55 (slightly more nonzeros than fill-in) to 1.0 (only nonzeros, no fill-in).
- VBL (variable): own implementation according to [3], with and without intrinsics.
- CSX (variable): library taken from the authors of the original work on CSX [18] [28], no influence on implementation.
- BCSR (fixed): own implementation according to [12], with and without intrinsics, supported block dimensions: 2×2, 3×3, 4×4

For all experiments, the SpMV operation was executed 100 times and the median of these execution times was taken as the resulting execution time, to exclude uncertainty of the measurements. Subsequently, this is referred to as execution time.

```
for (int i = 0; i < nonZeroBlocks; ++i){
  //general SpMV for any blocksize
  for (int ii = 0; ii < blockRow[i]; ++ii){
    double s = 0.0;
    int jj =  blockStart[i] + (blockColumn[i]*ii) ;
      for (int j = 0 ; j < blockColumn[i]; ++j, ++jj){
        s += values[jj] * x[columnIndex[i]+j];
      }
      y[rowIndex[i]+ii]+=s;
  }
}
```

Figure 3: SpMV implementation of DynB for general blocks.

V. Results

In this section we present selected results of the executed experiments. When boxplots are shown, the quartiles over the results for all 111 matrices are given, whiskers extend to the last datapoint within $1.5 \times$ *interquartile range* and outliers are drawn as points.

Fig. 4 shows the execution times of the SpMV for the implemented formats with different configurations, if possible. For all formats the SpMV was executed with compiler optimization level `O0`, `O3` and `fast` and an implementation using intrinsics (with `fast`). For DynB only the results for selected configurations are presented. For the CSX only one result is presented, because the library settings could not be controlled. Overall it can be seen that, using compiler optimization `O0` (no optimization and vectorization) and `O3` results in slower execution times than using `fast` and intrinsics, which confirms the results found in [14]. This can be explained, because with the compiler option `fast` processor specific code is generated. Hence, with `fast` and intrinsics the CPU specific vector instructions can be used. Moreover, the difference between `fast` and intrinsics for DynB and BCSR seems to be marginal. For DynB, there seem to be hardly any differences dependent on the threshold T, except when looking at the outliers. For BCSR, the compiler with the `fast` option does even a better optimization than handwritten intrinsics. For the VBL format, the intrinsic implementation performed better than the `fast` optimization. Comparing the VBL intrinsics with the CSX shows that these two versions are on a similar level. However, the (one-time) creation times for the VBL format were much shorter than for the CSX format, due to the simpler heuristics used in VBL. For the DynB format the implementation of the heuristic is currently a prototype and needs improvement in runtime. A possible reason for the better performance of the 1D VBL format compared to the 2D formats DynB and BCSR could be, that for 1D blocks there are no jumps within the result vector y of the multiplication $Ax = y$. Thus, 1D blocks may benefit from better spatial locality, while still being large enough to use vector units efficiently.

Fig. 5 shows the coefficient of variation of the SpMV execution time for the DynB format for the 111 test matrices, over all thresholds (optimization `fast`). It can be seen that, for some matrices varying the threshold T has a significant impact on the execution time. This is due to the different blocks that were found by the heuristic. Fig. 6 shows the found blocks and their execution times according to the threshold for the *nlpkkt80* matrix. This matrix has the highest coeffiecient of variation. It can be seen that, for several thresholds the same blocksizes were found. Consequentliy, the execution times for

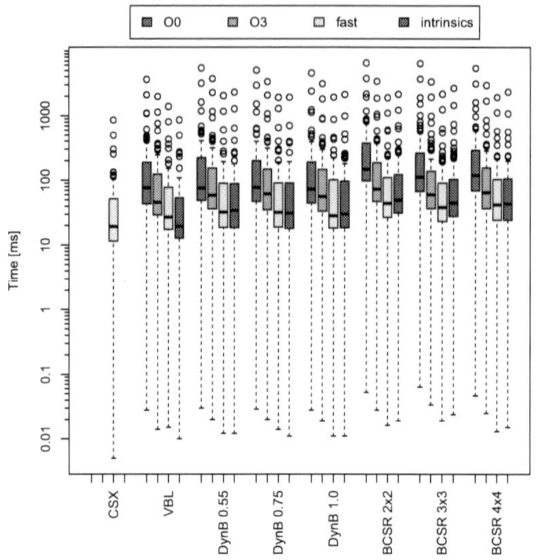

Figure 4: SpMV with all Blocking Formats, Different Configurations.

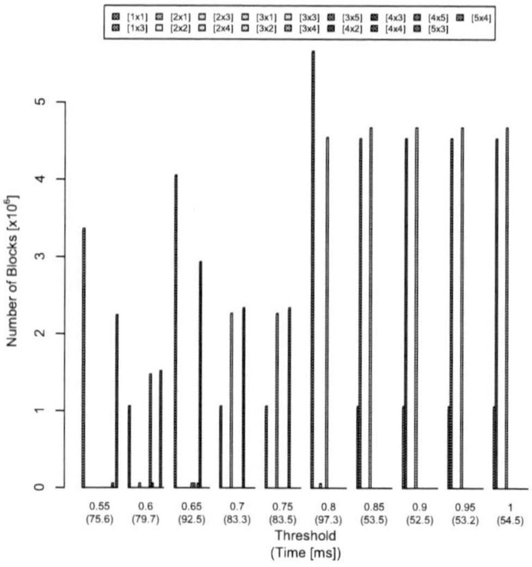

Figure 6: Blocks Found for DynB with Different Thresholds, *nlpkkt80* Matrix.

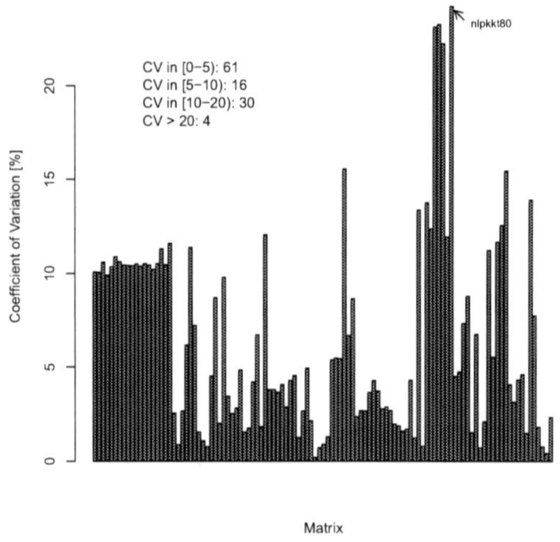

Figure 5: Coefficient of Variation of SpMV with DynB over all Thresholds per Matrix.

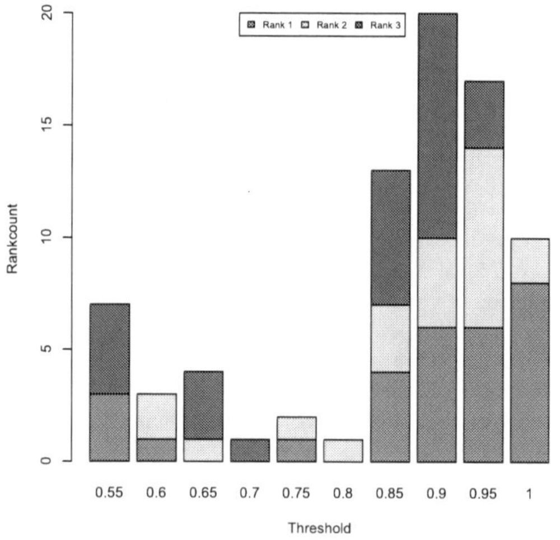

Figure 7: Ranking of DynB Thresholds.

same blocksizes do not differ. Moreover, when blocksize 1×1, i.e., the block consists of a single nonzero, is predominant the execution times are highest. Here, a lot of overhead arises due to the indices that have to be stored for only single values. The best execution times are achieved, when the threshold is higher, i.e., less fill-in occurs, and (for this matrix) a lot of 1D blocks are found. For the *G3_circuit* matrix the results are similar, but its coefficient of variation is lower, what can be explained by the lower number of nonzeros, so execution time is primarily lower. The matrix with the lowest coefficient of varience is the *kkt_power*. For this matrix, changing the threshold did not result in different blocks, due to its structure. Hence, the execution time was the same for all thresholds.

Fig. 7 shows the count of the ranking (rank 1 to rank 3, related to time) of the thresholds across all matrices (optimization `fast`), i.e, how often a threshold resulted in the fastest, 2nd fastet and 3rd fastest time. Overall it can be seen that, a threashold of 0.9 could lead mostly to a ranking. Although a threshold of 0.9 more often lead to rank three, this might be a good indicator that this is a well enough threshold for general use. A threshold between 0.7 and 0.8 did not result in a good ranking for the testmatrices. A lower threshold of 0.55 (adding more fill-in) could, in some cases, result in better rankcounts again.

This is further shown in Fig. 8. Here, the normalized times ($Time \in [0.0, 1.0]$), for selected matrices with different

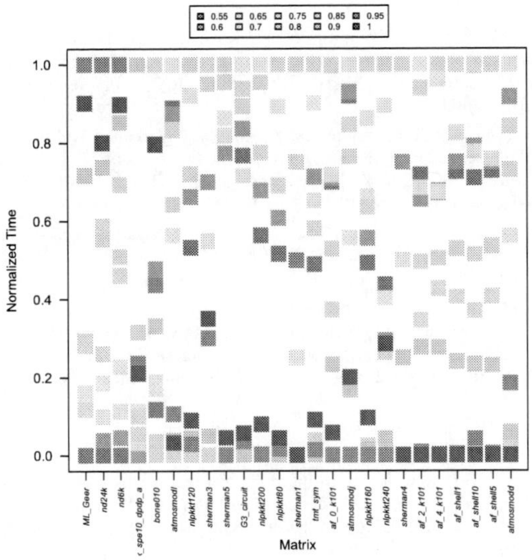

Figure 8: Normalized Times for selected Matrices with DynB, Different Thresholds.

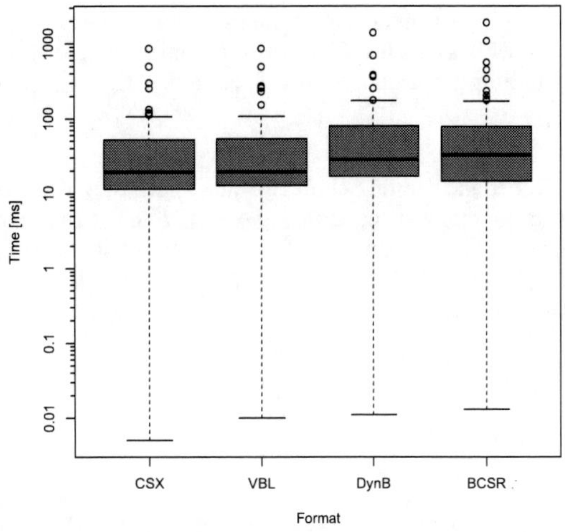

Figure 9: SpMV with all Blocking Formats, Best Results.

TABLE I: Selected DynB Times for ML_Geer

Threshold	Predominant Block	Compileroption	Time [ms]
0.55	8×8	`fast`	175.2
		`O0`	554.5
0.95	2×2	`fast`	251.0
		`O0`	513.9

structures, is given for different thresholds (optimization `fast`). It can be seen that, not for all matrices a higher threshold leads to short execution times of the SpMV operation. For example, the matrix *ML_Geer* shows the best results with lowest threshold (thus more fill-in). Table I shows the absolute results for this matrix. With a higher amount of fill-in it is possible to find more 8×8 blocks. Looking at the times dependent on compileroptions, it can be seen that, when `fast` (and thus vectorization) is used SpMV is faster when using vectorization. Moreover, the `fast` works better when the 8×8 blocks are predominant. Thus this matrix has shortest SpMV execution times with a threshold of 0.55 and compileroption `fast`. Another interesting fact that can be derived fom Table I is, when `O0` is used the higher threshold with predominant 2×2 blocks is faster than the lower threshold with 8×8 blocks.

Finally, Fig. 9 shows a summary for all formats. Here, only the minimal execution time of a format (over all configurations) is given. It can be seen, that the varible formats perform better than the static BCSR for these matrices without explicit blockstructure. For the variable formats, CSX and VBL perform best. Table II shows the different outliers of the formats. It can be seen that *nlpkkt160*, *nlpkkt200*, *nlpkkt240* and *HV15R* are outliers across all formats. These matrices have the biggest ammount of nonzeros ($> 200,000,000$) in the testset. The other outliers are mostly different between the formats.

TABLE II: Outliers of SpMV in Fig. 9

Matrix	CSX	VBL	DynB	BCSR
circuit5M				x
Cube_Coup_dt0	x			
dielFilterV2real		x		x
dielFilterV3real		x	x	x
Flan_1565	x		x	
HV15R	x	x	x	x
matrix_spe5Ref_dpdp_a	x			
matrix_spe5Ref_dpdp_b	x			
matrix_spe5Ref_dpdp_c	x			x
matrix_spe5Ref_dpdp_d	x			x
matrix_spe5Ref_dpdp_e	x			
ML_Geer	x			
nlpkkt120				x
nlpkkt160	x	x	x	x
nlpkkt200	x	x	x	x
nlpkkt240	x	x	x	x

VI. Conclusions

In this paper, an overview of different variable and fixed blocking techniques for SpMV was given. Moreover, a new matrix format for storing variable sized 2D blocks, called DynB, was introduced. For this format, a prototype algorithm for finding variable blocks and an implementation of the SpMV operation was presented. Furthermore, several optimization techniques, such as using vector intrinsics, were examined. For this, the execution time of SpMV using DynB and three other blocking formats was measured. Results showed, for a test set of 111 matrices, that using the `fast` option of the Intel Compiler could lead to good results, by effectively using CPU specific vector instructions. Using vector intrinsics with hand tuned code for the use of vector units did not result in better performance compared to just using the compiler option `fast`. Furthermore, variable blocking techniques showed better performance than static blocking techniques for these matrices. For the DynB format, the structure of the matrix can have a significant impact on the dimension of the found blocks and thus on the execution time of the SpMV operation. Moreover, the choice of an appropiate threshold for DynB is dependent on the matrix structure. Future work on the DynB format will include improvements in finding variable sized rectangular blocks as well as further optimization and parallelization of block handling inside the SpMV operation.

ACKNOWLEDGEMENTS

Jan Ecker and Simon Scholl at Bonn-Rhein-Sieg University helped us in many discussions. We would like to thank the CMT team at Saudi Aramco EXPEC ARC for their support and input. Especially we want to thank Ali H. Dogru for making this research project possible.

REFERENCES

[1] Y. Saad, Iterative Methods for Sparse Linear Systems, 2nd ed. SIAM, 2003.

[2] E.-J. Im, K. Yelick, and R. Vuduc, "Sparsity: Optimization framework for sparse matrix kernels," The International Journal of High Performance Computing Applications, vol. 18, no. 1, pp. 135–158, 2004.

[3] A. Pinar and M. T. Heath, "Improving performance of sparse matrix-vector multiplication," in Proc. ACM/IEEE Conference on Supercomputing (SC'99), pp. 30 – 39. IEEE, Nov. 1999.

[4] S. Williams et al., "Optimization of sparse matrix-vector multiplication on emerging multicore platforms," in Proc. ACM/IEEE Supercomputing 2007 (SC'07), pp. 1–12. IEEE, 2007.

[5] R. W. Vuduc, "Automatic performance tuning of sparse matrix kernels," Ph.D. dissertation, University of California, Berkeley, 2003.

[6] R. Kannan, "Efficient sparse matrix multiple-vector multiplication using a bitmapped format," in Proc. 20th International Conference on High Performance Computing (HiPC), pp. 286–294. IEEE, 2013.

[7] M. Belgin, G. Back, and C. J. Ribbens, "Pattern-based sparse matrix representation for memory-efficient smvm kernels," in Proc. 23rd International Conference on Supercomputing (SC'09), ser. ICS '09, pp. 100–109. ACM, 2009.

[8] A. Buluc, J. T. Fineman, M. Frigo, J. R. Gilbert, and C. E. Leiserson, "Parallel sparse matrix-vector and matrix-transpose-vector multiplication using compressed sparse blocks," in Proc. 21th Annual Symp. on Parallelism in Algorithms and Architectures (SPAA'09), pp. 233–244. ACM, 2009.

[9] A. Buluc, S. Williams, L. Oliker, and J. Demmel, "Reduced-bandwidth multithreaded algorithms for sparse matrix-vector multiplication," in Proc. Intl. Parallel and Distributed Processing Symposium (IPDPS'2011), pp. 721–733. IEEE, 2011.

[10] V. Karakasis, G. Goumas, and N. Koziris, "A comparative study of blocking storage methods for sparse matrices on multicore architectures," in Proc. 12th IEEE Intl. Conference on Computational Science and Engineerging (CSE-09), pp. 247–256. IEEE, 2009.

[11] Y. Saad, "Sparskit: a basic tool kit for sparse matrix computations," http://www-users.cs.umn.edu/~saad/software/SPARSKIT/, 1994, [retrieved: August, 2016].

[12] R. Barrett et al., Templates for the Solution of Linear Systems: Building Blocks for Iterative Methods, 2nd ed. SIAM, 1994.

[13] User and Reference Guide for the Intel C++ Compiler 15.0, https://software.intel.com/en-us/compiler_15.0_ug_c ed., Intel Corporation, 2014, [retrieved: August, 2016].

[14] R. Berrendorf, M. Weierstall, and F. Mannuss, "Program optimization strategies to improve the performance of SpMV-operations," in Proc. 8th Intl. Conference on Future Computational Technologies and Applications (FUTURE COMPUTING 2016), pp. 34–40. IARIA, 2016.

[15] S. Yan, C. Li, Y. Zhang, and H. Zhou, "yaSpMV: yet another SpMV framework on GPUs," in Proc. 19th ACM SIGPLAN Symposium on Principles and Practice of Parallel Programming (PPoPP'14), pp. 107–118. ACM, 2014.

[16] R. W. Vuduc and H.-J. Moon, "Fast sparse matrix-vector multiplication by exploiting variable block structure," in Proc. First Intl. Conference on High Performance Computing and Communications (HPCC'05), pp. 807–816. Springer-Verlag, 2005.

[17] V. Karakasis, G. Goumas, and N. Koziris, "Performance models for blocked sparse matrix-vector multiplication kernels," in Proc. 38th Intl. Conference on Parallel Processing (ICPP'09), pp. 356 – 364. IEEE, 2009.

[18] V. Karakasis, T. Gkountouvas, K. Kourtis, G. Goumas, and N. Koziris, "An extended compression format for the optimization of sparse matrix-vector multiplication," IEEE Transactions on Parallel and Distributed Systems, vol. 24, no. 10, pp. 1930–1940, Oct. 2013.

[19] K. Kourtis, G. Goumas, and N. Koziris, "Optimizing sparse matrix-vector multiplication using index and value compression," in Proc. 5th Conference on Computing Frontiers (CF'08), pp. 87–96. ACM, 2008.

[20] M. Martone, S. Filippone, S. Tucci, P. Gepner, and M. Paprzycki, "Use of hybrid recursive csr/coo data structures in sparse matrix-vector multiplication," in Computer Science and Information Technology (IMCSIT), Proceedings of the 2010 International Multiconference on, pp. 327–335. IEEE, 2010.

[21] M. Martone, S. Filippone, M. Paprzycki, and S. Tucci, "Assembling recursively stored sparse matrices." in IMCSIT, pp. 317–325, 2010.

[22] ——, "On the usage of 16 bit indices in recursively stored sparse matrices," in Symbolic and Numeric Algorithms for Scientific Computing (SYNASC), 2010 12th International Symposium on, pp. 57–64. IEEE, 2010.

[23] M. Martone, S. Filippone, S. Tucci, M. Paprzycki, and M. Ganzha, "Utilizing recursive storage in sparse matrix-vector multiplication-preliminary considerations." in CATA, pp. 300–305, 2010.

[24] GCC, the GNU Compiler Collection, Free Software Foundation, https://gcc.gnu.org/, [retrieved: August, 2016].

[25] Intel® Haswell, Intel, http://ark.intel.com/products/codename/42174/Haswell, [retrieved: August, 2016].

[26] T. A. Davis and Y. Hu, "The University of Florida Sparse Matrix Collection," ACM Trans. Math. Softw., vol. 38, no. 1, pp. 1:1–1:25, Nov. 2010.

[27] SPE Comparative Solution Project, Society of Petroleum Engineers, http://www.spe.org/web/csp/, [retrieved: August, 2016].

[28] V. Karakasis, T. Gkountouvas, and K. Kourtis, CSX libryry v0.2, https://github.com/cslab-ntua/csx, [retrieved: August, 2016].

A Genetic Algorithm Solution for the Doctor Scheduling Problem

Abir Alharbi and Kholood AlQahtani
Mathematics Department, King Saud University, Riyadh, Saudi Arabia
e-mail:abir@ksu.edu.sa , 432201096@student.ksu.edu.sa

Abstract—In this study, we present a genetic algorithm solution to the scheduling problem for doctors in the Pediatric Department of Prince Sultan Military Medical City (PSMMC) in Riyadh Saudi Arabia. The genetic algorithm approach uses a cost bit matrix where each cell indicates any violation of constraints. The experimental results show that the suggested method generated a doctor schedule faster and with less violated constrains compared to the traditional manual methods.

Keywords- Doctor Scheduling Problem, Genetic Algorithms, cost bit matrix.

I. INTRODUCTION

A hospital providing around-the-clock services divides its daily work into consecutive shifts, and a shift is a period of time in which a group of employees is in-service. A doctor is assigned to a set of shifts, and this assignment satisfies several constraints that may be set up by staffing requirements, rules by the administration, and labor contract clauses. In a Doctor Scheduling Problem (DSP), each doctor is assigned to the set of shifts and rest days in a timetable called a doctor roster. DSP was proven to be NP-hard even with only a subset of real world constraints [4]. In the literature, many research works were done on DSP or the similar Nurse Scheduling Problem (NSP). Miller et al. [13], and Warner et al. [14] formulated Nursing Schedule Problem as the selection of a timetable that minimized an objective function that balanced the trade-off between staffing coverage and nurses' preferences. Abdannadher et al. [2], applied Constraint Logic Program (CLP) framework and Li et al. [11], employed Bayesian optimization algorithm. Jan et al. [9], and Aickelin et al. [3] applied the genetic algorithms (GA) to NSP. Kundu et al. [10] applied genetic algorithm and simulated annealing to the same problem instances and compared their performances with others, and [6] applied coloring graph theory to solve NSP.

In DSP, there are many constraints and there can be several different instances with different set of constraints. In this study, we consider the cyclic Doctor Scheduling Problem with the following constraints. An instance includes three components:

(1) the personal preference of each doctor to work on particular days and shifts,

(2) the minimal coverage constraints of the minimal required number of doctors per shift and per day,

(3) the case-specific constraints specified by personal time requirements, specific workplace conditions, etc.

The objective of this problem is to satisfy doctors' requests as much as possible while fulfilling the employers' requirements. In this paper, we apply a genetic algorithm with a cost bit matrix that penalizes the solution of the DSP if the constrains are violated, and hence find a schedule solution that optimizes the doctors' roasters and satisfies the constraints. In the next section, we will briefly introduce the genetic algorithms, DSP, its cost function, and the cost bit matrix. In Section III the GA results are discussed. Finally, conclusions and future work are discussed in Section IV.

II. GENETIC ALGORITHMS

Genetic Algorithms (GA) are adaptive heuristic search algorithms [12] premised on the evolutionary ideas of natural selection and genetics. The basic concepts of the GA were designed to simulate those processes in natural evolution system, and survival of the fittest. GA are a powerful tool to solve optimization problems with multiple variables [1][7]. GA were applied to several scheduling problems [3][5][8][9]. GA use a search algorithm to simulate the process of natural selection. GA start with the set of potential solutions called population and evolves toward more optimal solutions. The solutions are evaluated by a fitness function. The fitness value represents the quality measure of a solution so that the algorithm can use it to select ones with better genetic material for producing new solutions and further generations. The selection chooses superior solutions in every generation and assures that inferior solutions become extinct. The crossover operator chooses two solutions from the current population and generates a new solution based on their genetic material. Selection and crossover operators will expand the good features of superior individuals through the whole population. They will also direct the search process towards a local optimum. The mutation operator changes the value of some genes in a solution and helps to search other parts of the problem space. The main disadvantage of GA is the requirement for a large computation time.

A. Doctor Scheduling Problem

DSP consists of creating weekly or monthly schedules for N doctors by assigning one out of a number of possible shift patterns to each doctor. These schedules have to satisfy working contracts and meet the requirements for the number of doctors of different grades for each shift, while being seen to be fair by the staff concerned. Therefore, DSP is essentially a scheduling problem that suits a number of constraints. The constraints are usually categorized into two categories: soft and hard constraints. Hard constraints should always be satisfied in any working schedule so that there will be no breaches. Any schedule that does not satisfy all of the hard constraints cannot be a feasible one. Possible examples include restrictions on the number of doctors for each shift; the maximum number of shifts in a week, a month, etc. On the contrary, soft constraints can be violated but as minimal as possible. In other words, the soft constraints are expected to be satisfied, but violation does not make it an infeasible solution. We confined the constraints as follows:

(a) Hard constraints

(i) There are constraints on the number of doctors for each working shift per day. The number of doctors for morning, evening, and night shift should be between the minimum and maximum values.

(ii) There are constraints for the working patterns. Morning after night shift, evening after night, morning after evening shift and three consecutive night shifts are restricted combination of working patterns.

(b) Soft constraints

There are constraints for the total number of off-days (o), night (n), morning (m) and evening (e) shifts during a certain period of days for each doctor.

In this project, we consider a scheduling problem for the Pediatric Department of Prince Sultan Military Medical City (PSMMC) in Riyadh/ Saudi Arabia. Monthly doctors' rosters are made manually before the end of each month. Figure 1 shows original hospital roasters for the month of February 2016. Even though making monthly rosters manually required great effort and time, it did not resolve all conflicts, and sometimes it had created more tedious adjustments to accomplish needed tasks. There are consultants, senior and junior doctors working in this department. This project is concerned with scheduling shifts for junior doctors in two of the department wards for one month only. A major problem with any scheduling problem is the allocation of resources in an effective way, and violating constraints will be affecting the quality of the solution.

B. The Cost Function

We have to define a cost function which, after optimization, will obtain optimal schedules for each doctor. Let N, D be the number of doctors and days. Then, DSP may be represented as a problem to find a schedule matrix, so that each element of the matrix, X_{ij} expresses that doctor i works on day j where X_{ij} =(m e, n, o).

(a) To evaluate the violation of hard constraint (i), we define m, e, n as the total number of doctors for morning, evening, and night shift on day j. If any of these numbers are not between the minimum and maximum number of doctors for each shift (mmin, mmax, emin, emax, nmin, nmax), cost C_1 will be incremented by l.

(b) To evaluate the violation of hard constraint (ii), working patterns are examined. Any violation of the working patterns specified (such as n after m, e after n, m after e, or consecutive n, n, n) will increment cost C_2 by l.

(c) To evaluate the violation of soft constraint, we define M, E, N, O as the total number of the corresponding shifts, morning, evening and night and off-days for doctor i during the period of D and Mreq , Ereq, Nreq, Oreq as the required number of morning, night and night shifts and off-days for all doctors during the period of D. If any of these numbers M, E, N, O does not meet, Ereq, Nreq, Oreq respectively, cost C_3 will be incremented by 1.

Different weight values can be assigned for the costs C_l, C_2 and C_3. Then, the final cost function is

$$f= C_1*w_1 + C_2*w_2+ C_3*w_3$$

where w_l, w_2 and w_3 are weight values for C_l, C_2 and C_3, respectively. Our goal is to minimize the cost function f so as to find an optimal doctor schedule. The simplest method to find the solution is a brute force approach (manually) evaluating all possible doctor schedules and finding the feasible one with the minimum cost among them. However, if the number of all possible doctor's increase, this approach is intractable. This is a class of problems schedules for which it is believed that no efficient algorithm exists, called NP-hard. In other words, the algorithms that guarantee to find an optimal solution with the size of D and N in reasonable time may not exist. To overcome this problem, we use a genetic algorithm which is an approximation algorithm. GA provide an approximate solution rather than an optimal one in acceptable time.

C. GA Paramreters for Selction and Crossover

The initial population (n), are the first n schedules for doctors that are NxD matrices, is generated randomly assigning each doctor to one of the three shifts with a day-off on each day, Table I shows a sample of a week schedule for 5 doctors (a 5x7 matrix). The costs of these schedules are calculated by cost functions C_l, C_2 and C_3. The method of selection in this study, is the roulette wheel selection that is the most common type of selection method. Two schedules, P1 and P2, are chosen randomly based on their costs and are used to produce an offspring. One schedule can be selected for a parent more than once. The crossover between the two chosen parents genome is done at a single point randomly chosen with probability 0.8 to produce the new generation offspring, and with 0.01 Mutation rate. The remaining initial parameters are set as given by the PSMMC hospital for Feb 2016, N=24, D=29, mmin=8, mmax=10, emin=6, emax=10, nmin=6, nmax=10, and soft constrains for each week Mreq=Ereq=Nreq=2, and Oreq=1. The method was activated to reach an optimum cost=0 (f=0) using Matlab genetic algorithm toolbox with Intel Core ™ i5-250M 2.5 Ghz CPU and 4GB.

TABLE I. SAMPLE WEEK OF HOSPITAL SCHEDULE FOR 5 DOCTORS

Doctor	M	T	W	TH	F	S	SU
1	m	e	n	o	m	m	n
2	e	m	m	n	o	m	n
3	n	n	o	m	e	e	e
4	m	m	e	e	n	o	m
5	e	e	e	n	m	n	o

III. GA RESULTS

The genetic algorithm started with a population size of 60 individuals, with the size of each genome NxD matrix (24 doctors for 29 days). The algorithm terminates when the maximum number of generations reaches 300, or when the increase in fitness of the best individual over five successive generations falls below a certain threshold, set at 2×10^{-6}. Our fitness function f is set to the final cost function as $f = 5C_1 + 5C_2 + C_3$, which penalizes systems violating the constrains with the assigned weights. The GA runs throughout the generations to find the best genome in this population. The best genome is the one, which violates the least number of constrains. After all 300 generations (repeated 50 times), the genetic algorithm finds the optimum genome; hence, it finds the best doctor schedule table which violates the least constrains. The proposed GA results are compared to the hospital manual roaster tables derived from Fig. 1. Table III shows the incident matrix for the 24 doctors in PSMMC for the month of February, 2016. Fig. 2 shows the GA results as plots of the best fitness value over the generations, and average distance between individuals for the 4 weeks. The best doctor schedule produced from the GA is given in Table IV. Table II shows a comparison of the performance results of the two methods. Both methods solved each of the given problem instances and the results did not violate any of hard constraints in all periods. GA generated schedules with optimal cost in all periods, also, the optimal costs from GA is smaller than that of the manual tables. The average execution time of GA is around 3.45 minutes which is much faster than those of manual tables which takes a few hours to accomplish. Hence, GA are very effective compared to traditional manual methods based on on time and least constrains violation.

TABLE II. COMPARISONS OF GA AND TRADITIONAL HOSPITAL SCHEDULE

period	Method	f_{opt}	T (min)
1week	GA	2	2.6
	Manual	7	
2weeks	GA	5	3.2
	Manual	11	
3weeks	GA	4	3.75
	Manual	12	
4weeks	GA	3	3.96
	Manual	10	

IV. CONCLUSION AND FUTURE WORK

In this paper, we proposed a Genetic Algorithm approach with a cost bit matrix to solve a DSP in PSMMC hospital. The genetic algorithm found solutions satisfying all the constraints. This approach generated a doctor schedule faster in speed and better in quality than traditional manual methods. Although we have presented this work in terms of doctor scheduling, it should be noted that the main idea of the approach could be applied to many other scheduling problems. Future research aims at experiments on the nurse's schedule in PSMMC hospital with more constraints and a diversity of requirements. Our future plans also include producing a software that helps hospitals design schedules with their constrains for their doctors and nurses with simple inputs and less time to avoid manual schedule making.

ACKNOWLEDGMENT

This research project was supported by a grant from the "Research Centre of the Female Scientific and Medical Colleges", Deanship of Scientific Research, King Saud University.

REFERENCES

[1] Alharbi A, Rand W, Rolio R , et al (2007), Understanding the Semantics of Genetic Algorithms in Dynamic Environments A case Study Using the Shaky Ladder Hyperplane-Defined Functions, Workshop on Evolutionary Algorithms in Stochastic and Dynamic Environments, incorporated in Evo Conferences Valencia, Spain.

[2] S. Abdennadher and H. Schienker, "Nurse Scheduling using Constraint Logic Programming", Proc. AAAI '99/IAAI '99, (1999), pp. 838-843.

[3] U. Aickelin and K. A. Dowsland, "An indirect Genetic Algorithm for a Nurse-Scheduling Computers & Operations Research, vol. 31, no. 5, (2004) April, pp. 761-778.

[4] U. Aickelin and K. A. Dowsiand, "Exploiting Problem structure roistering problem", Journal of Scheduling, vol. 3, (2000), pp. 139-153.

[5] A. Brezulianu, F. Monica and F. Lucian, "A Genetic Algorithm Approach for a Constrained Employee Scheduling Problem as Applied to Employees at Mall Type Shops", IJAST, vol. 14, (2010), pp. 1-14.

[6] A. Gideon, A Nurse Scheduling Using Graph Coloring. Master thesis submit- ted, Mathematics Department, Kwame Nkrumah University, Ghana, 2013.

[7] D. E. Goldberg, "Genetic Algorithms in Search, Optimization and Machine Learning", Addison Wesley (1989) .

[8] H. Heidari and A. Chalechale, "Scheduling in Multiprocessor System Using Genetic Algorithm", IJAST, vol 43, (2012), pp.81-94.

[9] A. Jan, M. Yamamoto and A. Ohuchi, "Evolutionary Algorithms for Nurse Scheduling Evolutionary Computation, 2000. Proc. The 2000 Congress, (2000), pp. 196-203.

[10] S. Kundu, M. Mahato, B. Mahanty and S. Acharyya, "Comparative Performance of Simulated Annealing and Genetic Algorithm in Solving Nurse Scheduling Problem", Proc. Int'l Multi Conference of Engineers and Computer Scientists 2008 1, (2008) January, pp. 1-5.

[11] J. Li and U. Aickelin, "A Bayesian Optimization Algorithm for the Nurse Scheduling Evolutionary Computation, 2003. In: CEC '03.

[12] Michalewicz , Z. Genetic Algorithms +Data Structures= Evolution Programs, 3rd edition, Springer-Verlag, (1996).

[13] H. E. Miller, W. P. Pierskalla and G. J. Rath, "Nurse Scheduling using Mathematical Programming,"Operations Research, vol. 24, no. 5, (1976), pp. 857-870.

[14] D. M. Warner and J. Prawda, "A Mathematical Programming Model for Scheduling Nursing Personnel in a Hospital", Management Science, vol. 19 (4-Part-1), (1972) December, pp. 411-422.

GENERAL PAEDIATRIC ON-CALL ROTA

February 2016

Date	Day	1st On-Call (Bleep 0344)		2nd On-Call (Bleep 0271)	1st On-Call (Bleep 0240)	1st On-Call (Bl eep 0340)	2nd On-Call (Bleep 0304)	Consultant	
		PGICU 3.1	PGICU 1.6	PGICU 1.6 & 3.1	Admission & A&E Interns (Bleep 0232)	Wards 3.3, 4.1, 4.2 & 4.3 Interns (Bleep 0236)	Admission/ Wards	General	PGICU
1	Mon	ELGAWHARAH	MALIK	Rizwan	AZIZ MUSAINED	ALANOUD M	FARHOOD	A Hilwa	Chehab
2	Tues	QASSIM	KHALED	Warwar	HEBA	HAMZAH	MARAM	A Fawaz	Chehab
3	Wed	M. ASIRI	HAMDAN	Yacoub	HISHAM	FAHAD	GHADAH	R Asiri	Chehab
4	Thu	GRACE	NOURAH	Inayat	FADIAH	ALANOUD K	MANAR	H Ahmari	Mohaimeed
5	Fri	TAGHREED	A. JABER	Rizwan	BASHAYER M	ALANOUD M	BIN HUSSAIN / FARHOOD	H Ahmari	Mohaimeed
6	Sat	ELGAWHARAH	MALIK/ Asim S	Ahmed	KHALED	AZIZ MUSAINED	MARAM / GHADAH	H Ahmari	Mohaimeed
7	Sun	AMAL	HISHAM	Warwar	HAMZAH	HEBA	M. ASIRI	A Hilwa	Thabet
8	Mon	NADA ALHARBI	NOURAH	Yacoub	ALANOUD K	FADIAH	NOUR	R Asiri	Thabet
9	Tues	RAED	Asim S	Inayat	ALANOUD M	BASHAYER M	FARHOOD	M Hijazi	Thabet
10	Wed	BODOUR	HISHAM	Rizwan	FAHAD	AZIZ MUSAINED	BIN HUSSAIN	H Ahmari	Thabet
11	Thu	MUJAHID	MALIK	Yaser	HAMZAH	HEBA	SAEED	A Hilwa	Bafaqih
12	Fri	NADA	KHALED	Warwar	AHMED	ALANOUD K	GHADAH / MARAM	A Hilwa	Bafaqih
13	Sat	ESRAA M	HAMDAN	Yacoub	FAHAD	A. JABER	M. ASIRI / FARHOOD	A Hilwa	Bafaqih
14	Sun	EBTISAM	Asim S	Inayat	ALANOUD M	FADIAH	RAED	H Ahmari	Mohaimeed
15	Mon	TAGHREED	MALIK	Rizwan	BASHAYER M	AZIZ MUSAINED	NOUR	A Fawaz	Mohaimeed
16	Tues	NADA	KHALED	Yaser	ALANOUD K	HAMZAH	MARAM	R Asiri	Mohaimeed
17	Wed	QASSIM	NOURAH	Yacoub	FADIAH	HEBA	GHADAH	M Hijazi	Mohaimeed
18	Thu	ESRAA M	Asim S	Ahmed	ALANOUD M	BASHAYER M	MANAR	R Asiri	Thabet
19	Fri	MUJAHID	FAHAD	Inayat	NADA ALHARBI	HANEM	RAED / NOUR	R Asiri	Thabet
20	Sat	SARAH F	GRACE	Warwar	HISHAM	AHMED	QASSIM / BIN HUSSAIN	R Asiri	Thabet
21	Sun	RAED	Asim S	Rizwan	AHMED	ALANOUD K	GHADAH / MARAM	A Hilwa	Bafaqih
22	Mon	TAGHREED	MALIK	Ahmed	BASHAYER M	AZIZ MUSAINED	NOUR	H Ahmari	Bafaqih
23	Tues	AMAL	HISHAM	Inayat	ALANOUD K	FADIAH	NOUR	A Fawaz	Bafaqih
24	Wed	QASSIM	KHALED	Warwar	HAMZAH	HEBA	M. ASIRI	M Hijazi	Bafaqih
25	Thu	NADA ALHARBI	NOURAH	Rizwan	FADIAH	ALANOUD K	MANAR	A Fawaz	Chehab
26	Fri	EBTISAM	Asim S	Yacoub	BASHAYER M	AZIZ MUSAINED	NOUR	A Fawaz	Chehab
27	Sat	MUJAHID	FAHAD	Yaser	HISHAM	AHMED	QASSIM / BIN HUSSAIN	A Fawaz	Chehab
28	Sun	QASSIM	NOURAH	Inayat	AZIZ MUSAINED	ALANOUD M	FARHOOD	R Asiri	Chehab
29	Mon	M. ASIRI	HAMDAN	Warwar	HEBA	HAMZAH	MARAM	A Hilwa	Chehab

Department of Paediatrics									
Paediatric ICU Team									
Division Mobile: 0504585767		Febrauary 2016							
		1-6 PICU On- call Team A 08:00-08:00			3-1 PICU service Team B 08:00 – 16:00			PRRT & Transportation 08:00-08:00 Team C	
Date	Day	Consultant	Fellow / Registrar	Resident	Consultant	Fellow	Registrar/Resident	Consultant	Fellow /Registrar
1	Mon	Chehab	Rizwan	ELGAWHARAH	Mohaimeed	Rizwan	NOUR S	Mohaimeed	Rizwan
2	Tues	Chehab	Warwar	QASSIM	Mohaimeed	Rizwan	NOUR S	Mohaimeed	Rizwan
3	Wed	Chehab	Yacoub	M. ASIRI	Mohaimeed	Rizwan	NOUR S	Mohaimeed	Rizwan
4	Thu	Mohaimeed	Inayat	GRACE	Mohaimeed	Inayat	GRACE	Mohaimeed	Inayat
5	Fri	Mohaimeed	Rizwan	TAGHREED	Mohaimeed	Rizwan	TAGHREED	Mohaimeed	Rizwan
6	Sat	Mohaimeed	Ahmed	ELGAWHARAH	Mohaimeed	Ahmed	ELGAWHARAH	Mohaimeed	Ahmed
7	Sun	Thabet	Warwar	AMAL	Bafaqih	Warwar	MALIK	Bafaqih	Warwar
8	Mon	Thabet	Yacoub	NADA ALHARBI	Bafaqih	Warwar	MALIK	Bafaqih	Warwar
9	Tues	Thabet	Inayat	RAED	Bafaqih	Warwar	MALIK	Bafaqih	Warwar
10	Wed	Thabet	Rizwan	BODOUR	Bafaqih	Warwar	MALIK	Bafaqih	Warwar
11	Thu	Bafaqih	Yaser	MUJAHID	Bafaqih	Yaser	MUJAHID	Bafaqih	Yaser
12	Fri	Bafaqih	Warwar	NADA	Bafaqih	Warwar	NADA	Bafaqih	Warwar
13	Sat	Bafaqih	Yacoub	ESRAA M	Bafaqih	Yacoub	ESRAA M	Bafaqih	Yacoub
14	Sun	Mohaimeed	Inayat	EBTISAM	Chehab	Inayat	HAMDAN	Chehab	Inayat
15	Mon	Mohaimeed	Rizwan	TAGHREED	Chehab	Inayat	HAMDAN	Chehab	Inayat
16	Tues	Mohaimeed	Yaser	NADA	Chehab	Inayat	HAMDAN	Chehab	Inayat
17	Wed	Mohaimeed	Yacoub	QASSIM	Chehab	Inayat	HAMDAN	Chehab	Inayat
18	Thu	Thabet	Ahmed	ESRAA M	Thabet	Ahmed	ESRAA M	Thabet	Ahmed
19	Fri	Thabet	Inayat	MUJAHID	Thabet	Inayat	MUJAHID	Thabet	Inayat
20	Sat	Thabet	Warwar	SARAH F	Thabet	Warwar	SARAH F	Thabet	Warwar
21	Sun	Bafaqih	Rizwan	RAED	Thabet	Yaser	Abdullah S	Thabet	Yaser
22	Mon	Bafaqih	Ahmed	TAGHREED	Thabet	Yaser	Abdullah S	Thabet	Yaser
23	Tues	Bafaqih	Inayat	AMAL	Thabet	Yaser	Abdullah S	Thabet	Yaser
24	Wed	Bafaqih	Warwar	QASSIM	Thabet	Yaser	Abdullah S	Thabet	Yaser
25	Thu	Chehab	Rizwan	NADA ALHARBI	Chehab	Rizwan	FATIMAH	Chehab	Rizwan
26	Fri	Chehab	Yacoub	EBTISAM	Chehab	Yacoub	HALA	Chehab	Yacoub
27	Sat	Chehab	Yaser	MUJAHID	Chehab	Yaser	NADA ALHARBI	Chehab	Yaser
28	Sun	Chehab	Inayat	QASSIM	Mohaimeed	Ahmed	Yosef	Mohaimeed	Ahmed
29	Mon	Chehab	Warwar	M. ASIRI	Mohaimeed	Ahmed	Yosef	Mohaimeed	Ahmed

Figure 1. Example of a Hospital Manual Doctor schedule.

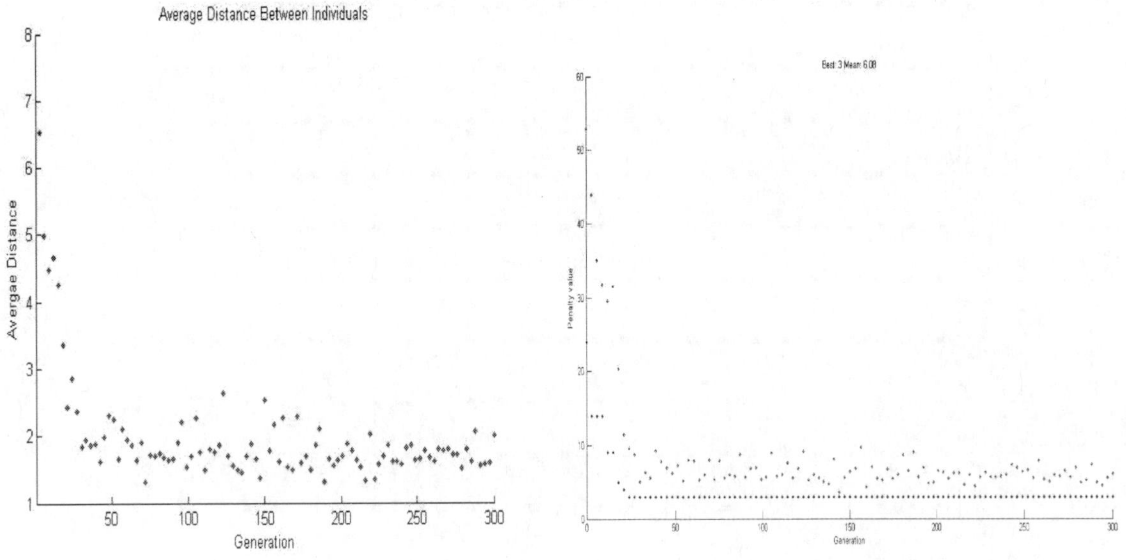

Figure 2. GA results showing the average distance between the indivisuals, and the best fitness value for 4 weeks.

TABLE III. THE HOSPITAL INCIDENT MATRIX FOR DOCTORS WORKING IN SAME GROUP AND WARD FOR N=25.

	$R3_1$	$R4_1$	$R1_1$	$R1_5$	$R2_4$	SUB_1	$R3_2$	$R4_2$	$R1_2$	$R2_1$	$R2_5$	SUB_2	$R3_3$	$R4_3$	$R1_3$	$R2_2$	$R2_6$	SUB_3	$R3_4$	$R4_4$	$R1_4$	$R2_3$	$R2_7$	SUB_4
$R3_1$	■	▮	▮	▮	▮	▮	■	■	■	■	■	■	■	■	■	■	■	■	■	■	■	■	■	■
$R4_1$	▮	■	▮	▮	▮	▮	■	■	■	■	■	■	■	■	■	■	■	■	■	■	■	■	■	■
$R1_1$	▮	▮	■	▮	▮	▮	■	■	■	■	■	■	■	■	■	■	■	■	■	■	■	■	■	■
$R1_5$	▮	▮	▮	■	▮	▮	■	■	■	■	■	■	■	■	■	■	■	■	■	■	■	■	■	■
$R2_4$	▮	▮	▮	▮	■	▮	■	■	■	■	■	■	■	■	■	■	■	■	■	■	■	■	■	■
SUB_1	▮	▮	▮	▮	▮	■	■	■	■	■	■	■	■	■	■	■	■	■	■	■	■	■	■	■
$R3_2$	■	■	■	■	■	■	■	▮	▮	▮	▮	▮	■	■	■	■	■	■	■	■	■	■	■	■
$R4_2$	■	■	■	■	■	■	▮	■	▮	▮	▮	▮	■	■	■	■	■	■	■	■	■	■	■	■
$R1_2$	■	■	■	■	■	■	▮	▮	■	▮	▮	▮	■	■	■	■	■	■	■	■	■	■	■	■
$R2_1$	■	■	■	■	■	■	▮	▮	▮	■	▮	▮	■	■	■	■	■	■	■	■	■	■	■	■
$R2_5$	■	■	■	■	■	■	▮	▮	▮	▮	■	▮	■	■	■	■	■	■	■	■	■	■	■	■
SUB_2	■	■	■	■	■	■	▮	▮	▮	▮	▮	■	■	■	■	■	■	■	■	■	■	■	■	■
$R3_3$	■	■	■	■	■	■	■	■	■	■	■	■	■	▮	▮	▮	▮	▮	■	■	■	■	■	■
$R4_3$	■	■	■	■	■	■	■	■	■	■	■	■	▮	■	▮	▮	▮	▮	■	■	■	■	■	■
$R1_3$	■	■	■	■	■	■	■	■	■	■	■	■	▮	▮	■	▮	▮	▮	■	■	■	■	■	■
$R2_2$	■	■	■	■	■	■	■	■	■	■	■	■	▮	▮	▮	■	▮	▮	■	■	■	■	■	■
$R2_6$	■	■	■	■	■	■	■	■	■	■	■	■	▮	▮	▮	▮	■	▮	■	■	■	■	■	■
SUB_3	■	■	■	■	■	■	■	■	■	■	■	■	▮	▮	▮	▮	▮	■	■	■	■	■	■	■
$R3_4$	■	■	■	■	■	■	■	■	■	■	■	■	■	■	■	■	■	■	■	▮	▮	▮	▮	▮
$R4_4$	■	■	■	■	■	■	■	■	■	■	■	■	■	■	■	■	■	■	▮	■	▮	▮	▮	▮
$R1_4$	■	■	■	■	■	■	■	■	■	■	■	■	■	■	■	■	■	■	▮	▮	■	▮	▮	▮
$R2_3$	■	■	■	■	■	■	■	■	■	■	■	■	■	■	■	■	■	■	▮	▮	▮	■	▮	▮
$R2_7$	■	■	■	■	■	■	■	■	■	■	■	■	■	■	■	■	■	■	▮	▮	▮	▮	■	▮
SUB_4	■	■	■	■	■	■	■	■	■	■	■	■	■	■	■	■	■	■	▮	▮	▮	▮	▮	■

TABLE IV. GENETIC ALGORITHM BEST DOCTOR SCHEDULE N=24, D=29.

Dr #/day	1	2	3	4	5	6	7	8	9	10	11	12	13	14	15	16	17	18	19	20	21	22	23	24	25	26	27	28	29
1	m	e	n	o	m	m	n	m	e	n	o	m	m	n	m	e	n	o	m	m	n	m	e	n	o	m	m	n	m
2	e	m	m	n	o	m	n	e	m	m	n	o	m	n	e	m	m	n	o	m	n	e	m	m	n	o	m	n	e
3	n	n	o	m	e	e	e	n	n	o	m	e	e	e	n	n	o	m	e	e	e	n	n	o	m	e	e	e	n
4	m	m	e	e	n	o	m	m	m	e	e	n	o	m	m	m	e	e	n	o	m	m	m	e	e	n	o	m	m
5	e	e	e	n	m	n	o	e	e	e	n	m	n	o	e	e	e	n	m	n	o	e	e	e	n	m	n	o	e
6	m	e	n	o	m	m	n	m	e	n	o	m	m	n	m	e	n	o	m	m	n	m	e	n	o	m	m	n	m
7	e	m	m	n	o	m	n	e	m	m	n	o	m	n	e	m	m	n	o	m	n	e	m	m	n	o	m	n	e
8	n	n	o	m	e	e	e	n	n	o	m	e	e	e	n	n	o	m	e	e	e	n	n	o	m	e	e	e	n
9	m	m	e	e	n	o	m	m	m	e	e	n	o	m	m	m	e	e	n	o	m	m	m	e	e	n	o	m	m
10	e	e	e	n	m	n	o	e	e	e	n	m	n	o	e	e	e	n	m	n	o	e	e	e	n	m	n	o	e
11	m	e	n	o	m	m	n	m	e	n	o	m	m	n	m	e	n	o	m	m	n	m	e	n	o	m	m	n	m
12	e	m	m	n	o	m	n	e	m	m	n	o	m	n	e	m	m	n	o	m	n	e	m	m	n	o	m	n	e
13	n	n	o	m	e	e	e	n	n	o	m	e	e	e	n	n	o	m	e	e	e	n	n	o	m	e	e	e	n
14	m	m	e	e	n	o	m	m	m	e	e	n	o	m	m	m	e	e	n	o	m	m	m	e	e	n	o	m	m
15	e	e	e	n	m	n	o	e	e	e	n	m	n	o	e	e	e	n	m	n	o	e	e	e	n	m	n	o	e
16	m	e	n	o	m	m	n	m	e	n	o	m	m	n	m	e	n	o	m	m	n	m	e	n	o	m	m	n	m
17	e	m	m	n	o	m	n	e	m	m	n	o	m	n	e	m	m	n	o	m	n	e	m	m	n	o	m	n	e
18	n	n	o	m	e	e	e	n	n	o	m	e	e	e	n	n	o	m	e	e	e	n	n	o	m	e	e	e	n
19	m	m	e	e	n	o	m	m	m	e	e	n	o	m	m	m	e	e	n	o	m	m	m	e	e	n	o	m	m
20	e	e	e	n	m	n	o	e	e	e	n	m	n	o	e	e	e	n	m	n	o	e	e	e	n	m	n	o	e
21	m	e	n	o	m	m	n	m	e	n	o	m	m	n	m	e	n	o	m	m	n	m	e	n	o	m	m	n	m
22	e	m	m	n	o	m	n	e	m	m	n	o	m	n	e	m	m	n	o	m	n	e	m	m	n	o	m	n	e
23	n	n	o	m	e	e	e	n	n	o	m	e	e	e	n	n	o	m	e	e	e	n	n	o	m	e	e	e	n
24	m	m	e	e	n	o	m	m	m	e	e	n	o	m	m	m	e	e	n	o	m	m	m	e	e	n	o	m	m

Lyapunov's inequality for a fractional differential equation subject to a non-linear integral condition

Maysaa Al-Qurashi
Department of Mathematics
College of Science, King Saud University
Riyadh, Saudi Arabia
Email: maysaa@ksu.edu.sa

Lakhdar Ragoub
College of Computers and Information Systems
Al Yamamah University
Riyadh, Saudi Arabia
Email: radhkla@hotmail.com

***Abstract*—In this paper, we investigate a Lyapunov's inequality for a non-linear fractional differential equation, subject to the non linear integral boundary condition. Such boundary conditions are different from the ones widely considered for a class of Lyapunov's inequality. The main tools are the Fubini's theorem and the construction of the Green function which corresponds to the given problem in consideration. In order to illustrate this result, we give an example where we show that the non existence of non trivial solutions of an appropriate eigenvalue fractional boundary value problem obey this necessary integral condition.**

***Index Terms*—Lyapunov's inequality, non linear boundary condition, Caputo fractional derivative, Green function.**

I. Introduction

In this paper, we present a Lyapunov's inequality for the following boundary value problem:

$$\begin{cases} ({}_cD^\alpha u)(t) + q(t)u(t) = 0, \\ a < t < b, \quad 0 < \alpha \leq 1, \\ u(a) + \mu \int_a^b u(s)q(s)\, ds = u(b), \end{cases} \tag{1}$$

where q is a continuous function defined on $[a, b]$ to R, a and b are consecutive zeros of the solution u and μ is positive. ${}_cD^\alpha$ stands for the Caputo derivative. It is evident to the reader to see that $u = 0$ is a trivial solution, and therefore only non-negative solutions are taken in consideration.
We prove that problem (1) has a non-trivial solution for $\alpha \in (0, 1]$ provided that the real and continuous function q satisfies

$$\int_a^b |q(t)|\, dt > \frac{\Gamma(\alpha)\mu^\alpha(b-a)}{\alpha(b-a+\mu)(\alpha\mu+1)^{(\alpha-1)}} \tag{2}$$

The investigation of Lyapunov's inequalities has begun very recently, where the first differential equation is based on fractional differential operators as well as that of Ferreira. In order to start with this new result, let us dwell with some references.

$$\begin{cases} u''(t) + q(t)u(t) = 0, \quad a < t < b \\ u(a) = u(b) = 0, \end{cases}$$

where a and b are consecutive zeros of u and the function $q \in C([a, b]; \mathbb{R})$. Lyapunov [1] showed the following necessary condition of existence of non-trivial solutions

$$\int_a^b |q(t)|\, dt > \frac{4}{b-a}. \tag{3}$$

Once this result is proved, similar type inequalities have been obtained for other kind of differential equations and boundary conditions see [2], [3], [4], [5].
Concerning differential equation with fractional derivative's in [6], Ferreira derived Lyapunov's inequality for the problem

$$\begin{cases} ({}_aD^\alpha u)(t) + q(t)u(t) = 0, \\ a < t < b, \ 1 < \alpha \leq 2, \\ u(a) = u(b) = 0, \end{cases} \tag{4}$$

where $q \in C([a, b], \mathbb{R})$, a and b are consecutive zeros of u, and ${}_aD^\alpha$ is the Riemann-Liouville fractional derivative of order $\alpha > 0$ defined for an absolute continuous function on $[a, b]$ by

$$({}_aD^\alpha f)(t) = \frac{1}{\Gamma(1-\alpha)} \frac{d^n}{dt^n} \int_a^t (t-s)^\alpha f(s)\, ds$$

where $n \in \mathbb{N}, n < \alpha \leq n+1$ (For more details of fractional derivatives see [7]). The corresponding necessary condition of existence that he proved in [6] reads

$$\int_a^b |q(t)|\, dt > \Gamma(\alpha) \left(\frac{4}{b-a}\right)^{\alpha-1} = \Gamma(\alpha) \left(\frac{2^{2(\alpha-1)}}{(b-a)^{(\alpha-1)}}\right), \tag{5}$$

which in the particular case $\alpha = 2$ corresponds to Lyapunov's classical inequality (1) see [1].

Then, Ferreira [8] dealt with fractional differential boundary value problems with Caputo's derivative which is defined for a function $f \in AC^n[a, t]$ by

$$({}_a^C D^\alpha f)(t) = \frac{1}{\Gamma(1-\alpha)} \int_a^t (t-s)^\alpha f^{(n)}(s)\, ds.$$

For the boundary value problem

$$\begin{cases} ({}_a^C D^{\alpha}u)(t) + q(t)u(t) = 0, \\ a < t < b,\ 1 < \alpha \le 2, \\ u(a) = u(b) = 0, \end{cases} \tag{6}$$

where $q \in C([a, b]; \mathbb{R})$ and a and b are consecutive zeros of u, Ferreira [6] proved that if (6) has a nontrivial solution, then the following necessary condition is satisfied

$$\int_a^b |q(t)|\, dt > \frac{\Gamma(\alpha)\alpha^{\alpha}}{[(\alpha-1)(b-a)]^{\alpha-1}}. \tag{7}$$

For more details on this subject, one may see [2], [6], [8], [3], [4] and the references therein.

II. Main results

The aim of this section is to investigate the necessary condition of existence of non trivial solutions of the given boundary value problem (1). To do this, we need to use the two following auxiliary lemmas.

Lemma 1: [7], [5] Let $\alpha > 0$, then the differential equation

$${}_c D^{\alpha} h(t) = 0$$

has solutions $h(t) = c_0 + c_1 t + c_2 t^2 + ... + c_{n-1} t^{n-1}$, $c_i \in R, i = 0, 1, 2, ..., n-1$, $n = [\alpha] + 1$.

Lemma 2: [7], [5] Let $\alpha > 0$, then

$$I_c^{\alpha} D^{\alpha} h(t) = I^{\alpha} h(t) + c_0 + c_1 t + c_2 t^2 + ... + c_{n-1} t^{n-1}$$

for some $c_i \in R, i = 0, 1, 2, ..., n-1$, $n = [\alpha] + 1$.

III. A Lyapunov-type inequality for problem (1)

In order to prove the corresponding Lyapunov-type inequality for the non linear integral fractional boundary value problem (1), let us re-write the considered problem in its equivalent integral form. Indeed, the next lemma formulates this fact.

Lemma 3: The solution u of (1) can be written in the integral form as

$$u(t) = \int_a^t G(t,s)q(s)u(s)\, ds + \int_t^b G(t,s)q(s)u(s)\, ds,$$

where the Green function $G(x, t)$ is defined by

$$\Gamma(\alpha)G(t,s) = \begin{cases} \frac{(t-s)^{\alpha-1}}{\Gamma(\alpha)} - \frac{(b-s)^{\alpha}}{b-a\alpha\Gamma(\alpha)} \\ + \frac{(b-s)^{\alpha-1}}{\mu(b-a)\Gamma(\alpha)}, \\ a \le s \le t, \\ \\ -\frac{(b-s)^{\alpha}}{(b-a)\alpha\Gamma(\alpha)} + \frac{(b-s)^{\alpha-1}}{\mu(b-a)\Gamma(\alpha)}, \\ t \le s \le b. \end{cases} \tag{8}$$

$$= \begin{cases} \frac{(t-s)^{\alpha-1}}{\Gamma(\alpha)} - g(t,s), & a \le s \le t \le b, \\ -g(t,s) \end{cases} \tag{9}$$

where $g(t,s) := \frac{(b-s)^{\alpha}}{(b-a)\alpha\Gamma(\alpha)} - \frac{(b-s)^{\alpha-1}}{\mu(b-a)\Gamma(\alpha)}$, for $a \le t \le s \le b$.

For the proof of Lemma 3, we use Lemma 1 and 2 to express $u(t)$ as

$$u(t) = c_0 + c_1(t-a) + c_2(t-a)^2 + ... + c_{n-1}(t-a)^{n-1},$$

for some $c_i \in R, i = 0, 1, 2, ..., n-1$, from one side. From another side, we have

$$I_c^{\alpha} D^{\alpha} u(t) = I^{\alpha} u(t) + c_0 + c_1 t + c_2 t^2 + ... + c_{n-1} t^{n-1}.$$

In particular for $0 < \alpha \le 1$, we obtain

$$u(t) = I^{\alpha} u(t) - c_0 = \int_a^t \frac{(t-s)^{\alpha-1}}{\Gamma(\alpha)} h(s)ds - c_0, \tag{10}$$

where $h(s) = u(s)q(s)$, for some constant c_0 in R.
We make integration of each side of (10) between a and b, and using Fubini's integral theorem, we get

$$\int_a^b h(s)\, ds = \int_a^b \frac{(b-\tau)^{\alpha}}{\alpha\Gamma(\alpha)} h(\tau)d\tau - c_0(b-a). \tag{11}$$

Employing the boundary condition (1), we obtain

$$u(a) = -c_0, \tag{12}$$

and

$$u(b) = \int_a^b \frac{(b-s)^{\alpha-1}}{\Gamma(\alpha)} h(s)ds - c_0. \tag{13}$$

Now combining (1), (11) and (13) we get

$$\begin{aligned} c_0 &= \frac{1}{b-a}\int_a^b \frac{(b-s)^{\alpha}}{\alpha\Gamma(\alpha)} h(s)ds \\ &- \frac{1}{\mu(b-a)}\int_a^b \frac{(b-s)^{\alpha-1}}{\Gamma(\alpha)} h(s)ds. \end{aligned} \tag{14}$$

Making insertion of (14) into (10) we find

$$\begin{aligned} u(t) &= \frac{1}{b-a}\int_a^t \frac{(t-s)^{\alpha-1}}{\Gamma(\alpha)} h(s)ds \\ &- \frac{1}{b-a}\int_a^b \frac{(b-s)^{\alpha}}{\alpha\Gamma(\alpha)} h(s) \\ &+ \int_a^b \frac{(b-s)^{\alpha-1}}{\Gamma(\alpha)} h(s)ds. \end{aligned} \tag{15}$$

Therefore the Green function of the given fractional boundary problem is obtained as described in (9). The next theorem is an essential tool to prove the main theorem of the paper

Theorem 1: The Green function G satisfies:

(1) $G(t,s) \ge 0$ for all $a \le t,\ s \le b$.
(2) $\max_{t \in [a,b]} G(t,s) = G(b,s), \quad s \in [a,b]$,
(3) $G(b,s)$ has a unique maximum given by:

$$\max_{s \in [a,b]} G(b,s) = \frac{\alpha(b-a+\mu)(\alpha\mu+1)^{(\alpha-1)}}{\mu^{\alpha}(b-a)\alpha\Gamma(\alpha)},$$

provided that

$$0 < \mu(b-a) < \alpha.$$

For the proof of Theorem 1, we start by deriving the function $G(t,s)$ with respect to t, for $s \le t$, as follows

$$\frac{\partial G}{\partial t} = -\frac{(\alpha-1)(t-s)^{\alpha-2}}{\Gamma(\alpha)}, \tag{16}$$

which is positive since $0 < \alpha \leq 1$. Thus, the Green function G is increasing as a function of t. We have

$$G(s,s) < G(t,s) < G(b,s).$$

Let us start with the right hand side of this last inequality which is $G(b,s)$, and denote it by $H(s)$. Then, we have

$$\begin{aligned} H(s) := G(b,s) &= \frac{(b-s)^{\alpha-1}}{\Gamma(\alpha)} - \frac{(b-s)^{\alpha}}{(b-a)\alpha\Gamma(\alpha)} \\ &+ \frac{(b-s)^{\alpha-1}}{\mu(b-a)\alpha\Gamma(\alpha)}\Gamma(\alpha). \end{aligned}$$

Deriving H with respect to s, we get

$$H'(s) = (\alpha\mu+1)(b-s)^{\alpha-1} - \mu(b-s)^{\alpha}.$$

We may observe that H' is equal to zero for $s = b - \frac{\alpha\mu+1}{\mu} := s^*$, and H' is positive for $s < s^*$ and negative for $s > s^*$. We conclude that the maximum of H is achieved at $s = s^*$. To this end the maximum of the Green function G is attained at $s = s^*$ and therefore

$$\max_{s\leq t} G(b,s) = G(b,s^*) = \frac{\alpha(b-a+\mu)(\alpha\mu+1)^{(\alpha-1)}}{\mu^{\alpha}(b-a)\alpha\Gamma(\alpha)}.$$

For the positivity of G, we consider $G(s,s)$ as a function of s defined by:

$$K(s) := G(s,s) = -\frac{(b-s)^{\alpha}}{(b-a)\alpha\Gamma(\alpha)} + \frac{(b-s)^{\alpha-1}}{\mu(b-a)\Gamma(\alpha)}.$$

Deriving K with respect to s, we obtain

$$K'(s) = \frac{\mu\alpha(b-s)^{\alpha-1} - \alpha(\alpha-1)(b-s)^{\alpha-2}}{\mu(b-a)\alpha\Gamma(\alpha)}$$

which is positive in view of $0 < \alpha \leq 1$, and $\mu > 0$. In other terms, the function K is an increasing function of s and therefore K satisfies

$$K(s) > K(a) := \frac{\mu\alpha(b-a)^{\alpha-1} - \alpha(\alpha-1)(b-a)^{\alpha-2}}{\mu(b-a)\alpha\Gamma(\alpha)}.$$

Now, in light of the assumption of the Theorem 1, $h(a)$ is a positive function in a which leads the Green function G to be positive. We note, in turn, that we derive $G(t,s)$ with respect to t for $s \geq t$, we obtain:

$$\frac{\partial G}{\partial t} = -\frac{\partial g}{\partial t} = 0. \tag{17}$$

Thus, the maximum of G is achieved at $s = s^*$ for all s, t in $[a,b]$.

Finally, we are now ready to prove the aim of this paper which is Lyapunov's inequality for the non integral boundary fractional boundary problem (1).

Theorem 2: Let u be a non trivial solution satisfying the following boundary value problem

$$\begin{cases} ({}_aD^{\alpha}u)(t) + q(t)u(t) = 0, \\ a < t < b,\ 0 < \alpha \leq 1, \\ u(a) + \mu\int_a^b h(s)\,ds = u(b), \end{cases} \tag{18}$$

where a and b are two consecutive zeros of u and μ is a positive constant in R. Then (18) has a non-trivial solution provided that the real and continuous function q satisfies the following integral condition

$$\int_a^b |q(t)|\,dt > \frac{\Gamma(\alpha)\mu^{\alpha}(b-a)}{\alpha(b-a+\mu)(\alpha\mu+1)^{(\alpha-1)}}, \tag{19}$$

provided that

$$0 < \mu(b-a) < \alpha.$$

For the proof of Theorem 2, we equip the Banach space $C[a,b]$ with the Chebychev norm $||u|| = \max_{t\in[a,b]} |u(t)|$.
As

$$u(t) := \int_a^b G(t,s)q(s)u(s)\,ds,$$

we have

$$||u|| \leq \int_a^b \max_{t,s\in[a,b]} |G(t,s)|\,|q(s)|\,ds\ ||u||.$$

Then since u is a non trivial solution, in view of Theorem 1, we get

$$1 \leq \int_a^b \frac{1}{\Gamma(\alpha)}\left(\frac{\alpha(b-a+\mu)(\alpha\mu+1)^{(\alpha-1)}}{\mu^{\alpha}(b-a)}\right)|q(s)|\,ds.$$

Using the properties of G, the inequality (19) is obtained.

IV. Application

In order to illustrate Theorem 2, we give an application of Lyapunov-type inequality (19) for the following eigenvalue problem and we will get a bound for λ for which the boundary value problem in consideration has a non trivial solution. Precisely, we will show how the necessary condition of existence can be employed to determine intervals for the real zeros of the Mittag-Leffeler function.

$$\begin{aligned} E_{\alpha}(z) &= \Sigma_{k=0}^{\infty}\frac{z^k}{k\alpha+\alpha}, \\ z \in \mathcal{C}, &\quad \text{and } \mathcal{R}(\alpha) \text{ is positive.} \end{aligned} \tag{20}$$

By setting $a = \frac{1}{2}$, $b = 1$, $\mu = \alpha$, and taking into consideration the Sturm-Liouville eigenvalue problem

$$\begin{cases} ({}_{\frac{1}{2}}D^{\alpha}u)(t) + \lambda u(t) = 0, \\ 0 < t < \frac{1}{2}, \quad 0 < \alpha \leq 1, \\ u(\frac{1}{2}) + \alpha\int_{\frac{1}{2}}^{1} u(s)\,ds = u(1). \end{cases} \tag{21}$$

Theorem 3: If λ is an eigenvalue of the fractional boundary value problem (21) then the following inequality holds

$$|\lambda| \geq \frac{\Gamma(\alpha)\alpha^{\alpha-1}}{(\alpha+2)(\alpha^2+1)}. \tag{22}$$

For the proof of Theorem 3, it is sufficient to use the integral inequality (19). We assume that, if λ is an eigenvalue of the boundary value problem (21), then there exists only one non-trivial solution depending on λ such that the following inequality is satisfied

$$\int_{\frac{1}{2}}^{1} |\lambda|\, dt \geq \frac{\Gamma(\alpha)\alpha^{\alpha}(b-a)}{\alpha(b-a+\alpha)(\alpha^2+1)^{\alpha}}, \tag{23}$$

or equivalently, we have

$$|\lambda| \geq \frac{\Gamma(\alpha)\alpha^{\alpha-1}}{(\alpha+2)(\alpha^2+1)}. \tag{24}$$

which completes the proof.

ACKNOWLEDGMENT

This research project was supported by a grant from the Research Center of the Female Scientific and Medical Colleges Deanship of Scientific Research, King Saud University.

REFERENCES

[1] A. M. Lyapunov, "Problème général de la stabilité du mouvement," *Ann. Fac. Sci. Univ. Toulouse*, vol. 2, pp. 203–407, 1907.

[2] M. Al-Qurashi and L. Ragoub, "Nonexistence of solutions to a fractional differential boundary value problem," *J. Nonlinear Sci. Appl.*, vol. 9, pp. 2233–2243, 2016.

[3] M. Jleli, L. Ragoub, and B. Samet, "On a Lyapunov-type inequality for a fractional differential equation under a Robin boundary condition," *J. of functions space*, 2014.

[4] S. Sitho, S. K. Ntouyas, W. Yukunthorn, and J. Tariboon, "Lyapunov type inequalities for hybrid fractional differential equations," *Journal of Inequalities and Applications*, 2016.

[5] S. Zhang, "Positive solutions for boundary-value problems of nonlinear fractional diffrential equations," *Electron. J. Differential Equations*, vol. 36, 2006.

[6] R. A. C. Ferreira, "A Lyapunov-type inequality for a fractional boundary value problem," *Fract. Calc. Appl. Anal.*, vol. 16 (4), pp. 978–984, 2013.

[7] A. A. Kilbas, H. M. Srivastava, and J. J. Trujillo, "Theory and applications of fractional differential equations," *North-Holland Mathematics Studies, Elsevier, Amsterdam, The Netherlands*, vol. 204, 2006.

[8] R. A. C. Ferreira, "On a Lyapunov-type inequality and the zeros of a certain Mittag-Leffler function," *J. Math. Anal. Appl.*, 2014.

Graph Coloring Applied to Medical Doctors Schedule

Ferdous M O Tawfiq, Kholoud Khalid S Al-qahtani

King Saud University- Riyadh. Saudi Arabia

e-mails: {ftoufic@ksu.edu.sa, 432201096@student.ksu.edu.sa}

***Abstract*— Scheduling shifts is a tiresome and time consuming task in any business, and particularly in hospitals where errors are costly, rules are plentiful and changes are rapid. The person performing this function (Rota Organizer) will have to keep track of all the employees concerned, distributing hours fairly and avoiding collisions. Rules regulating working hours and breaks have to be followed and the qualifications of individual employees need to be considered. Hours are spent every day on this task in every ward. The goal of this paper is to solve Doctors Scheduling Problem (DSP) and initialize a fair roster for two wards of Pediatric Department (PD) in Prince Sultan Military Medical City (PSMMC) in Saudi Arabia. So, to find a solution to DSP, we used Graph Coloring which is one of the methods mostly used to solve this problem.**

Keywords- graph coloring; doctors roster; greedy algorithm.

I. INTRODUCTION

In the study of graphs, which are mathematical structures used to model pair wise relations between objects, a "graph" is made up of vertices (or nodes) and lines, called edges, that connect them.

Graphs can be used to model many types of relations and processes in physical, biological, social and information systems. Graph coloring has been studied extensively for the past decades. The surge for studying graph coloring in recent times has resulted in countless real-life problem applications, which include scheduling problems. The research presented in this paper aims to provide an effective procedure for solving Doctors Scheduling Problem (DSP) related to their shifts. DSP is a major problem faced by many hospitals all over the world. We tried in two wards of PSMMC to establish a roster for one month as a beginning to achieve a general procedure for every month. After exploring relevant references, the problem will be described in detail, followed by the formulation of the relevant coloring problem and its solution with recent results.

II. RELATED WORK

Nurses' rostering problem has been studied in the literature by many researchers, for example [1] [4] [6]. Kumara et al. [6] used graph coloring for scheduling with a specific different algorithm (other than greedy algorithm). [1] [4] used graph coloring to make the schedule by greedy algorithm, but for a few number of nurses. In this paper graph coloring is used to solve doctors' scheduling problem (DSP) related to their shifts for one month in two wards of PSMMC. Realizing that establishing a general procedure to create a roster for every month has not been done yet for any hospitals in Saudi Arabia, this work might lead to a follow up by more research. For the advantages of this procedure to be clear, a needed comparison will be done.

III. STATEMENT OF THE PROBLEM

In this paper, we consider a scheduling problem for Pediatric Department of Prince Sultan Military Medical City (PSMMC) in Riyadh/ Saudi Arabia. It is considered one of the top governmental hospitals with almost twenty seven departments. There are more than five thousand doctors in the hospital. We communicated with Dr. Nawaf Al khayat (Dr.N.A.,) in PD of PSMMIC; he is a consultant and supervisor of resident doctors training in PSMMIC.

Usually, monthly doctors roster are made manually before the end of each month. Rota organizer has the responsibility to publish next month's roster. Even though making monthly rosters manually requires great effort, it does not resolve all conflicts. Instead, it has created more tedious adjustments to accomplish needed tasks. There are consultants, senior and junior doctors working in this department. This paper is concerned with scheduling shifts for junior and senior doctors in two of the department wards for one month only.

There are three types of doctors: Consultants, Seniors (R3 & R4) and Juniors (R1 & R2), where the number indicates trainee year. In PSMMC pediatric department, which has thirteen wards, there are thirty eight resident doctors; R1, R2, R3 and R4. It has been specified for us to work on scheduling shifts for only two wards: PG (Pediatrics General) and PGICU (Pediatrics General Intensive Care Unit) wards. In addition, we were given the following information:

1. Each working day consists of eight to eight and half hours.
2. Each shift consists of twenty four hours.
3. Every doctor who has participated in a shift will not be given anther shift for the next three days.
4. There are twenty two junior and sixteen senior doctors.
5. In each working month, there are doctors who are

excluded from participating in shifts due to other responsibilities or personal circumstances.

We chose September 2016 to be the month we consider for scheduling. In September, only eighteen doctors are excluded which is the least number of doctors, compared with the remaining months. From the list of names given to us by Dr.N.A., we have listed doctors who will participate in September shifts (S.S.). There are twelve juniors and eight seniors available. In the proposed solution for DSP (Doctors Scheduling Problem), we need to assign doctors to shifts.

IV. FORMULATION OF A GRAPH COLORING PROBLEM

First, we divided the doctors into four shift groups. Each group has two seniors and four juniors, based on department daily requirement, and the fact that we only have twelve juniors and eight seniors in this month. Since both PG and PGICU involved doctors cannot accomplish needed shifts while meeting restrictions of the department, we had several options.

We chose to involve one doctor outside PG and PGICU, each day of September to complement needed shifts. So we had A, B, C and D groups to cover first four consecutive days which will represent the same groups for the following four days, and so on. This implies a need for additional four juniors {SUB.1, SUB.2, SUB.3, SUB.4}, (SUB.1 refer to first substitute for a junior), to complement the required number of doctors (8 seniors and 16 juniors in condition 3 above).

TABLE I. GROUPS OF SEPTEBER SECHDULE DOCTORS(S.S.D.).

Group	Doctors
A	$R3_1$, $R4_1$, $R1_1$, $R1_5$, $R2_4$, SUB_1.
B	$R3_2$, $R4_2$, $R1_2$, $R2_1$, $R2_5$, SUB_2.
C	$R3_3$, $R4_3$, $R1_3$, $R2_2$, $R2_6$, SUB_3.
D	$R3_4$, $R4_4$, $R1_4$, $R2_3$, $R2_7$, SUB_4

By using above data, an incident matrix is initiated for S.S.D. It is a 24 × 24 matrix. If any two doctors are in same group then ij-th entry is 1 otherwise it is 0. Now, since the incident matrix is a big matrix, we had to divide it into 4 submatrices (blocks) which include all nonzero entries (for the sake of presenting results in appropriate template).

	$R3_1$	$R4_1$	$R1_1$	$R1_5$	$R2_4$	SUB_1
$R3_1$	0	1	1	1	1	1
$R4_1$	1	0	1	1	1	1
$R1_1$	1	1	0	1	1	1
$R1_5$	1	1	1	0	1	1
$R2_4$	1	1	1	1	0	1
SUB_1	1	1	1	1	1	0

Frist submatrix $[a^1_{ij}]$.

	$R3_2$	$R4_2$	$R1_2$	$R2_1$	$R2_5$	SUB_2
$R3_2$	0	1	1	1	1	1
$R4_2$	1	0	1	1	1	1
$R1_2$	1	1	0	1	1	1
$R2_1$	1	1	1	0	1	1
$R2_5$	1	1	1	1	0	1
SUB_2	1	1	1	1	1	0

Second submatrix $[a^2_{ij}]$.

	$R3_3$	$R4_3$	$R1_3$	$R2_2$	$R2_6$	SUB_3
$R3_3$	0	1	1	1	1	1
$R4_3$	1	0	1	1	1	1
$R1_3$	1	1	0	1	1	1
$R2_2$	1	1	1	0	1	1
$R2_6$	1	1	1	1	0	1
SUB_3	1	1	1	1	1	0

Third submatrix $[a^3_{ij}]$.

	$R3_4$	$R4_4$	$R1_4$	$R2_3$	$R2_7$	SUB_4
$R3_4$	0	1	1	1	1	1
$R4_4$	1	0	1	1	1	1
$R1_4$	1	1	0	1	1	1
$R2_3$	1	1	1	0	1	1
$R2_7$	1	1	1	1	0	1
SUB_4	1	1	1	1	1	0

Fourth submatrix $[a^4_{ij}]$.

Each block is $a\ 6 \times 6$ submatrix, for first block say $[a^1_{ij}]$ where $1 \leq ij \leq 6$. 1st column is for $R3_1$, 2nd column is for $R4_1$, …, and last column (6th column) is for SUB_1. Rows has been delt with in same way. So $[a^2_{ij}]$, $[a^3_{ij}]$ and $[a^4_{ij}]$ are 6×6 submatrices in the same way. ($[a_{ij}]$ is a 24×24 matrix). By using the incident matrix $[a_{ij}]$, a graph is constructed with S.S.D. as vertices. If two doctors are in same group, then they are linked by an edge.

Next, we colored the graph by using Greedy algorithm. We started with red as color number one and took color number two to be yellow. Color number three is gray, also color number four is orange and color number five is green. We needed six colors, so the last color is going to be blue.

Now we will start with vertices representing seniors; first senior of each day will be colored in red. The second senior adjacent to the first one will be colored yellow. Since every day there are four juniors adjacent to each other and to the red and yellow seniors, the first one of these juniors every day will be colored gray, the second one is orange, third one is green, and last one is blue. See Figure 1. Above, we have included substitutes in the coloring scheme to organize needed shifts. This means the first day group will be repeated in fifth day, second group will be repeated in sixth day, third group will be repeated in seventh day and fourth group will be repeated in eighth day. So, to finish up the process the cycle will be repeated every four days.

TABLE II. GROUPS AFTER APPLYING GRAH COLORING

Group	**Doctors**
$G1$	$R3_4, R4_2, R4_3, R3_1$
$G2$	$R4_1, R4_4, R3_3, R3_2$
$G3$	$R1_4, R1_2, R1_1, SUB_3$
$G4$	$R1_5, R2_5, SUB_4, R2_6$
$G5$	$R2_4, R1_3, SUB_2, R2_7$
$G6$	$R2_3, R2_2, R2_1, SUB_1$

Accordingly, we formulated a table where S.S.D. doctors in G1,G2,…, G6 should be in the same ward if they are in the same group. Based on restrictions specified in Section 4 concerning the problem of making doctors roster for September 2016 in PD of PSMMC, we have divided doctors into shift groups.

Then, we applied the graph theory to these groups so that each vertex represents a doctor and there is an edge between any two doctors in one shift group, see section 3.1 for details.

After graphing, we used Greedy Algorithm to color. We used six colors for twenty four vertices, where each four vertices have one color.

In the graph, doctors represented by vertices of the same color are grouped as one since they will be working in the same ward. The shift groups (Table I) are then used to form a 24×2 matrix. The elements of first columns represent numbering of doctors and element of second column represent colors of these doctors which are numbering like that (1 is red, 2 is yellow, 3 is gray, 4 is orange, 5 is green and 6 is blue). We used this matrix to create code by Matlab. The output of this code is distribution in the wards.

V. RESULTS

Table III shows the first phase of result: distribution of doctors in wards. We note that each element represents the participation of a specific doctor in a shift, i.e.,

$$\begin{cases} 1 & \text{if doctor is alternating.} \\ 0 & \text{if doctor is not alternating.} \end{cases}$$

TABLE III. DISTRIBUTION OF DOCTORS IN WARDS AFTER CONVERTING RESULT FROM MATLAB.

A	B	C	D	E	F
$R3_1$	$R4_1$	SUB_1	$R2_4$	$R1_5$	$R1_1$
$R4_2$	$R3_2$	$R2_1$	SUB_2	$R2_5$	$R1_2$
$R4_3$	$R3_3$	$R2_2$	$R1_3$	$R2_6$	SUB_3
$R3_4$	$R4_4$	$R2_3$	$R2_7$	SUB_4	$R1_4$

In this paper, we have finalized a roster for September 2016 shifts of two wards PG and PGICU in PD of PSMMC. This roster has taken into consideration departmental restrictions. In doing so, we are hoping to have saved PG and PGICU from getting into misunderstandings, as well as any other relevant troubles. Instead of wasting time and effort to generate doctors roster, the staff can concentrate on other important medical duties.

At the end, we can confirm that steps leading to a roster of September 2016, as detailed in Section 4, can be used and applied for other months, and for nurses, as well as doctors.

TABLE IV. THE FINAL ROSTER FOR THE PD.

Date	Day	A	B	C	D	E	F
4 Sep.	Sun.	$R3_1$	$R4_1$	SUB_1	$R2_4$	$R1_5$	$R1_1$
5	Mon.	$R4_2$	$R3_2$	$R2_1$	SUB_2	$R2_5$	$R1_2$
6	Tue.	$R4_3$	$R3_3$	$R2_2$	$R1_3$	$R2_6$	SUB_3
7	Wed.	$R3_4$	$R4_4$	$R2_3$	$R2_7$	SUB_4	$R1_4$
8	Thu.	$R3_1$	$R4_1$	SUB_1	$R2_4$	$R1_5$	$R1_1$
9	Fri.	$R4_2$	$R3_2$	$R2_1$	SUB_2	$R2_5$	$R1_2$
10	Sat.	$R4_3$	$R3_3$	$R2_2$	$R1_3$	$R2_6$	SUB_3
11	Sun.	$R3_4$	$R4_4$	$R2_3$	$R2_7$	SUB_4	$R1_4$
12	Mon.	$R3_1$	$R4_1$	SUB_1	$R2_4$	$R1_5$	$R1_1$
13	Tue.	$R4_2$	$R3_2$	$R2_1$	SUB_2	$R2_5$	$R1_2$
14	Wed.	$R4_3$	$R3_3$	$R2_2$	$R1_3$	$R2_6$	SUB_3
15	Thu.	$R3_4$	$R4_4$	$R2_3$	$R2_7$	SUB_4	$R1_4$
16	Fri.	$R3_1$	$R4_1$	SUB_1	$R2_4$	$R1_5$	$R1_1$
17	Sat.	$R4_2$	$R3_2$	$R2_1$	SUB_2	$R2_5$	$R1_2$
18	Sun.	$R4_3$	$R3_3$	$R2_2$	$R1_3$	$R2_6$	SUB_3
19	Mon.	$R3_4$	$R4_4$	$R2_3$	$R2_7$	SUB_4	$R1_4$

20	Tue.	$R3_1$	$R4_1$	SUB_1	$R2_4$	$R1_5$	$R1_1$
21	Wed.	$R4_2$	$R3_2$	$R2_1$	SUB_2	$R2_5$	$R1_2$
22	Thu.	$R4_3$	$R3_3$	$R2_2$	$R1_3$	$R2_6$	SUB_3
23	Fri.	$R3_4$	$R4_4$	$R2_3$	$R2_7$	SUB_4	$R1_4$
24	Sat.	$R3_1$	$R4_1$	SUB_1	$R2_4$	$R1_5$	$R1_1$
25	Sun.	$R4_2$	$R3_2$	$R2_1$	SUB_2	$R2_5$	$R1_2$
26	Mon.	$R4_3$	$R3_3$	$R2_2$	$R1_3$	$R2_6$	SUB_3
27	Tue.	$R3_4$	$R4_4$	$R2_3$	$R2_7$	SUB_4	$R1_4$
28	Wed.	$R3_1$	$R4_1$	SUB_1	$R2_4$	$R1_5$	$R1_1$
29	Thu.	$R4_2$	$R3_2$	$R2_1$	SUB_2	$R2_5$	$R1_2$
30	Fri.	$R4_3$	$R3_3$	$R2_2$	$R1_3$	$R2_6$	SUB_3
1 Oct.	Sat.	$R3_4$	$R4_4$	$R2_3$	$R2_7$	SUB_4	$R1_4$

VI. FUTURE WORK

Many hospitals take a long time to prepare a doctors roster which is fair to everybody. Instead of wasting time in generating it, we hope to generalize in future work a software, where minimum data is required to have a roster for any month.

ACKNOWLEDGEMENT

Thanks to Deanship of Scientific Research at King Saud University (KSU) for funding this work through undergraduate students research support program project on (USRSP).

REFERENCES

[1] Amponsah, S.K, Agyeman, E., Okran, K.G., Graph Coloring, an Approach to Nurses Scheduling. American-Eurasian Journal of Scientific Research 6(1). Ghana, 2011, 1-5.

[2] Butt, R., Introduction to Numerical Analysis Using Matlab. USA, 2007.

[3] Diestel, R., Graph Theory. Springer-Verlag, New Your, 2000, 98-103.

[4] Gideon, A., A Nurse Scheduling Using Graph Coloring. Master thesis submitted, Mathematics Department, Kwame Nkrumah University, Ghana, 2013, 1-4, 35, 53-77.

[5] Harju, T., Graph Theory. Lecture Notes in Mathematics, Finland, 2011, 53-60.

[6] Kumara, B.T.G.S., Perera, A.A.I, Automated System For Nurse Scheduling Using Graph Coloring. Indian Journal of Computer Science and Engineering (IJCSE), 2011, 476-485.

[7] Rosen, K., Discrete Mathematics and It's Applications. New York, 2012.

[8] Rosen, K., Chromatic Graph Theory. Michigan, 2009.

[9] Shekhar, S., Graph Theory. Lecture Notes in Mathematics, US, 2012, 137-139.

[10] Skogvold, A.; Saether, T.; Moseby, S.; Westby, P., Flexible Duty Roster for Doctors in Hospital, 2009, 1-3.

[11] West, D., Introduction to Graph Theory. New Jesey, 2001.

[12] Wilson, R., Introduction to Graph Theory. England, 1996.

[13] Wren, A., Scheduling, Timetabling and Rostering- a Special Relationship?. Lecture Notes in Computer Science. Springer-verlag, Berlin, 1996, 46-75.

[14] Dharwardker,A., 2006. The Vertex Coloring Algorithm. Available at: < http://www.dharwadker.org/vertex_coloring/>, (March 2016).

[15] Greedy Coloring Algorithm. August 2015. Available at:

[16] < https://www.youtube.com/watch?v=vGjsi8 NIpSE > (March 2016).

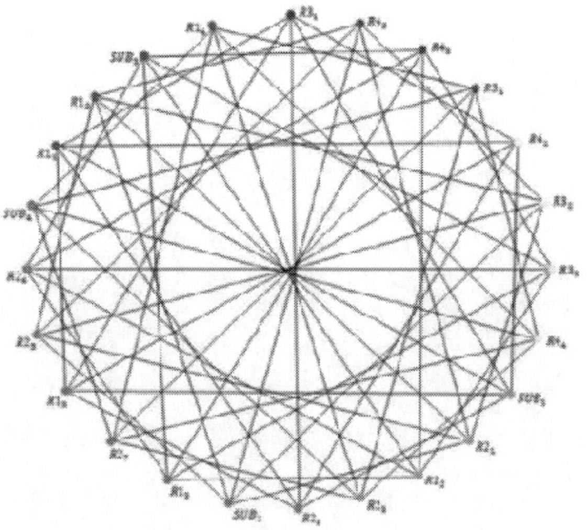

Figure 1. A colored graph of the doctors

AUTHOR INDEX